321 PAT

**Access to History
for the IB Diploma**

MW01278024

Communism in crisis 1976–89

Rakesh Pathak
Yvonne Berliner

T 67610

DISCARDED
PROPERTY OF
MULGRAVE SCHOOL
LIBRARY

HODDER
EDUCATION
AN HACHETTE UK COMPANY

The material in this title has been developed independently of the International Baccalaureate®, which in no way endorses it.

The Publishers would like to thank the following for permission to reproduce copyright material:

Photo credits pp26, 82, 83 AFP/Getty Images; **pp29, 53, 69** International Institute for Social History (Amsterdam); **pp50, 120***b* Getty Images; **pp119, 120***t***, 137** RIA Novosti; **pp144, 145, 179** Nicholas Garland/British Cartoon Library; **p148** Peter Turnley/Corbis; **p168** Telegraph Syndication/British Cartoon Library; **p172** Wally McNamee/Corbis; **pp174, 192** Bettmann/Corbis; **p181** Robert Wallis/SIPA/Corbis; **p187** David Turnley/Corbis.

Acknowledgements are listed on page 220.

Every effort has been made to trace all copyright holders, but if any have been inadvertently overlooked the Publishers will be pleased to make the necessary arrangements at the first opportunity.

Although every effort has been made to ensure that website addresses are correct at time of going to press, Hodder Education cannot be held responsible for the content of any website mentioned in this book. It is sometimes possible to find a relocated web page by typing in the address of the home page for a website in the URL window of your browser.

Hachette UK's policy is to use papers that are natural, renewable and recyclable products and made from wood grown in sustainable forests. The logging and manufacturing processes are expected to conform to the environmental regulations of the country of origin.

Orders: please contact Bookpoint Ltd, 130 Milton Park, Abingdon, Oxon OX14 4SB. Telephone: +44 (0)1235 827720. Fax: +44 (0)1235 400454. Lines are open 9.00a.m.–5.00p.m., Monday to Saturday, with a 24-hour message answering service. Visit our website at www.hoddereducation.co.uk

© Rakesh Pathak and Yvonne Berliner 2012

First published in 2012 by
Hodder Education,
An Hachette UK Company
338 Euston Road
London NW1 3BH

Impression number   10 9 8 7 6 5 4 3 2 1
Year   2016 2015 2014 2013 2012

All rights reserved. Apart from any use permitted under UK copyright law, no part of this publication may be reproduced or transmitted in any form or by any means, electronic or mechanical, including photocopying and recording, or held within any information storage and retrieval system, without permission in writing from the publisher or under licence from the Copyright Licensing Agency Limited. Further details of such licences (for reprographic reproduction) may be obtained from the Copyright Licensing Agency Limited, Saffron House, 6–10 Kirby Street, London EC1N 8TS.

Cover image © Images.com/Corbis
Illustrations by Gray Publishing
Typeset in 10/13pt Palatino and produced by Gray Publishing, Tunbridge Wells
Printed in Italy

A catalogue record for this title is available from the British Library

ISBN 978 1444 156386

Contents

Dedication

Keith Randell (1943–2002)

The original *Access to History* series was conceived and developed by Keith, who created a series to 'cater for students as they are, not as we might wish them to be'. He leaves a living legacy of a series that for over 20 years has provided a trusted, stimulating and well-loved accompaniment to post-16 study. Our aim with these new editions for the IB is to continue to offer students the best possible support for their studies.

Introduction

This book has been written to support your study of prescribed subject 3: Communism in crisis 1976–89 of the IB History Diploma Route 2. This first chapter gives you an overview of:

✪ the content you will study for Communism in crisis 1976–89

✪ how you will be assessed for Paper 1

✪ the different features of this book and how these will aid your learning.

What you will study

The period from 1976 to 1989 is a fascinating era of history. At a global level, it includes the end of the Cold War and how that process began in a world where the conclusion of the tension between the communist and capitalist systems seemed impossible to contemplate. Within the USSR and its satellites in central and eastern Europe, as well as in the People's Republic of China, the development and challenges of the communist system led to severe problems. The USSR faced its challenges through the rule of its Communist Party, but, as the crisis deepened, it was unable to hold the party and eventually the USSR together, leading to disintegration and the rise of new nations. China also faced internal challenges that were met by the ruling Communist Party in different ways, leading to reform and the survival of both the party and the nation. These significant events caused political and economic changes across the world, contributing to a new world order after 1989.

Communism in theory and practice

Your study will include the following:

- Key features of communist ideology in Chapter 1.
- Establishment of communist states in China up to 1964 and Russia up to 1976 in Chapter 1.

China's challenges

Your study will include the following:

- A detailed review of the struggle for the leadership of the Communist Party in China after the death of Mao Zedong in 1976 in Chapter 2.
- Economic policies under Deng Xiaoping from 1979 to 1989 in Chapter 3.
- Political changes under Deng Xiaoping from 1979 to 1989 in Chapter 4.

The USSR's challenges

Your study will include the following:

- Domestic and foreign problems of the Brezhnev era in Chapter 5.
- Gorbachev's reforms and the consequences for the Soviet state in Chapter 6.
- The relations between the superpowers from 1985 to 1989 in Chapter 7.
- The consequences of Gorbachev's policies for eastern European reform movements in Chapter 7.

How you will be assessed

The IB History Diploma can be studied to either Standard or Higher Level. It has three papers in total: Papers 1 and 2 for Standard Level and a further Paper 3 for Higher Level. It also has an internal assessment that all students must do.

- For Paper 1 you need to answer four source-based questions on a prescribed subject. This counts for 20 per cent of your overall marks at Higher Level, or 30 per cent of your overall marks at Standard Level.
- For Paper 2 you need to answer two essay questions on two different topics. This counts for 25 per cent of your overall marks at Higher Level, or 45 per cent of your overall marks at Standard Level.
- For Paper 3 you need to answer three essay questions on two or three sections. This counts for 35 per cent of your overall marks at Higher Level.
- For the Internal Assessment you need to carry out a historical investigation. This counts for 20 per cent of your overall marks at Higher Level, or 25 per cent of your overall marks at Standard Level.

Prescribed subject 3: Communism in crisis 1976–89 is assessed through Paper 1. Paper 1 of the IB History Diploma examination has five sources and four questions. The sources are from primary and secondary sources and, while the majority are written, visual sources are almost always present. The visual source could be a chart, graph, table, map, cartoon, poster, stamp or photograph.

Examination questions

The four questions on the examination paper assess different skills and knowledge. You must answer all four and have one hour to do so. The question types are as follows.

Question 1: Direct questions
Question 1 is worth 5 marks and has two parts, both of which test your reading comprehension abilities on two different sources. You need to

answer both parts of the question by reviewing the source material and paraphrasing information from the sources. There is detailed guidance on how to answer question 1 on pages 37–42. Examples of this type of question might be:

Example 1
What, according to Source C, were the justifications for the arrest of the Gang of Four?

Example 2
What does Source E say about the central political role of the Communist Party of the Soviet Union?

Question 2: Comparing and contrasting sources
Question 2 is worth 6 marks and asks you to compare and contrast two sources. Comparing means that you explain the similarities between the sources, while contrasting explains how they are different. You should aim to have about three similarities and three differences. There is detailed guidance on how to answer question 2 on pages 91–3. Examples of this type of question might be:

Example 1
Compare and contrast the views of Sources A and B regarding the struggle for power after the death of Mao Zedong.

Example 2
Compare and contrast the reasons for the failure of the Warsaw Pact as expressed by Sources C and D.

Question 3: Origins, purpose, value, limitations
Question 3 is worth 6 marks and asks you to explain the value and limitations of two sources with reference to their origin and purpose.

- The origin of a source is its author or creator. This should also include the date, publisher and type of delivery, which could be a book, speech, propaganda poster or diary entry.
- The purpose of the source explains what the author was trying to do, such as explaining the impact of an event or conveying a certain type of information.

The values and limitations will vary according to each source. A value could be that the author of the source witnessed the event or is an acknowledged scholar. An example of a limitation could be that an author was involved in events and therefore may be less objective. You should try to explain at least two values and two limitations per source, although this may not always be possible. There is detailed guidance on how to answer question 3 on pages 130–3. Examples of this type of question might be:

Example 1
With reference to their origin and purpose, assess the value and limitations of Source A and Source B for historians studying the Gang of Four.

Example 2
With reference to their origin and purpose, discuss the value and limitations of Source D and Source E for historians studying the impact of *glasnost* and *perestroika*.

Question 4: Essays integrating knowledge and sources
Question 4 is worth 8 marks and requires you to use all the sources in the examination and to integrate them into an essay that also contains your own knowledge. There is detailed guidance on how to answer question 4 on pages 160–5. Examples of this type of question might be:

Example 1
Using these sources and your own knowledge, explain why Deng Xiaoping revived the Four Modernizations.

Example 2
Using these sources and your own knowledge, discuss the extent to which you agree that the Soviet economy stagnated under Brezhnev.

The appearance of the examination paper

Cover
The cover of the examination paper states the date of the examination and the length of time you have to complete it: one hour. Please note that there are two routes in history. Make sure your paper says Route 2 on it. Instructions are limited and simply state that you should not open it until told to do so and that all questions must be answered.

Sources
Once you are allowed to open your examination paper, you will note that there are five sources, each labelled with a letter. There is no particular order to the sources, so Source A could potentially be a map, a speech, a photograph or an extract from a book. Source A is no more or less important than Source B and so on. If you see brackets, [ ], then this is an explanation or addition to the source by the creators of the examination and not part of the original source. Sometimes sources are shortened and you will see an ellipsis, three full stops or periods […] when this happens.

Questions
After the five sources, the four questions will appear. You need to answer all of them. It is better to answer the questions in order, as this will familiarize you with all the sources to be used in the final essay on Question 4, but this is not required. Be sure to number your questions correctly. Do not use bullet points to answer questions, but instead write in full sentences when possible. Each question indicates how many marks each question is worth.

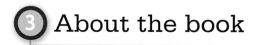
③ About the book

Coverage of course content

This book addresses the key areas listed in the IB History Guide for Route 2: Twentieth-century world history prescribed subject 3: Communism in crisis 1976–89. Chapters start with an introduction outlining the key questions they address. They are then divided into a series of sections and topics covering the course content. Throughout the chapters you will find the following features to aid your study of the course content:

Key and leading questions

Each section heading in the chapter has a related key question that gives a focus to your reading and understanding of the section. These are also listed in the chapter's introduction. You should be able to answer the questions after completing the relevant section.

Topics within the sections have leading questions that are designed to help you focus on the key points within a topic and give you more practice in answering questions.

Key terms

Key terms are the important terms you need to know to gain an understanding of the period. These are emboldened in the text the first time they appear in the book and are defined in the margin. They also appear in the glossary at the end of the book.

Sources

Each chapter contains several sources. These sources follow the labelling format of a Paper 1 examination. The sources have accompanying exam-style questions for you to practise. The sources are also used with the exam-style questions at the end of the chapters. The range of sources used will expose you to many different types of sources that you may find in the examination.

Key debates

Historians often disagree on historical events and this historical debate is referred to as historiography. Knowledge of historiography is helpful in reaching the upper mark bands when you take your IB History examinations. There are a number of debates throughout the book to develop your understanding of historiography.

Theory of Knowledge (TOK) questions

Understanding that different historians see history differently is an important element in interpreting the connection between the IB History Diploma and Theory of Knowledge. Alongside most historiographical debates is a Theory of Knowledge-style question that makes that link.

Summary diagrams

At the end of each section is a summary diagram that gives a visual summary of the content of the section. It is intended as an aid for revision.

Chapter summary

At the end of each chapter is a short summary of the chapter. This is intended to help you revise and consolidate your knowledge and understanding of the content.

Skills development

At the end of Chapters 2–7 are the following:

- Examination guidance on how to answer different question types, accompanied by a sample answer and commentary designed to help you focus on specific details.
- Examination practice in the form of Paper 1-style questions.
- Suggestions for learning activities, including ideas for debate, essays, displays and research which will help you develop Paper 1 skills and a deeper understanding of the content.

These are all intended to help you develop the following skills in order to achieve examination success.

- Source analysis.

This book allows you to become familiar with the works of many historians and primary source material. It teaches you to analyse all types of sources and gives you the opportunity to review their strengths, weaknesses, origins, purpose, values and limitations.

- Integrating sources into essays.

Integrating sources into essays requires that you know how to write a good essay. This book gives guidance on writing good essays that integrate sources.

End of the book

The book concludes with the following sections.

Timeline

This gives a timeline of the major events covered in the book that is helpful for quick reference or as a revision tool.

Glossary

All the key terms in the book are defined in the glossary.

Further reading

This is a list of books, websites, films and other resources that may help you with further independent research and presentations. It may also be helpful when further information is required for internal assessments and extended essays in history. You may wish to share the contents of this area with your school or local librarian.

Internal assessment

All IB History diploma students are required to write a historical investigation that is assessed internally. The investigation is an opportunity for you to dig more deeply into a subject that interests you. There is a list of possible topics at the end of the book that could warrant further investigation to form part of your historical investigation.

Communism in the USSR and China

This chapter investigates the key features of communism as a political ideology in order to provide a historical context for the evaluation of the period 1976–89. It also provides a brief explanation of the establishment and early history of the two dominant communist states in the twentieth century: the USSR and the People's Republic of China. You need to consider the following questions throughout this chapter:

✪ What are the key features of communist ideology?
✪ What were the key features of the communist state established in the USSR up to 1964?
✪ What were the key features of the communist state established in China up to 1976?

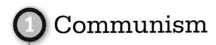 Communism

▶ *Key question:* What are the key features of communist ideology?

 KEY TERM

Communism Political and economic system in which the working class is the only class, there is no private ownership of property, and usually the government directs all aspects of the economy.

Capitalism An economic system in which wealth is largely in private hands, and goods and services are exchanged in order to generate profit.

Marxism–Leninism The original teachings of Marx which were adjusted by Lenin to deal with the economic, social and political conditions of Russia.

Communism is a political and economic system in which the working class is the only class, there is no private ownership of property and usually the government directs all aspects of the economy. It developed out of the writings of several people, primarily Karl Marx, Friedrich Engels and Vladimir Lenin.

Karl Marx, appalled at the conditions of industrial workers in the nineteenth century, came to believe that **capitalism** exploited and abused people, helping only a small group of people who benefited from the labour of others. He thought, along with Friedrich Engels, that a new economic (as well as political and social system) should exist. Marx and Engels presented these ideas in *The Communist Manifesto*, published in 1848, and Marx's views came to be known as Marxism. Vladimir Lenin, a Russian Marxist, added to Marx's teachings to fit the economic and social conditions of Russia in the late nineteenth and early twentieth centuries. These were combined into a communist philosophy known as **Marxism–Leninism**. Some of their main views are outlined on page 10.

Proletariat Marx's term for the industrial working class, primarily factory workers.

Bourgeoisie The middle class, particularly business interests, who Marx believed benefited most from the existing capitalist economic system.

Nationalism Political ideology which favours individuals associating with other members of a nation or national group, in order to promote the interests and coherent collective identity of that group.

Dictatorship of the proletariat A term used by Marx to suggest that following the overthrow of the bourgeoisie, government would be carried out by and on behalf of the working class.

? How do the language and tone of Source A reflect the revolutionary aspect of communism?

- Many institutions have been created to control, exploit and enslave the industrial workers, known as the **proletariat**, including:
  - laws that benefit the **bourgeoisie** – those who benefit from the labour of others
  - labour unions that have the proletariat negotiating with the bourgeoisie for minor benefits
  - religion that teaches people to be obedient and wait for heavenly reward so that they can continue to labour peacefully for others
  - **nationalism** that divides the world's workers, who actually have more in common with people of their economic class in other places than the wealthy of their own country.
- Economic competition within the bourgeoisie means that this class will shrink in time so that a constantly growing proletariat will eventually support only a small number of people.
- The proletariat should rise up and end their exploitation at the hands of the bourgeoisie.
- Eventually the bourgeoisie will, and should, end as a class so that there is only one social, economic and political class: the proletariat. Once this occurs, the world will have a completely equal society where people's requirements are produced, greed ends and there is no unemployment, among other utopian benefits.
- In order to ensure that this system is established, there will be a transition phase after the end of the bourgeoisie where a so-called **dictatorship of the proletariat** will form to guide the new system. This will include the control of all economic and financial resources; essentially government ownership of all property and means of production. This will eventually be unnecessary and will be dissolved leading to a communist utopia.

SOURCE A

Excerpts from *The Communist Manifesto* by Karl Marx and Friedrich Engels, originally published in German in 1848 and translated into English by Samuel Moore in co-operation with Friedrich Engels in 1888. Online version found at: http://www.anu.edu.au/polsci/marx/classics/manifesto.html by Dr Rick Kuhn, Researcher at Australia National University in Canberra, Australia.

You are horrified at our intending to do away with private property. But in your existing society, private property is already done away with for nine-tenths of the population; its existence for the few is solely due to its non-existence in the hands of those nine-tenths. You reproach us, therefore, with intending to do away with a form of property, the necessary condition for whose existence is the non-existence of any property for the immense majority of society …

The Communists disdain to conceal their views and aims. They openly declare that their ends can be attained only by the forcible overthrow of all existing social conditions. Let the ruling classes tremble at a communist revolution. The proletarians have nothing to lose but their chains. They have a world to win …

Proletarians of all countries, unite!

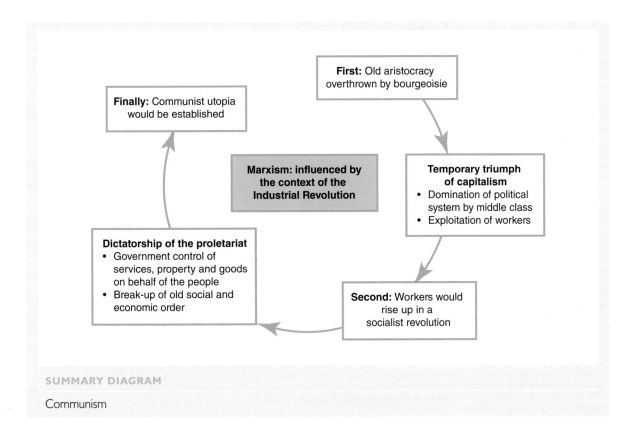

SUMMARY DIAGRAM

Communism

The USSR from Lenin to Brezhnev

▶ *Key question: What were the key features of the communist state established in the USSR up to 1964?*

Communism was established in most of the Russian Empire between 1917 and 1921 as a result of economic, social and political unrest that resulted from Russia's involvement in the First World War. After the **Bolshevik** Revolution in October 1917, and the subsequent Russian Civil War, which ended in Bolshevik victory in 1921, the Union of Soviet Socialist Republics (**USSR**) was formed.

The USSR had a series of strong leaders who theoretically worked with others in the leading party committee, the **Politburo**. In reality, however, these individuals dominated the state in varying degrees.

 **KEY TERM**

Bolshevik The Russian Communist Party. It seized power in a revolution in October 1917.

USSR The Union of Soviet Socialist Republics was established in 1922, the biggest and most influential of which was Russia. Also known as the Soviet Union.

Politburo The Political Bureau of the Central Committee of the Communist Party of the Soviet Union whose members made most of the key policy and political decisions in the USSR.

Lenin

Following the October Revolution, Lenin quickly took steps to establish a one-party Bolshevik state in Russia. Lenin believed that the political destiny of the new state should be in the hands of a disciplined, dedicated party leadership who were best able to judge the true interests of the working class. While various bodies existed in the new government, it was the Politburo that held real power. Lenin chaired this body, as well as chairing Sovnarkom, a government body made up of commissars, each of whom was responsible for different policy areas.

War Communism

For the period of the Russian Civil War (1917–21) Lenin enforced an economic system called **War Communism**. In this system:

- currency was abolished along with private property
- all means of production were owned by the state
- all workers, soldiers and peasants were required to follow all decisions of the government or face severe consequences, including execution
- production focused almost exclusively on weapons so that the civil war could be won
- food grown by peasants was to be seized without compensation.

New Economic Policy (NEP)

While Lenin and the Communist Party won the war, millions starved and the repressive measures led to mutiny within the military. Once the war was successfully concluded, and facing a potential rebellion because of the harsh War Communism programme, Lenin established the New Economic Policy (**NEP**):

- Banks and large industries would be owned by the government while smaller factories could be held privately.
- Currency was reintroduced.
- Peasants would pay their taxes with grain, amounting to 50 per cent of their production, while any other farm products could be sold on the open market in exchange for currency and/or consumer goods.
- The state concentrated on the production of consumer goods so that peasants would be encouraged to produce more grain which they could sell in order to get money to purchase these goods. This grain would feed industrial workers in the cities and could also be exported to other countries in return for hard currency to purchase modern industrial equipment in order to continue the **Soviet Union**'s industrialization.

The NEP continued after Lenin's death in 1924, ending in late 1928 with a new economic system introduced by Stalin.

Foreign policy

Lenin was committed to world-wide revolution, with Russia being merely the starting point in a revolutionary chain reaction, and established

🗝 KEY TERM

War Communism Soviet economic policies applied by Lenin and the Bolsheviks during the Russian Civil War.

NEP Mixed capitalist and strict Marxist economic system instituted by Lenin in 1921 to improve food and industrial production in the new communist state.

Soviet Union The Union of Soviet Socialist Republics was established in 1922, the biggest and most influential of which was Russia. Also known as the USSR.

Comintern. However, the reality was that rather than exporting Marxism to the world, Lenin's time in power was dominated by the need to overcome internal enemies in the Russian Civil War. After the civil war, Russia was in no condition to attack other nations and had no desire to provoke others to attack it either.

Stalin

Following Lenin's death in 1924, the Soviet state became even more totalitarian in nature under the rule of Josef Stalin. Stalin removed political opponents from the Politburo, replacing them with supporters. By the mid-1930s, he was all-powerful with a **cult of personality** encouraged by the government in which thousands of statues of him were erected and cities named in his honour. While he crushed all political opposition and dominated all aspects of the government and Communist Party, he introduced major economic and social changes with the **Five Year Plans** and collectivized agriculture.

Five Year Plans

Beginning in 1929, but backdated to 1928, the state focused on rapid industrialization. This ignored the production of consumer goods and concentrated on building national infrastructure such as railways, developing sources of energy such as coal, petroleum and hydroelectric power, and building huge factories in the country's interior. While not all industrial targets were reached, there is no doubt that the country had become a major economic power within a decade, helping the state to survive a major German attack in the Second World War and then propelling it to an overwhelming victory.

Collectivization

In conjunction with the Five Year Plans, **collectivization** was introduced, where peasants were forced to abandon farming private plots and instead work together in large, government-controlled farms where everyone was supposed to share their tools, seed and labour. To break any resistance to this major social and economic change, prosperous, successful farmers were eliminated through forced labour and execution. Poor peasants also resisted, but also suffered from lack of commitment, equipment, food and seed. Millions died of starvation, especially in the countryside, as the government seized crops for export and industrial workers. The USSR had to import food for most of the rest of its existence.

Foreign policy

Until involvement in the Second World War, Soviet foreign policy and initiatives concentrated mostly on preventing interference in their internal affairs by other nations through a series of non-aggression pacts. When Germany invaded the USSR in 1941, bringing it into the Second World War, Stalin was forced to take a more active approach in relations with other states.

What were the key features of the Stalinist state?

🔑 KEY TERM

Comintern A communist organization set up in Moscow in 1919 to co-ordinate the efforts of communists around the world to achieve a global revolution.

Cult of personality The active encouragement of intense devotion and adulation of a political leader, for the purpose of maintaining power.

Five Year Plan A series of economic development plans imposed by Stalin between 1928 and 1941 that concentrated all industry under state control.

Collectivization Centrally planned and managed farming where peasants farm communally on large areas of land rather than for themselves individually.

The strategic consequence of the Second World War, which ended in victory for the Soviet Union and its allies in 1945, was to allow the USSR to dominate eastern Europe, where it established communist governments in order to create a buffer zone to make the USSR secure from future threats of invasion (see Source B).

SOURCE B

Europe in 1958.

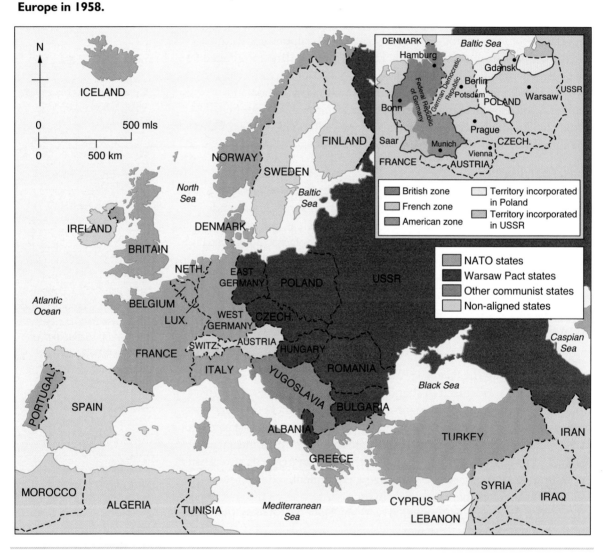

? Which areas came within the Soviet sphere of influence after the Second World War, according to Source B?

The Soviet hold over these **satellite states** was cemented by **COMECON** and, later, the **Warsaw Pact**. Both were dominated by the USSR. However, this eastern European empire was not without its cracks since Stalin and later Soviet leaders failed to impose their will on Yugoslavia.

With the Second World War over, the ideological differences between the wartime allies now came out into the open. In February 1946, Stalin made a speech in which he claimed that capitalism made another world war inevitable. In 1947, US President Truman announced plans to contain communism and, for his part, Stalin was becoming concerned about what he regarded as the premature revival of German economic power by the USA and its allies.

The division of Germany

Much of this mistrust stemmed from post-war events. After the Second World War, Germany had been divided into four zones managed by Britain, the USA, France and the USSR. Positioned within the Soviet zone, the city of Berlin was also divided into four zones administered by the four powers. In 1948, the three western zones carried out currency reform by introducing the Deutschmark. The Soviets, disapproving of any move to make Germany strong again, responded to this with the Berlin Blockade, which prevented any goods coming into the western zones of Berlin from West Germany via land. This meant that the entire population had to be supplied by air. After 11 months the blockade was called off in May 1949, but this event more than any other symbolized the beginning of the **Cold War**. In its aftermath, Germany was divided into two states: the capitalist Federal Republic (**FRG**) and the communist German Democratic Republic (**GDR**).

Asia

The East–West rift continued to spread to Asia. In January 1950, Stalin endorsed the idea of the communist leader of North Korea, Kim Il Sung, of an invasion of South Korea. Stalin's hope was that a war in the Korean peninsula would cost the USA much financially and militarily and thus weaken it militarily in other parts of the world. The war was fought to a stalemate and by 1953 the USA had suffered 142,000 fatalities in Korea, while over a million Koreans were killed. The country was divided in half, much like it had been before the conflict.

Khrushchev

By 1956, Nikita Khrushchev, a member of the post-Stalin Politburo, had taken control of the USSR. He condemned Stalin for perverting the principles of the Communist Party, and for purging some of its key figures. Khrushchev worked to rid the Soviet political system of some of the worst excesses of Stalinism as part of his project to return the USSR to 'Lenin's main road' or the essence of Marxism–Leninism, which included:

 **KEY TERM**

Satellite state A country which, while theoretically independent, is dominated by another.

COMECON A communist trading bloc established in eastern Europe in response to the Soviet perception of growing US economic influence in Europe.

Warsaw Pact A military alliance set up in 1955 between the USSR and its satellite states. The member countries were the USSR, East Germany, Poland, Czechoslovakia, Hungary, Romania, Bulgaria and Albania.

Cold War A tense 40-year strategic and ideological confrontation between the superpowers, USA and USSR, after the Second World War. It is named 'cold' because there was never a direct conflagration between the two opposing powers.

FRG Federal Republic of Germany, a capitalist state set up in 1949, amalgamating the British, US and French zones of occupation.

GDR German Democratic Republic, a communist state set up in 1949 in the Soviet zone of occupied Germany.

What did Khrushchev want to achieve?

- establishment of the political power of the working class under the leadership of the Marxist–Leninist party
- strengthening of the working class
- establishment of state ownership of the principal means of production
- socialist organization of agriculture
- planned development of the economy
- constant reference to Marxist–Leninist revolutionary theory
- defence of the socialist revolution from the attacks of capitalist, imperialistic states.

Khrushchev's economic policies

Khrushchev did make some attempt to address the fundamental issue of raising Soviet standards of living by building more houses between 1955 and 1964 and making paid holidays and medical care more widely available for Soviet workers. Nevertheless, his key domestic reforms such the **Virgin Lands Scheme**, failed to make the Soviet economy more efficient. By 1963, following two poor harvests, food shortages and rationing, there were significant social tensions. The USSR had to import wheat from Canada and the USA.

KEY TERM

Virgin Lands Scheme
Khrushchev's failed plan to farm more than 70 million acres of virgin land in Siberia and Kazakhstan in order to surpass the USA in agricultural production.

Superpower Term used to denote the USA and the USSR during the Cold War, as these were the first two nations to develop nuclear arms.

? According to Source C, how was the USSR inferior to capitalist countries?

SOURCE C

Extract from Joseph Stalin, 'Industrialization of the country and the right deviation in the C.P.S.U., November 19, 1928,' in J.V. Stalin, *Works*, Vol. 11, 1928 to March 1929, published by Foreign Languages Publishing House, Moscow, 1954, pages 257–8, 261–3. Online version found at www.fordham.edu/halsall/mod/1902lenin.asp. This text is part of the Internet Modern History Sourcebook Project by Paul Halsall at Fordham University, New York, USA. The Sourcebook is a collection of public domain and copy-permitted texts for introductory level classes in modern European and world history.

Look at the capitalist countries and you will see that their technology is not only advancing, but advancing by leaps and bounds, outstripping the old forms of industrial technique. And so we find that, on the one hand, we in our country have the most advanced system, the Soviet system, and the most advanced type of state power in the world, Soviet power, while, on the other hand, our industry, which should be the basis of socialism and of Soviet power, is extremely backward technically. Do you think that we can achieve the final victory of socialism in our country so long as this contradiction exists? What has to be done to end this contradiction? To end it, we must overtake and outstrip the advanced technology of the developed capitalist countries.

Khrushchev's foreign policy

At first, Khrushchev seemed to offer a less confrontational approach towards relations with the USA and its allies. In a nuclear age in which both **superpowers** possessed many nuclear bombs, he called for peaceful coexistence. Khrushchev, who was sometimes impulsive in character, remained convinced of the superiority of communism as a political and social system. He therefore consistently upheld Soviet military hegemony in eastern Europe. For example, when Imre Nagy's government in Hungary in 1956 seemed to be about to break away from Soviet domination, Khrushchev showed no hesitation in sending in Soviet troops to suppress this. For Khrushchev, as much as Stalin, eastern Europe remained a Soviet sphere of influence. In 1961, he also sanctioned the construction of the Berlin Wall, dividing the city to prevent the constant flow of East Germans into the western capitalist and democratic side.

However, in several Cold War crises, Khrushchev did show a pragmatic capacity to make some compromises in his stand-offs with the USA. In March 1959, he withdrew his ultimatum demanding that US troops withdraw from West Berlin and in the same year became the first Soviet leader to visit the USA. More significantly, in 1962, he proved willing to forge a compromise with US President Kennedy by removing Soviet missiles from Cuba, in return for the dismantling of US missile sites in Turkey.

By 1963 there were signs of a 'thaw' as the USSR, the USA and the UK signed a nuclear test ban treaty and the USA and the USSR set up a telephone line to resolve conflicts directly. A new, warmer era in the Cold War seemed to occur when Khrushchev was replaced as General Secretary of the Communist Party by Leonid Brezhnev, with Aleksey Kosygin as Prime Minister. Chapter 5 will discuss the extent to which the new Soviet rulers improved East–West relations.

Bolshevik Revolution, October 1917			
	Politics	**Economic and social system**	**Foreign policy**
Lenin 1917–24	One-party state: Politburo, key political body	• War Communism (until 1921) • New Economic Policy (NEP)	Comintern: world-wide revolution
Stalin 1924–53	• Purges: removal of political opponents • Cult of personality	• Five Year Plans • Collectivization	• 1930s: non-aggression pacts • 1941–5: Second World War • 1946–7: Start of Cold War • 1948–9: Berlin Blockade • 1950–3: Korean War
Khrushchev 1956–64	• Return to 'Lenin's main road' • Rejection of Stalinism	• Virgin Lands Scheme	• Peaceful coexistence • 1956: Hungarian uprising • 1961: Berlin Wall built • 1962: Cuban Missile Crisis

SUMMARY DIAGRAM

The USSR from Lenin to Brezhnev

Mao's China 1949–76

> ▶ *Key question: What were the key features of the communist state established in China up to 1976?*

On 1 October 1949, Mao Zedong's communists defeated the Nationalists after a long civil war, founding the People's Republic of China (PRC). The defeated Nationalists withdrew to the island of **Taiwan**. The PRC developed various programmes and policies to develop the state economically, while attempting to eradicate class divisions. A series of dramatic economic and social plans, often followed by Chinese Communist Party (CCP) purges, were initiated during Mao's life. After his death, the state continued to be dominated by those who had joined the CCP earliest, many of whom survived a particularly difficult ordeal known as the **Long March**.

Mao's rule of China 1949–76

As in the USSR, the most powerful political institution in the PRC was the Politburo of the CCP, whose five-man **Standing Committee** was chaired by Mao. The key government institution was the **State Council**, which possessed wide-ranging legislative and executive powers, again chaired by Mao. From 1949 onwards, the party controlled all aspects of the state and its citizens. Committee branches were established, for example, to extend state control to every neighbourhood.

Mass campaigns

One of the main features of Mao's rule was the use of mass campaigns in which the state encouraged millions to join various movements and actions. Some of these included:

- Campaigns to remove foreign residents from the PRC.
- The Five Antis Campaign against various offences such as fraud and bribery, but also to remove former Nationalists; this resulted in the deaths of many people.
- The Hundred Flowers Campaign, which encouraged people to criticize the CCP. Mao then used this to remove government officials who opposed his policies and those who had dared to criticize the government.
- Campaigns to reform agriculture by killing up to five million landlords and their families; reorganizing farmland into co-operative groups of varying sizes.
- The **Great Leap Forward**, which reorganized society throughout the PRC into communes and encouraged industrialization such as mining and iron smelting, even in areas where this was not feasible, to the neglect of agriculture. This led to the deaths of many tens of millions of people through starvation.

KEY TERM

Taiwan An island off south-east China to which Chiang Kai-shek retreated when the communists took over the mainland. It has been known as the Republic of China since 1949.

In what ways did Mao and the CCP transform China up to 1976?

KEY TERM

Long March An evacuation of southern China by the CCP in 1934 as a response to Nationalist attacks. Only 10 per cent of those beginning the march survived when it concluded a year later in northern China.

Standing Committee A small, élite decision-making body within the Politburo of the CCP.

State Council The main administrative body of the PRC government.

Great Leap Forward Ambitious and ultimately disastrous programme of industrialization and social revolution embarked on by Mao from 1958.

While Mao had been occasionally challenged by those who favoured a more ordered approach on the Soviet model, he was successfully sidelined briefly after the disaster of the Great Leap Forward. His main critics by 1958 were Liu Shaoqi and Deng Xiaoping. Liu eased Mao out of his position as Head of State in December 1958, although Mao's hold over the CCP and the **Military Affairs Commission** remained. Private agricultural plots in the countryside now began to be discreetly revived outside the co-operative system, although this did not prevent a major famine that resulted from the Great Leap Forward.

The Cultural Revolution

In the aftermath of the Great Leap Forward, the dedicated Mao supporter Lin Biao was appointed to command the People's Liberation Army (**PLA**). Lin moved to cement Mao's ideological hold over the army by compiling the quotations of Mao into the **Little Red Book**. This, and other publications, helped to lay the ideological groundwork for the cult of personality that would reach its peak during the **Cultural Revolution**. **Maoists** like Lin opposed Deng Xiaoping and Liu Shaoqi as they believed, rightly, that these men opposed Mao's version of **socialism**.

Mao encouraged a national rebellion against the central government in 1966 in an article: 'Bombard the HQ [headquarters]'. In August 1966, a Central Committee meeting called for a battle against Mao's enemies, labelled '**capitalist roaders**', and crowds of young people packed into Tiananmen Square in central Beijing chanting Mao's name. He urged students to form another mass movement to destroy the 'four olds': 'old culture, old thoughts, old customs and old habits'.

The result was social and political chaos on an unprecedented scale. Teenage cadres, known as **Red Guards**, took control of the streets, sometimes beating to death people that they regarded as 'reactionaries'. Liu Shaoqi died in 1969 in prison after being refused medical treatment. Under the direction of Mao's wife, Jiang Qing, aspects of Chinese culture were swept away. All western music was banned, as well as traditional Chinese opera. The country seemed on the verge of civil war as various groups of Red Guards competed for power.

In 1967, Mao began to rein in this anarchy. The PLA helped to bring the population back under control. Red Guards were encouraged to go and live in the countryside in order to redirect their revolutionary energies and over 12 million did so by 1972. The Cultural Revolution was Mao's attempt to regain power over the entire CCP by removing all possible rivals, in particular Liu; many other government officials were imprisoned, sent to work in factories or on farms, or were killed.

In 1971, Lin Biao died in a plane crash while fleeing the PRC to escape punishment from Mao; Mao believed he had too much power in the PLA. The PLA, however, was now a powerful political force with many generals in the Politburo.

 **KEY TERM**

Military Affairs Commission A key political body which controlled the People's Liberation Army.

PLA The People's Liberation Army, the military force of the CCP, which became the army of the Chinese state in 1949.

Little Red Book The informal name commonly used in the West for the pocket-size edition of *Quotations from Chairman Mao Zedong*, where he summarizes his wisdom.

Cultural Revolution Mao's attempt from 1966 to revolutionize Chinese society and the CCP, while at the same time dealing with political rivals.

Maoist A dedicated supporter of Mao's radical policies.

Socialism Political and economic system in which a nation's resources and means of production are controlled by the government to prevent extremes in wealth or poverty.

Capitalist roader The epithet used against those who criticized Mao's interpretation of communism.

Red Guards Maoist students who were trained to lead attacks against class enemies. They were the most dedicated supporters of the Cultural Revolution.

Mao and the control of the CCP

As he aged, Mao began to plan for a time when he would no longer be in control. Through the 1970s, he continued to maintain a collective party leadership, rejecting the cult of personality by having some of his statues taken down. He also analysed international affairs, dividing the world into three groups: underdeveloped nations, developed nations, and the USA and the USSR – the two superpowers. China's position was to be the leader of the Third World, another name for the underdeveloped group. Mao supported closer relations with the USA, receiving President Richard Nixon in Beijing in 1972, since he feared the USSR, which aimed to be the world's leading communist state at the PRC's expense.

Mao eventually re-established pragmatic politicians like Deng Xiaoping, who had been labelled as a 'capitalist roader' at the height of the Cultural Revolution. By 1975, Deng was Vice-Chairman of the CCP and a member of the CCP Standing Committee. More pragmatic communists, such as **Zhou Enlai** and Deng Xiaoping were far more popular with the public than supporters of the Cultural Revolution like Jiang Qing. When Zhou died in January 1976, it was used as an opportunity by many to go to Tiananmen Square to lay wreaths and make speeches praising his leadership, implicitly criticizing those who had opposed Zhou and Deng. These actions on the part of ordinary people reached a crescendo in early April 1976 during the Qing Ming festival, a point in the Chinese calendar when the dead are traditionally commemorated. These crowds were dismissed as '**rightists**' by the CCP's leadership and dispersed by force in the **Tiananmen Incident** (see page 24). Two days later, Deng Xiaoping was removed from political office. The CCP had become more divided.

Mao died in 1976, rightly credited as the creator of the PRC. It was not immediately clear who would replace him.

(see page 24)

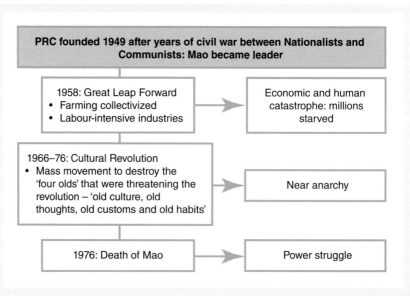

KEY TERM

Zhou Enlai Leading figure in the CCP, premier (1949–76) and foreign minister (1949–58).

Rightist The more moderate wing of the CCP leadership led by Zhou Enlai until his death and thereafter by Deng Xiaoping.

Tiananmen Incident Political disturbances in Beijing following the death of Zhou Enlai (not to be confused with the 1989 student protests).

SUMMARY DIAGRAM

Mao's China 1949–76

Chapter summary

Communism in the USSR and China

In the nineteenth century, Karl Marx developed a radical alternative to the capitalist social and economic order. He believed that the destruction of the middle classes' private businesses and property was inevitable and desirable. Instead, a state dominated by the working class, in which economic power was no longer in the hands of the middle class, would come into being. From this socialist state would evolve a communist utopia in which money would no longer be necessary.

Marxist ideas first began to be put into practice in Russia after 1917. A one-party state evolved in which occasional compromises with capitalism were possible, as shown by Lenin's NEP. Stalin dominated the politics of the USSR after Lenin's death in 1924, introducing a series of Five Year Plans and collectivization to bring the economic life of the country completely under state control. Critics were silenced through a series of purges. The Second World War led to the deaths of millions of Soviet soldiers and civilians but the defeat of Germany allowed Stalin and his successors to dominate eastern Europe. Khrushchev condemned Stalinism in 1956, but the failure of his economic reforms meant that major domestic problems would confront his successors.

Mao Zedong's victory in the Chinese Civil War in 1949 led to the establishment of a communist state in China. As in the USSR, class enemies like landowners were dealt with harshly and Five Year Plans were used to try and achieve rapid industrialization. The population was controlled through the use of mass campaigns. Mao's attempt during the Great Leap Forward to achieve an economic breakthrough, as well as a fundamental shift towards a communal way of life, was a catastrophic failure. A famine resulted in millions of dead. This led to the temporary political eclipse of Mao, but the Cultural Revolution allowed him to stage a spectacular political comeback. Pragmatic rivals like Liu Shaoqi were purged and the control of the party élite was shaken. For a time, there was anarchy in China, but by the time of Mao's death, it was clear that there would be a struggle for power between Maoists like Jiang Qing and more pragmatic figures like Deng Xiaoping.

CHAPTER 2

The struggle for power following Mao Zedong's death

This chapter analyses Mao's legacy and the power struggle within the Chinese Communist Party that took place in the aftermath of his death in 1976, including the ideological and factional struggles. You need to consider the following questions throughout this chapter:

✪ Who were the Gang of Four and why did they fall from power so quickly?

✪ What were the key policies of Hua Guofeng and why was he not able to establish a permanent hold on power?

✪ How was Deng Xiaoping able to re-emerge as a dominant force in Chinese politics?

 **KEY TERM**

Gang of Four A term allegedly coined by Mao himself to describe a group of influential leftist politicians who became powerful as radical activists defending strict Maoism in the mid-1960s during the Cultural Revolution and continued in power until after Mao's death in 1976.

How influential were the Gang of Four?

 **KEY TERM**

Leftist The more extreme wing of the CCP, typified by the Gang of Four, committed to a radical interpretation of Mao's ideas.

Maoism A form of Marxism developed by Mao that advocated development of communism through the peasantry with elements of Chinese nationalism.

 ## The Gang of Four and their fall from power

▶ **Key question:** Who were the Gang of Four and why did they fall from power so quickly?

Following Mao's death on 9 September 1976, there was a struggle for power, principally between Deng Xiaoping and the **Gang of Four**. This section looks at the Gang of Four's influence and how they were defeated.

The Gang of Four in power

Who were the Gang of Four?

The Gang of Four were four **leftist** members of the Politburo who had been the most enthusiastic supporters of the Cultural Revolution and tolerated no criticism of **Maoism** whatsoever. They were Jiang Qing, Zhang Chunqiao, Yao Wenyuan and Wang Hongwen.

Jiang Qing

Jiang, a former film star and Shanghai socialite, was Mao's fourth wife. She consolidated political power by adopting an extreme Maoist stance. She played a key role in encouraging a rejection of Confucianism and destroying any work of art and literature that did not adhere strictly to Maoism during the Cultural Revolution (see page 19). From 1969, as Mao's health was declining, she was a member of the Politburo in charge of artistic matters, ideology and propaganda.

Zhang Chunqiao

Zhang had previously been the head of the Communist Party in Shanghai during the Cultural Revolution and had supported radical groups like the **Red Rebels**. He became a member of the Politburo in 1973, and the inner-circle Politburo Standing Committee.

Yao Wenyuan

Yao was a CCP journalist. In the 1960s, he had supported Mao and Jiang Qing in devising a response to an opera that had subtly criticized Mao's actions in the Great Leap Forward called 'Hai Rui Dismissed from Office'. In November 1965, he wrote a critical review of the opera in the major Shanghai newspaper *Wenhui Bao*. He was then elected to the Politburo in 1969 where he worked on propaganda.

KEY TERM

Red Rebels During the Cultural Revolution, young people who were not accepted into the Red Guards joined radical splinter groups called Red Rebels.

SOURCE A

Excerpt from 'Reassessing the starting point of the Cultural Revolution' by Hao Ping, *China Review International*, March 1996, Vol. 3, Issue 1, pages 66–86. Professor Hao, of Beijing University, has written about the start of the Cultural Revolution in China. *China Review International* has been published by the University of Hawaii, USA, since 1994 and reviews works regarding China from all over the world.

It is now well accepted by scholars both in China and abroad that the publication of Yao Wenyuan's article 'On the New Historical Peking Opera Hairui Dismissed from Office' in Wenhui Bao *on November 10, 1965, was the beginning of the Cultural Revolution. This point of view was first expressed by Mao Zedong in 1967 when he met with a military delegation from Mali.*

According to Source A, what started the Cultural Revolution?

Wang Hongwen

Wang was a former Shanghai textile worker who had come to prominence during the Cultural Revolution as a trade union leader. He was the youngest member of the Gang. He accepted that the aims of the Cultural Revolution could not be achieved without purging opponents. He was elected to the Politburo in 1973, and was Party Vice-Chairman at 39 years of age. Jiang Qing insistently pushed for him to succeed Mao.

The Gang of Four's ideology

The Gang of Four's members were passionate believers in Maoist ideology. They saw dangerous signs of 'bourgeois' thought in the ideas of Deng Xiaoping and Zhou Enlai, powerful figures in the CCP. Deng and Zhou questioned some aspects of orthodox communist doctrine and felt that Chinese communism needed to adapt in order to survive.

To the Gang of Four, Deng's and Zhou's support for export-led growth and the import of technology from the capitalist west, as well as their emphasis on urban industrial development, seemed to lack the ideological purity and emphasis on class struggle of the Cultural Revolution period. Instead, the Gang of Four, whose ideas many historians refer to as 'leftist', had a vision of a decentralized, self-sufficient economy of communes in which the revolutionary will of the masses, rather than technical expertise, would ensure progress.

The Gang of Four's influence

The heyday of the Gang of Four's influence spanned from 1965 and the start of the Cultural Revolution (see page 19) until 1976 after the death of Mao. As long as Mao was alive, the Gang of Four remained a very influential faction as it became responsible for propaganda, writing in the press about the necessity for purging critics of Maoism and inciting Red Guards to increasingly violent attacks. Its incendiary rhetoric was particularly vicious when directed at Deng Xiaoping and Zhou Enlai, two leading figures in the CCP. The Gang's slogans and political campaigns were also directed at party and army leaders perceived to be non-supportive of Mao or, ultimately, to be potential challenges to Mao's leadership.

The Gang of Four's influence was particularly strong in its links to local political leaders who led persecutions and trials in the name of strict Maoist political doctrine. However, even as Mao's health deteriorated, its main influence remained in the propaganda sphere rather than in areas of policy like transportation and economics.

The Tiananmen Incident

In January 1976, Zhou Enlai died. The Gang of Four tried to downplay his death, denouncing further displays of public mourning after the official memorial ceremony on 15 January. This led to mass demonstrations from people who insisted on honouring Zhou as a beloved statesman and, on 4 April 1976, hundreds of thousands of demonstrators gathered in Beijing's Tiananmen Square, ostensibly to mourn Zhou. Hundreds of demonstrators were beaten and arrested by police, although none were killed in what became known as the Tiananmen Incident. The Gang of Four used all means of propaganda to denounce the peaceful demonstrations of public fervour for Zhou and was instrumental in mobilizing security forces that violently beat the demonstrators in Tiananmen Square.

Power struggle

Deng, jockeying for a future leadership position, became increasingly the focus of the Gang's criticism. With propaganda under its control, the Gang of Four published articles and designed posters denouncing Deng as sympathetic to capitalism; his pragmatic economic policies were dismissed in official propaganda as capitalist and 'poisonous weeds'. Jiang Qing herself was influential enough to sway Mao to secure the temporary downfall of Deng through accusing him of being part of a conspiracy that had caused the demonstrations after Zhou's death. In April 1976, the Politburo officially dismissed him as Vice-Premier, and as Vice-Chairman of the CCP. He was removed from the Central Military Committee, and Mao was quoted as saying 'Leave him his party card to show to his descendants'.

Under the determined leadership of Jiang Qing, the Gang of Four began to push strongly for Wang Hongwen to succeed Mao, whose health was deteriorating. Even so, Mao did not relinquish power to Jiang Qing or the Gang of Four, or accept that Wang Hongwen would succeed him. Instead, he promoted Hua Guofeng, a mild political leader from Hunan, and named him Premier.

Public sentiment against the Gang's high-handed ways was increasingly present in local poetry and comments. A power struggle between the PLA under Defence Minister Marshal Ye Jianying (a Deng supporter) and the Gang of Four, with control of some military factions and an armed band in Shanghai, now began. Hua Guofeng remained aloof at first.

The Gang of Four's fall from power

On 9 September 1976, Mao died. He was buried in the Great Hall of the People in Tiananmen Square in Beijing. On 18 September 1976, Jiang Qing stood directly behind Premier Hua Guofeng while he delivered the official eulogy at Mao's funeral. In terms of political symbolism, this seemed to suggest that Jiang Qing was influential, but not pre-eminent. At the first Politburo meeting after the death of Mao, nobody stood up when Jiang Qing entered the room and other senior communists talked among themselves while she attempted to speak. Less than a month later, the Gang of Four was arrested.

> **Why did this most radical faction in the CCP lose influence?**

The Gang of Four's rapid descent from power

As Mao's official widow, despite their estrangement, Jiang Qing insisted on handling Mao's will. With Mao gone, she was now refused in her demands. As she mustered armed support, Jiang openly criticized Hua, who was supported by Marshal Ye and other key military figures in the PLA. In October 1976, at the meeting of the Standing Committee of the Politburo, Zhang Chunqiao, Yao Wenyuan and Wang Hongwen were arrested on the orders of Hua Guofeng. Jiang Qing was later arrested in her home, accused of planning to assassinate Hua.

The fact that the Gang of Four's downfall came so soon after the death of Mao suggests that without his support, its power base was very fragile. The Gang of Four lacked support in the 16-member Politburo and in the PLA. Only in Shanghai did security forces seem sympathetic to the Gang of Four, but this was not sufficient on its own. Beijing, rather than Shanghai, was the real centre of political power. Public sentiment against the Gang's imperious ways and total control of propaganda had made it most unpopular. Ultimately, by 1976, most **cadres**, and also the High Command of the PLA, wanted a return to some semblance of political normality after the chaos of the Cultural Revolution, whose biggest proponents were the Gang of Four members. All of these factors aided the downfall of the Gang of Four.

 **KEY TERM**

Cadres Professional revolutionaries willing to devote all their time and effort to the communist cause.

KEY TERM

Show trial A trial that is staged for the public, usually with the verdict decided well in advance.

The Gang of Four's trial

The Gang's members were put on trial in 1980. In an atmosphere that appeared at times to be close to that of a **show trial,** they were accused of various crimes. All four were blamed for the Cultural Revolution and for other destructive actions. Jiang Qing remained defiant throughout, insisting that during the Cultural Revolution she had simply acted on Mao's orders. As she was dragged from the courtroom, she shouted an old Cultural Revolution slogan, 'to rebel is justified'. She was clearly unrepentant. Zhang Chunqiao, too, refused to acknowledge the authority of the court to try him; Yao Wenyuan and Wang Hongwen made confessions. Jiang Qing and Zhang

? What is the importance of Source B in understanding the PRC after Mao?

SOURCE B

Jiang Qing, leader of the Gang of Four, fourth wife of Mao Zedong and radical supporter of the Cultural Revolution at her trial, 26 November 1980. Two armed guards flank her.

Chunqiao were sentenced to death, although this was commuted to life imprisonment. Jiang Qing remained in prison until her death by suicide in 1991. Zhang died of cancer in 2005. Yao Wenyuan was sentenced to 20 years and was released in 1996, while Wang Hongwen was sentenced for life and died in 1992.

SOURCE C

Excerpt from *The Search for Modern China* edited by Pei-kai Cheng, Michael Lestz and Jonathan D. Spence, published by W.W. Norton, New York, 1999, pages 615–16. Cheng is a Professor of History at Pace University in New York, USA. Lestz is Professor of History and Chairman of the History Department at Trinity College, in Connecticut, USA. Spence is a Professor of History at Yale University, USA.

All four radical leaders of the Cultural Revolution were suddenly arrested without warning by Hua Guofeng's orders on October 6th, and placed in detention at an unknown location. They were accused of having constituted a clique or 'Gang of Four' and of having persevered in their evil conduct despite stern warnings from Mao himself ... Cumulatively, they were accused of almost every possible crime in the political book, including factional attacks on Zhou Enlai forging Mao's statements, diluting the criticisms of Lin Biao to save their own skin, organizing their own armed forces ... [and] attacking worthy government cadres.

> What are the values and limitations of Source C in showing why the Gang of Four fell from power?

Who were in the Gang of Four?	• Jiang Qing • Zhang Chunqiao • Yao Wenyuan • Wang Hongwen
What did it believe?	• Maoist ideology • Decentralized, self-sufficient economy of communes • The revolutionary will of the masses would ensure progress
What influence did it have?	• Control of propaganda • Strong links to local political leaders • Incited Red Guard attacks
Why was it defeated?	• Tiananmen Incident • Mao promoted Hua Guofeng to Premier • Mao's death led to power struggle: Hua Guofeng succeeded him • Gang of Four lacked a strong political powerbase • Hua Guofeng ordered arrest for planning to assassinate him
What happened to the members?	• Show trial 1980 • Jiang, Zhang and Wang: life imprisonment • Yao: imprisoned until 1996

SUMMARY DIAGRAM

The Gang of Four and their fall from power

Hua Guofeng in power 1976–81

> ▶ *Key question:* What were the key policies of Hua Guofeng and why was he not able to establish a permanent hold on power?

The key policies of Hua Guofeng

How successful were Hua Guofeng's policies?

The main beneficiary of the downfall of the Gang of Four was Hua Guofeng. He was born into a peasant family in 1921 and had come to political prominence between 1949 and 1970, organizing collectivization in Hunan Province and providing Mao with favourable reports on the implementation of the Great Leap Forward there (see page 18). He was appointed to the Politburo in 1973, and in April 1976, he took over Zhou Enlai's role of State Premier. Mao perhaps hoped that he might be an uncontroversial figure committed to preserving his legacy. He allegedly said to Hua, after the Tiananmen Incident, that 'with you in charge I am at ease'.

However, Mao also commented that one of Hua's greatest political assets was that 'he is not stupid'! Despite such a mild endorsement, on 7 October 1976, he was appointed Chairman of the **Central Committee** and became the most powerful man in the PRC. He was formally endorsed by the 1977 **Party Congress** as Mao's successor. Yet he was in an unstable position. Although he had the Gang of Four arrested and blamed for the excesses of the Cultural Revolution, he had actually risen politically during the Cultural Revolution.

The 'Two Whatevers'

In power as Premier of the PRC, Hua Guofeng was slow to reinstate Deng to his previous party leadership positions and decided his best recourse was to remain devoted to the legacy of Mao, a policy known as the 'Two Whatevers'. In the words of Hua himself, 'whatever decisions Mao made we firmly support, whatever Mao instructed we unwaveringly follow'. Hua used an extensive propaganda campaign by posters to indicate clearly that he was Mao's chosen successor. This included publicly supporting a Mao Memorial in Tiananmen Square and publishing more of Mao's writings. He promoted festivals, dances, concerts and other forms of public displays of affection for Mao's memory and his own loyalty to Mao.

The Ten Year Plan

Hua did not just cultivate the Mao image, however. In February 1978, he pushed through an ambitious Ten Year Plan. This economic programme promoted over 100 projects in various areas of the economy, such as steel production, oil, electricity and transportation. However, after years of low production due to the chaos of the Cultural Revolution and the uncertainty

🔑 KEY TERM

Central Committee A key body within the CCP with membership of up to 300 people meeting at least twice a year, electing new members of the Politburo.

Party Congress A representative body of the entire membership of the CCP which usually meets every four to five years to formally elect the Central Committee.

SOURCE D

Propaganda poster of 1977, entitled 'Laying the Foundation' showing Hua Guofeng, with Marshal Ye at his side, laying of the foundations of Mao's mausoleum in Tiananmen Square, Beijing.

What information is conveyed by Source D about Hua?

surrounding Mao's illness and death, there was not enough revenue to support these ambitious projects. In a marked departure from Maoism, foreign investment from the capitalist world, in particular Germany and Japan, was now permitted. The plan also emphasized traditional aspects of Maoist ideology such as the role of the masses' revolutionary fervour in bringing about modernization.

Economic reality fell short of expectations. Targets, such as increasing steel production from the 21 million tonnes produced in 1973 to 60 million by 1985 and eventually 180 million tonnes by 1999, were not met. Optimistic assessments of increased oil production also proved to be unfounded. One reason for not being able to reach the targets set in the Ten Year Plan was that, in the aftermath of the Cultural Revolution, higher education in particular had been disrupted, with many students having had their studies interrupted. The consequence of this was that by the late 1970s, China lacked the professionals and trained experts necessary to make the plan a success.

Other initiatives

Hua's tenure as Premier included other initiatives as well. He:

- promoted family planning in China, which he voiced in the Fifth National People's Congress in 1980, to enforce a **one-child policy** for Chinese citizens (see page 78)
- released and **rehabilitated** nearly 100,000 prisoners by 1978 and 200,000 more in the 1980s, including high party officials supportive of Deng, artists and writers imprisoned during the Cultural Revolution and other political prisoners.

Former Chinese President Liu Shaoqi (see page 19) and his wife Wang Guangmei had a particularly poignant story (see Source E).

SOURCE E

Excerpt from 'Wang Guangmei's personal photo album (III) the days with Lui Shaoqi' by Luo Haiyan, 10 December 2010 in the online news service *China Today* at www.chinatoday.com.cn/ctenglish/se/txt/2010-11/04/ content_309588.htm. Luo Haiyan is a senior editor with the PRC's Xinhua News Agency, vice-president and editor at Xinhua Publishing House, and a published author of political and biographical books on China. *China Today* is published by the government of the PRC with the stated goal of presenting a positive image of the PRC to the outside world and has been published in various formats and under various titles since 1949.

But in 1967, early in the political turbulence of the cultural revolution, Wang Guangmei and [her husband] President Liu Shaoqi were criticized and denounced. Facing violent storms of humiliation and slander, she bravely stood by her husband, putting up firm resistance and never wavering in her trust in justice. If we say that Wang Guangmei's early love for Liu Shaoqi was born of a young intellectual's admiration for a full-time revolutionary, then their support of each other in a time of need and seeing each other through thick and thin could be called a model for revolutionary couples.

On September 13, 1967, Wang Guangmei was officially arrested. Two months later she was jailed in Qincheng Prison, and confined for more than 11 years. Liu Shaoqi was persecuted to death in 1969.

Immediately on her release on December 22, 1978, Wang Guangmei set about rehabilitating Liu Shaoqi's political reputation. In 1980, the Central Committee of the Chinese Communist Party announced the restoration of Liu Shaoqi's reputation, and held a solemn memorial meeting in the Great Hall of the People in Beijing, where Deng Xiaoping delivered a memorial speech. On May 19, Wang Guangmei and her sons and daughters scattered Liu Shaoqi's ashes on the Yellow Sea.

KEY TERM

One-child policy A policy introduced by the Chinese government to try to force married couples to have only one child to prevent population growth.

Rehabilitated Restored to previously held party and government positions.

? According to Source E, how was Liu Shaoqi's reputation restored?

Hua Guofeng's fall from power

The failure of Hua's Ten Year Plan certainly exposed him to criticisms from other senior communists. This weakened him politically, but his position as Mao's chosen successor was threatened once Deng returned to his party positions from Guangzhou in Guangdong Province. In the end, the loss of a political power base contributed more to Hua's downfall than his economic policies.

> Why was Hua Guofeng not able to establish a permanent hold on power?

SOURCE F

Excerpt from 'China's New Economic Policy under Hua Guofeng: Party consensus and party myths' by Frederick Teiwes and Warren Sun in *The China Journal*, July 2011, Issue 66, page 23. Dr Teiwes is Emeritus Professor of Chinese Politics at the University of Sydney and Dr Sun is a Professor at the School of Asian Languages and Studies at Monash University. Both universities are in Australia. They have collaborated in writing about Chinese politics for the Australian Research Council. *The China Journal* has been published by the Australian National University for over 30 years and features articles on various topics regarding modern China.

According to Source F, why was Hua considered politically weak?

Where Hua would have gone in policy terms had he retained authority is moot but, with regard to the early manifestations of reform, he was clearly a key supporter. In a striking private appraisal in the context of the April 1979 economic work conference, [CCP Chairman] Hu Yaobang observed that [CCP Vice-Chairman] Chen Yun, who was just recovering from health problems, had said little and Deng was preoccupied with non-economic matters, while 'Chairman Hua has a comparatively profound understanding of the necessity for economic system reform.' In any case, Hua's weakness did not lie in his policy program, and was certainly not due to a rigid adherence to 'whatever' Mao had endorsed. Rather, it was due to his low historical standing within the CCP. Compared to Deng and Chen Yun, who were regarded as true heroes of the 1949 revolution, Hua was a mere '1938 cadre' who came into the Party relatively late in its struggle. Without historical credentials, he was not able to prevail when events turned against him. This, however, does not contradict the fact that in economic policy, and on most other policy issues as well, Hua and Deng stood together in 1977–78.

Hua's weak political control

In August 1977, the Eleventh Party Congress met and confirmed Deng's rehabilitation to Vice-Premier and Vice-Chairman of the CCP. Deng was now also head of the PLA, further increasing his power. Deng was also given charge of implementing the Four Modernizations originally set out by Zhou Enlai in 1975 to give a new impulse to industry, agriculture, defence and technology. In addition, the Eleventh Party Congress announced the end of the Cultural Revolution, and Hua's past as Security Chief during the Cultural Revolution and his commitment to Maoism were beginning to seem out of step with the rest of the party.

Hua lost further support by the way in which he sought to emulate Mao by creating a cult of personality with an intense propaganda campaign as well as changing his hairstyle to resemble Mao's. At a time when rivals of Mao, like Deng, were staging a political comeback, such actions did nothing but increase Hua's political isolation. Deng and his allies began to portray Hua as blindly following Maoist ideas, regardless of whether or not they actually worked. At the **CCP Plenum** in 1978, the Tiananmen Incident was retrospectively declared to be 'revolutionary'. This was done to rectify the original CCP declaration in 1976 that it was 'counter-revolutionary' and therefore had had to be suppressed by security forces. This placed Hua, who had been responsible as Minister of Public Security for the repression of these protests after the death of Zhou Enlai, in a very awkward position indeed.

KEY TERM

CCP Plenum Discussion forums within the Central Committee usually guided by members of the Politburo.

Hua resigns

Hua continued to lose control of various divisions of the government. He was not purged, but his political power shrank rapidly. The Politburo was divided into three factions: Hua's, Deng's and Marshal Ye's, the latter of which often acted as the decisive faction in support of Deng. By 1980, isolated and under attack in Politburo meetings, Hua was no longer really a figure of any importance in PRC politics. A final political blow came in 1981 when the imprisonment of the Gang of Four further discredited those associated with Maoism, like Hua. Hua, a realistic man, recognized he no longer had political allies and resigned as Chairman of the CCP and Chairman of the Military Committee in 1981. Hu Yaobang, an associate of Deng, became Premier and Chairman, while Deng became Chairman of the Military Committee in June 1981. Hua was quietly demoted and died in relative obscurity in 2008.

? According to Source G, how significant a role did Hua play in Chinese history?

SOURCE G

Excerpt from *China Under Communism* by Alan Lawrance, published by Routledge, London, 1998, page 97. Lawrance was Visiting Research Fellow at the University of Hertfordshire in the UK and author of *Mao Zedong* (1991) and *China's Foreign Relations Since 1949* (1975).

How did Hua become Party Chairman when Mao died and survive at the head of the political system until 1981? He presided during a period of fundamental change but his place in history has been overshadowed, as his power was undermined, by the rise of Deng Xiaoping. If Hua's career as Chairman is described as one of slow failure, at least he can be credited with holding the ring during the transitional period when ideology gave way to a new era of pragmatic reforms.

What were the CCP's Politburo's criticisms of Hua?

Analysis of Hua's rule

Regarding economic policy, Hua recognized the importance of western technology and investment in revitalizing the PRC economy. It should also be noted that unlike more radical leftists, like the Gang of Four, he showed that he could work with pragmatic moderates like Deng and therefore a prolonged bout of CCP infighting was avoided. This occurred as China's politics and economics tried to find a new way to improve life for its citizens without giving up some important tenets of Maoism. In analysing Hua's tenure in office, it is important to view the official criticism of him by the Politburo of the CCP (see Source H).

SOURCE H

Excerpt from 'Hu Yaobang: New Chairman of the Chinese Communist Party' by Shu-shin Wang, *Asian Survey*, Vol. XXII, No. 9, September 1982, pages 811–12. Dr Shu-shin Wang is currently Professor of Political Science at Northeastern Illinois University, Chicago, Illinois, USA. *Asian Survey* is published by the University of California Press in the USA, covering international relations throughout Asia.

At an enlarged Politburo meeting in mid-November 1980, Hua was severely criticized for his incorrect commitments, including:

(1) *long-term persistence in the 'two whateverisms';*
(2) *implementation of a 'leftist' economic policy …*
(3) *resistance to Deng's political line that 'practice' was 'the sole criterion of truth';*
(4) *adoption of an ambiguous attitude toward the correction of false charges, wrong sentences, and frame-ups;*
(5) *opposition to the reversal of … the Tiananmen Incident;*
(6) *prevention of Deng and Chen Yun's rehabilitation; and*
(7) *creation of his own cult of personality.*

On the basis of these defects, the meeting declared that Hua's contribution to the overthrow of the Gang of Four should be affirmed, but he was no longer fit to be party chairman and chairman of the CCP Military Affairs Commission. Hua offered his resignation to the meeting and it was quickly accepted.

What can be inferred from Sources F (page 31) and H about the reasons for Hua Guofeng's downfall? Discuss the relative importance of economic and political reasons.

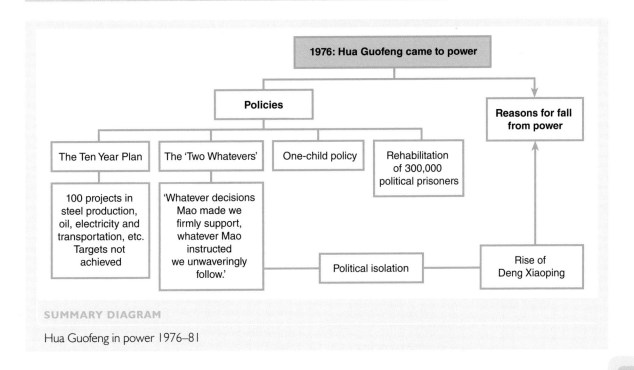

SUMMARY DIAGRAM

Hua Guofeng in power 1976–81

The re-emergence of Deng Xiaoping 1973–8

▶ *Key question: How was Deng Xiaoping able to re-emerge as a dominant force in Chinese politics?*

Deng Xiaoping was a long-time member of the CCP. His fortunes varied while Mao was alive but he was able to take control of the state within a few years after Mao's death, for a variety of reasons.

How did Deng survive the Cultural Revolution?

The political career of Deng Xiaoping 1973–6

Deng Xiaoping had been an influential member of the CCP since 1923. He was a veteran of the Long March (see page 18) and the Chinese Civil War and had been a key member of the ruling élite, especially in the period of reconstruction following the Great Leap Forward. Along with Liu Shaoqi (see page 19) he had been a victim of the Gang of Four during the Cultural Revolution and condemned as a 'capitalist roader'. For being critical of Mao's policies, Deng and his wife were exiled to Jiangxi Province in 1969 and placed under house arrest. Their son, a university physics student, had been badly beaten by Red Guards. Only in 1971 was he returned to Deng and his wife, paralysed. Deng's other children, who had been exiled in the countryside, were slowly allowed to return to their parents.

Deng was brought back into frontline politics by Mao in 1973, following the death of Lin Biao, Defence Minister between 1969 and 1971, and thought to be Mao's chosen heir at the time (see page 19). This was partly due to the influence of Zhou Enlai. By 1975, Deng had been appointed Vice-Premier and a member of the Standing Committee. He was also Vice-Chairman of the CCP and Chief of Staff of the armed forces.

Deng was mostly quiet about his years of exile and his family losses. His official biography in the *China Daily* is excerpted in Source I.

Deng suffered a brief setback in the aftermath of the Tiananmen Incident. The fact that he delivered the eulogy at Zhou's funeral led to his being labelled as a 'rightist' by Maoists in the Politburo and he was stripped of his political posts. However, Mao and the Gang of Four were not powerful enough to get rid of Deng entirely, especially as Deng enjoyed the support of powerful figures such as the Defence Minister, Marshal Ye Jianying.

SOURCE I

Excerpt from a biography of Deng Xiaoping from *China Daily* online at www.chinadaily.com.cn/english/doc/2004-06/25/content_342508.htm (25 June 2004). *China Daily* is one of the PRC's five top state news sites. Its purpose is to inform foreign readers in English of the latest news and background about the PRC.

In October 1969, when Lin Biao, in an attempt to seize party and state leadership, issued his 'No. 1 order' to prepare against war, Deng Xiaoping was sent under escort to Xinjian County, Jiangxi Province. Having already been dismissed from all his posts, he was taken to do manual labour at the county's tractor repairing plant every morning. He worked as a fitter, as he had learned to do in France in his youth, and found himself as proficient at the job as before. Living with him were his wife Zhuo Lin, who was often ill, and his aged stepmother Xia Bogen, the three of them having only one another to depend on. It was Deng Xiaoping who, at the age of 65, took care of cleaning the room, chopping the wood and breaking up the coal. When Deng Pufang [Deng's son] became paralyzed and needed help, after repeated requests by his parents and grandmother, he was sent to live with them; then his father took on the additional responsibility of nursing him. During this period Deng Xiaoping made the best use of his spare time, often reading late into the night. He read a great number of Marxist-Leninist works and many other books both Chinese and foreign, ancient and modern. The ordeal in Xinjian lasted for three years.

In September 1971 the collapse of Lin Biao's plot for a counter-revolutionary coup and his death in an air crash eventually led to the rehabilitation of Deng Xiaoping. In 1972 Mao Zedong began to consider letting Deng resume his work, and the following year, with the support of Zhou Enlai, he was restored to his post as Vice-Premier of the State Council.

> Analyse the language of this biography in Source I. What can you deduce about Deng's ordeal in Jiangxi Province?

The political career of Deng Xiaoping 1976–81

A sign of how much support Deng had among the cadres and the party hierarchy, in the aftermath of Mao's death, is that by 1977 the ***People's Daily*** was running pro-Deng articles. There were also pro-Deng demonstrations in Tiananmen Square on the first anniversary of the death of Zhou Enlai.

Deng's political comeback was sealed in 1977 when the Eleventh Congress of the CCP formally announced the end of the Cultural Revolution and he was granted all his previous posts (see page 31). Hua probably helped to restore him with the hope of gaining his support in the CCP.

What actually happened was that over the next few years Deng and the 'rightists' worked quietly to undermine Hua and the '**whateverists**'.

> How was Deng able to outmanoeuvre his political enemies?

 **KEY TERM**

People's Daily A Chinese newspaper with close links to the Central Committee of the CCP.

Whateverists A term used to describe supporters of Hua Guofeng who believed that Mao's economic and political legacy must be maintained.

Symbolic of the increasing dominance of Deng's faction was undoubtedly the Third Plenum of the Eleventh Central Committee of the CCP in December 1978 when the official line on the Tiananmen Incident was changed (see page 32) and victims of Mao's purges such as the former Defence Minister, Peng Dehuai, were formally rehabilitated. For the first time, it was admitted that Mao had not been immune from making mistakes. The economy was weak as a result of the Cultural Revolution since much production had ceased. Deng's famous quote 'poverty is not socialism' gave impulse to making Chinese economic development the top priority. Deng walked a fine line between criticizing Mao and at the same time reaffirming the Maoist dictum 'practice is the sole criterion of truth'.

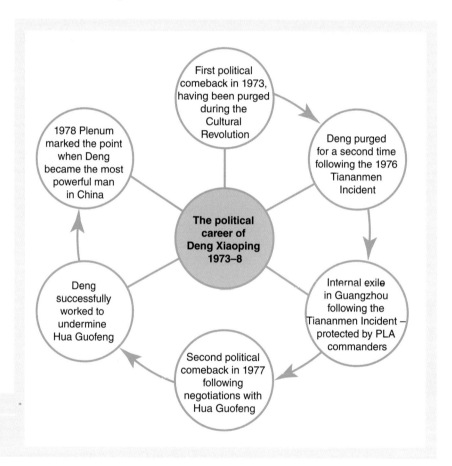

SUMMARY DIAGRAM

The re-emergence of Deng Xiaoping 1973–8

Chapter summary

The struggle for power following Mao Zedong's death

As Mao grew older and ill, he was increasingly under the influence of the 'leftist' faction of the CCP led by his wife Jiang Qing, who believed in doctrinaire Maoism, extolling agriculture and peasants and creating a vast propaganda machine to continue forcibly to support Mao's policies, regardless of their obvious failure. The failures were blamed by the 'leftists' on the 'rightist' factions. These were called 'capitalist roaders' or those who wanted China to follow a capitalist road to development, because the 'leftists' felt their emphasis on industrial and technological economic development smacked of capitalism.

The 'rightists,' most notably Deng Xiaoping and Liu Shaoqi, lost out from 1966 to 1976 during the purges of the Cultural Revolution. The campaign against any criticism of Mao was given free rein with the promotion of the radical Red Guards by Jiang Qing and the Gang of Four. Mao supported them, fearing the 'rightist' faction and aware that he was losing control. Still, in an effort to steer clear of the two factions, Mao decided on the relatively obscure, but loyal, Hua Guofeng as his successor.

The key event in the Gang's downfall, however, came with the Tiananmen Incident in April of 1976, when masses of demonstrators thronged the square to honour Zhou Enlai who had died in January. The Gang accused Deng of encouraging this and succeeded in having him removed temporarily, but by the end of the year Hua, after Mao's death, had the Gang of Four arrested and later tried and convicted to life sentences or long-term imprisonment.

Hua held on to power by promoting adherence to Maoist dogma, or the policy of 'whatever' Mao said was the right way to follow. He did display some flexibility in promoting the unsuccessful Ten Year Plan to advance industrial development. He slowly lost his positions in the CCP and PLA, while Deng Xiaoping emerged as the dominant force in Chinese politics.

 Examination advice

Paper 1 Question 1: how to answer direct questions

Question 1 on the IB History Diploma examination is in two parts. Each part involves comprehension and simply asks you to tell the examiner what the sources say. Each of the questions will ask only about one source. You will often see questions that ask you to convey the message or meaning of a source. This is asking you to explain what the source is saying.

Question 1 requires no prior knowledge, just the ability to understand sources. When you start your examination, you will receive five minutes of 'reading time' when you cannot actually touch your pen and start writing. Use the time wisely and read Question 1a to see which source it is asking about. Once you understand which source the question is about, read the source and then think of your response. When the five minutes are up, you may begin writing and you should be ready to answer the question immediately.

Question 1 is worth 5 marks out of the total of 25 for all Paper 1. This means it is worth about 20 per cent of the overall mark. Answering questions 1a and 1b should take five minutes or less of the actual examination time.

How to answer

In order to best answer the question, you first have to determine what the question is asking you about the source and what type of source it is. The vast majority of sources are fragments of speeches, quotes from various historians or historical figures, or any other type of written source. There are, however, visual sources that can be asked about as well, such as photographs, charts, maps, cartoons and diagrams.

When you start your answer it is good practice to use the wording in the question to help you focus your answer. For example:

Question	Begin your answer with …
According to Source X, what is the significance of Lin Biao?	The significance of Lin Biao, according to Source X, is …
What was the importance of the Gang of Four according to Source X?	The importance of the Gang of Four, according to Source X, was …
What was Deng Xiaoping's view on capitalism according to Source X?	According to Source X, Deng Xiaoping's view on capitalism was …

After starting your answer, understand that you should paraphrase what the original source stated. This means you should explain what the source says, but in your own words. Sometimes this is impossible because the words used in the source may be so specific that there is no other way to say them. If this occurs, make sure you put quotation marks around the phrases which you are copying from the source.

The total number of marks available for Question 1 is 5. One part is worth 3 marks and the other 2 and this will be clearly indicated on the examination. If a question is worth 2 marks, try to have at least two specific points to your answer. If a question is worth 3 marks, have at least three points.

Example

This question uses Sources C and F found on this chapter on pages 27 and 31.

a) According to Source C, of what crimes were the Gang of Four accused? (3 marks)

b) What information is conveyed by Source F? (2 marks)

Below is a good sample answer to the question.

> 1a) According to Source C, the Gang of Four were accused of forming a 'clique' or exclusive group and failing to heed Mao Zedong's warnings to desist in their 'evil' work. They were also accused of politically attacking Zhou Enlai, attacking government officials, and having their own armed forces.
>
> 1b) Source F indicates that Hua Guofeng was weakened by the fact that he had only joined the Chinese Communist Party in 1938. This is contrasted to at least two other leaders, Deng Xiaoping and Chen Yun, who had joined much earlier and therefore had more authority within the party, although they held lesser titles.

Each answer repeats part of the question, using phrases such as 'According to Source C …' and 'Source F indicates …', helping the answer focus on the question.

Both sources are paraphrased in the answers.

Both 1a and 1b are answered in full sentences and not bullet points.

Questions 1a and 1b were worth a combined 5 marks. Both answers indicate that the student read and understood what each source stated. Question 1a was worth 3 marks. The answer for 1a contains at least three different points to address the question. Question 1b was worth 2 marks. The answer has more than two points to answer the question.

Interpreting visual sources

Visual sources are often included on Paper 1 examinations and can be used in any of the questions. Visual sources include cartoons, maps, graphs, charts, tables, photographs, posters and potentially many other types of graphic art. Some visual sources are easier to understand than others.

Cartoons and posters

Cartoons and posters can be very similar in terms of symbolism, message and intended effect. Either can be intended to make fun of something, criticize a person or idea, try to get the viewer to agree with their point of view, or inform. They can be complex and should be treated very carefully and thoroughly.

Symbolism

First, we need to consider symbolism. The chart below gives some of the more common symbols used in cartoons and posters and their potential meanings. Not all of them refer to this chapter or book, but you should know them. Below are just some of the basics, but the list is almost endless.

Symbol	Represents	Symbol	Represents
Red star, five points	USSR, China, communism	Hammer and sickle	USSR, communism
Bear	Russia, USSR	Scales, blind-folded woman	Justice
Workers' cap	USSR, communism	Money bags, fat men	Wealth
Swastika	Nazi Germany	Crown of leaves, winged goddess	Victory
Red flag	USSR, China, communism	Statue of Liberty (one arm holding torch, other holding tablet)	Democracy, USA
The colour red	Communism	Uncle Sam	USA
Outstretched arm salute	Fascist salute	Olive branch, dove	Peace
Goddess of Freedom (two hands holding torch)	Freedom, democracy	Skull and crossed bones	Death
Star of David, six points	Jews, Judaism, Zionism, Israel after 1948	Hourglass	Time
Turtle	Slow movement	Factory, smokestack	Industry
Chains	Oppression	Bulldog, eagle	War, possibly a nation such as Britain for bulldog or eagle for the USA
Bomb	Disaster, war, major tension	Woman or baby crying	Misery, death, destruction

Representations of people

Additionally, significant people like Mao Zedong, Hua Guofeng, Deng Xiaoping, Leonid Brezhnev, Mikhail Gorbachev and others dealt with in this and other chapters in the book appear in cartoons and other visual sources. Mao always appears with swept-back hair and a rotund, benign smile; Brezhnev with bushy black eyebrows and so forth. Cartoons in this and other chapters in the book will help you to understand how individuals typically appear in cartoons.

Captions

Captions are the labels that accompany visual sources. These are very important, often informing you of the date of creation, name of artist and perhaps country of origin. All of this information helps to determine the message of the source. Often captions include a direct message that is easy to understand such as the message on the propaganda poster that clearly states that Hua Guofeng is 'Laying the Foundation' (Source D, page 29). Read captions carefully.

Example

Look at Source D (page 29) which is from 1977. 'Laying the Foundation' is the message to the Chinese people. You are aware after this chapter that Hua Guofeng had some important challenges to deal with, succeeding such a strong personality as Mao Zedong, who had founded the PRC and whose words were treated with utmost reverence. The words of the caption tell us that he is building a mausoleum for Mao, but he is also beginning the foundation of a post-Mao China. The message is directed at the Chinese people telling them that they should respect Mao, but that he is now in a mausoleum and a new person is their leader. The imagery promotes the message as well. Hua is in the forefront, shovel in hand, giving an impression of an energetic new start, in contrast to the last decade of Mao's illness and death. Behind him is Marshal Ye, symbolizing the tacit support of the army for Hua's new leadership. All around are happy, cheering people, eager to begin to build a renovated China. They are dressed in different costumes, representing the unity of different ethnic groups in China. Behind and above looms a placid, approving Mao, who is dead, but still an inspiration to his successors, amid red flags that symbolize the decided continuation of communism in China.

Photographs

Photographs are another visual source. Photographs can capture a specific moment. Sometimes photographs just record what the photographer saw at that particular moment, while many photographs, especially of political events, politicians and conferences, are usually ones in which everyone poses in a specific way for an intended effect.

Example

Source B (page 26) is a photograph recording the arrival of Jiang Qing at her trial on 26 November 1980. Two armed guards flank her. Notice that:

- Jiang is brought in with her hands handcuffed, looking grim and with her mouth set firmly, her lips pursed defiantly.
- The two guards are young and armed, in sharp contrast to the middle-aged prisoner.

These observations indicate that the picture was taken for an official reason. While this does not make the source any less valuable, we must realize that this was probably taken for political reasons, perhaps to be distributed to the press. This was perhaps intentional, designed to show that Hua would deal sharply with the Gang of Four, a policy that was quite popular as they were widely hated by many. Jiang was especially despised for her high-handed ways, so a portrayal of her public humiliation was important to convey the message of Hua's new leadership of the PRC.

How to answer

It is likely that you will be asked to analyse one of the visual sources that appear on your Paper 1 examination in Question 1. The questions are usually very straightforward, asking you to indicate what the message of the source is.

Example

This question uses Source D on page 29 in this chapter.

What information is conveyed by Source D about Hua? (3 marks)

- First, take note of any words. It is known that the poster is titled 'Laying the Foundation'. Review the analysis on page 40.
- Next, notice symbolism:
  - shovels = energy, industriousness
  - red flags = communism
  - military uniform = army support
  - different costumes = ethnic diversity
  - Mao's picture = tacit approval, continuation of Mao's ideas
  - tombstone = Mao's death, end of an era.
- Finally, write your answer to the question.

> The answer indicates which source is being analysed, the type of source and the date.

> The caption is thoroughly analysed, including its double meaning.

> All major elements depicted in the poster are discussed and analysed, including the shovels, red flags, people cheering, Marshal Ye and Mao's portrait.

> Terms and phrases such as 'likely' and 'may be' are used appropriately when presenting a hypothesis based on historical events and probability but where some other interpretation may be possible.

> The answer is summarized in the final sentence to make sure all points have been covered.

Source D is a Chinese political poster from 1977. The poster enthusiastically supports the new leadership of Hua Guofeng, as indicated by the cheering and clapping people and Mao's approving picture. The poster indicates that Hua, dressed in Maoist suit and cap, shovel in hand, will be able to lay the foundations for building his succession, while at the same time honouring Mao by burying him and building him a mausoleum. That is why the poster is titled 'Laying the Foundation'. The red flags are an obvious reference to communism which may convey that it will continue as the ideology of the PRC. Behind Hua stands Marshal Ye. It is important that he is behind Hua, not in the forefront, thereby likely symbolizing army support of Hua's leadership. The message of this propaganda poster is that Hua should be supported in order to continue to build up communism in China, after the death of Mao.

> The answer indicates that the question was understood. There are at least three points made about the poster. All points are clear, supported with evidence from the poster, and accurate. Good use of analysis and deduction.

Examination practice

Below are some exam-style questions for you to practise. Paper 1 exams are one hour long, not including five minutes of reading time at the exam's start when only reading is permitted. You may wish to only practise specific questions, and if this is the case, allow the following amounts of time per question:

Question 1:	5 minute
Question 2:	10 minutes
Question 3:	10 minutes
Question 4:	35 minutes

These questions relate to PRC politics between 1976 and 1979. The sources used are found within this chapter on the following pages:

- Source B (page 26)
- Source C (page 27)
- Source H (page 33)
- Source G (page 32)
- Source I (page 35)

1 **a)** What, according to Source C, were the justifications for the arrest of the Gang of Four? *(3 marks)*
(For guidance on how to answer this style of question see page 37.)

b) What message is conveyed by Source B? *(2 marks)*
(For guidance on how to answer this style of question see page 41.)

2 Compare and contrast the views expressed in Source G and H about Hua Guofeng. *(6 marks)*
(For guidance on how to answer this style of question see page 91.)

3 With reference to their origin and purpose, discuss the value and limitations of Source G and Source I for historians assessing Deng Xiaoping's rise to power. *(6 marks)*
(For guidance on how to answer this style of question see page 130.)

4 'Deng Xiaoping's rise to power had less to do with his own political strengths and more to do with the weaknesses and disunity of his opponents.' Using Sources B, C, G, H and I and your own knowledge assess the validity of this claim. *(8 marks)*
(For guidance on how to answer this style of question see page 160.)

 # Activities

1 One of the keys to understanding the intricacies of PRC politics between 1976 and 1979 is to understand three ideological terms: leftist, rightist and whateverist.

- Explain in as much detail as possible what is meant by these terms.
- Which of the politicians you have studied in this chapter were leftists?
- Which of the politicians you have studied in this chapter were rightists?
- Which of the politicians you have studied in this chapter were whateverists?

2 'Hua Guofeng deserves to be more than just a footnote in the history of modern China.' Write a 200-word evaluation of this statement, including as many supporting case studies as possible.

3 Based on what you have learned in this chapter, what qualities do you think were required by a successful ruler of the People's Republic of China? Were there any groups and institutions whose support was absolutely vital?

CHAPTER 3

China under Deng Xiaoping: economic policies and the Four Modernizations

This chapter analyses the economic policies embarked on by Deng Xiaoping from 1979 and the extent to which they amounted to a radical change of direction for China's economy. You need to consider the following questions throughout this chapter:

✪ Why were the Four Modernizations introduced?

✪ How did the Four Modernizations transform China politically and economically?

✪ How successful were Deng Xiaoping's economic policies?

1 The background to the Four Modernizations

▶ *Key question: Why were the Four Modernizations introduced?*

Deng appeared an unlikely figure to launch an economic revolution. He had barely survived the Cultural Revolution. By the time of the Third Plenum of the Eleventh Central Committee of the Chinese Communist Party (CCP) in 1978, he was over 70 years old. His long career in the CCP had been built on knowing how to navigate political controversy, although the Gang of Four and Mao's infirmity made this extremely challenging.

Many historians see Deng as a far-sighted realist. The most famous quote attributed to him is 'it does not matter if a cat is black or white, as long as it catches mice'. In other words, in terms of economic policy, Deng was more interested in outcomes than ideology. Armed with the knowledge that Maoist economic policies had failed (see page 19) and presiding over a rising population approaching one billion by 1978, a quarter of whom were living in a state of abject poverty, Deng decided to act. The consequences would be far reaching.

SOURCE A

Excerpt from a speech entitled 'The present situation and the tasks before us' given by Deng Xiaoping on 16 January 1980, from *Selected Works of Deng Xiaoping (1975–1982)*, published by Foreign Language Press, Beijing, 1984, p. 236. Deng is speaking at a meeting of cadres called by the Central Committee of the CCP.

The superiority [of the socialist system] should manifest itself in many ways, but first and foremost it must be revealed in the rate of economic growth and economic efficiency. Without political stability and unity, it would be impossible for us to settle down to construction. This has been borne out by our experience in more than twenty years since 1957 … In addition to stability and unity, we must maintain liveliness … when liveliness clashes with stability and unity, we can never pursue the former at the expense of the latter. The experience of the Cultural Revolution has already proved that chaos leads only to retrogression, not to progress.

> What can be deduced about Deng Xiaoping's economic and political outlook from Source A?

Political support for the Four Modernizations

> How did the Four Modernizations affect the PRC's politics?

The **Four Modernizations** were a set of economic priorities that had originally been established by Deng's political mentor, Zhou Enlai, at the Fourth National People's Congress in January 1975. Zhou stated that it was essential that significant resources be devoted to national defence, agriculture, science and industry. In part, Zhou's priorities reflected a concern of many Chinese politicians, including Deng Xiaoping and Hua Guofeng. It was realized that only by matching the West in terms of economic growth and technological advancement could China hope to emerge as a great power once again.

It would take all of Deng's political finesse to maintain the political priorities of the CCP as a communist system and at the same time apply the economically liberal reform policies needed to make the Four Modernizations work. It was at the Third Plenum of the Eleventh Central Committee of the CCP in 1978 that Deng's reforms gained political support to transform China. This was extraordinary, because for the first time class struggle as an ongoing focus took second place to economic reform, as the Four Modernizations led to the following political and economic changes:

 **KEY TERM**

Four Modernizations
The set of policies promoted by Deng Xiaoping after 1978 which introduced significant elements of capitalism into the Chinese economy.

- The political focus of the CCP should be the Four Modernizations and not class struggle.
- The continuation of revolution under the dictatorship of the proletariat now took second place to economic reform.
- The volume of trade needed to be increased by opening up China's internal market.
- China had to focus on export-oriented growth.
- Advanced technology and management expertise had to be acquired.

 **KEY TERM**

Open Door Policy
Allowing foreign investment in the PRC.

Reaching out to the West

Once he had succeeded in having the Four Modernizations and its political ramifications approved by the Central Committee in 1978, Deng implemented this programme. The economy was rapidly opened to foreign investors. This was known as the **Open Door Policy**. What motivated Deng was his awareness of the economic success of neighbouring capitalist economies like Hong Kong, Singapore and Taiwan. His pragmatic interest in economic policies that were successful, as opposed to following Marxist doctrine, meant Deng would consider some level of capitalism to help China to develop.

At a national science conference held in 1978, Deng indicated that he was willing to develop relations with the capitalist West to achieve his aims.

? According to Source B, in what ways did Deng Xiaoping wish to transform the PRC?

SOURCE B

Excerpt from 'China's "Four Modernizations" lead to closer Sino-U.S. science ties,' by Barbara J. Culliton, *Science*, New Series, Vol. 201, No. 4355, 11 August 1978, pages 512–13, published by American Association for the Advancement of Science. Culliton is a well-known journalist regarding science topics.

'The entire nation is embarking with tremendous enthusiasm on the march towards the modernization of science and technology. Splendid prospects lie before us,' declared Vice-Premier Teng Hsiao-ping [Deng Xiaoping], who is actively engaged in expanding China's contacts with foreign nations. On the theory that 'Backwardness must be perceived before it can be changed,' Teng spoke bluntly about China's state of affairs and her new determination to catch up with and even surpass the rest of the world, adhering 'to the policy of independence and self-reliance.' Then Teng went on to say, 'But independence does not mean shutting the door on the world, nor does self-reliance mean blind opposition to everything foreign.'

What ideological changes were needed to implement the Four Modernizations?

Communism vs pragmatism

The implementation of the Four Modernizations meant the start of a new period of ideological development in China. The ideological challenge consisted of integrating Marxism–Leninism with pragmatism in order to address the actual economic conditions of China.

In 1978, Deng Xiaoping stressed that the entire party should revisit Maoist doctrine without criticizing it, or as he put it, to 'seek truth from facts and unite as one'. The facts were undeniable, as China, despite decades of communism, was still an economically undeveloped country. By the time the Twelfth Central Committee convened in 1982, Deng formally put forward the proposition of 'building socialism with Chinese characteristics'.

Deng made a rather convoluted attempt to fit together capitalist policies with Marxism. He argued that a true socialist revolution could not occur until a bourgeois revolution had first taken place, which is, in fact, what Karl Marx had originally proposed in the middle of the nineteenth century (see page 10). Mao had discussed this with his followers in the early days of the CCP, but persevered with his idea of a peasant revolution, rather than wait for a proletarian one. Mao's programmes, however, failed to solve China's poverty and it took Deng and his carefully worded Four Modernizations to begin the process of economic reform.

SOURCE C

Excerpt from *Modern China*, third edition, by Edwin E. Moïse, published by Longman, UK, 1986, page 231. Moïse teaches History of Modern China, Japan and Vietnam at Clemson University in South Carolina, USA.

China's great problem remained its fundamental poverty. Most of the people still lived in poor villages, where they scraped out a living without enough machinery, fertilizer or land. Most villages were still not far above subsistence level; when crops failed through drought or flood, as they did in parts of two provinces in 1980, the peasants went hungry … In an effort to promote agricultural production, the government released many of the restrictions on the 'spontaneous capitalist tendencies' of the peasantry. The income of a family came to depend much more on the production of that family, rather than being the family's share of the production of a larger group. Experiments with the 'responsibility system', in which a family or a small group of families was given responsibility for a piece of land or an enterprise owned by their production team, brigade, or commune, occurred quite widely in 1979. Soon afterwards some of the provincial officials who had played a major role in these experiments were promoted to top positions in Beijing; Zhao Ziyang from Sichuan became Premier.

> What reasons does the author in Source C put forward to explain China's poverty? **?**

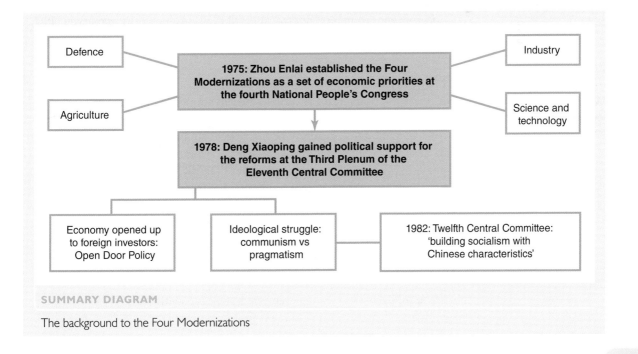

SUMMARY DIAGRAM

The background to the Four Modernizations

The Four Modernizations up to 1989

▶ *Key question: How did the Four Modernizations transform China politically and economically?*

From 1978, the Four Modernizations became more directly associated with Deng than with Zhou. Both men sought to modernize four areas of the PRC's economy: agriculture, industry, science and technology, and national defence.

Agriculture

> **How did the Four Modernizations aim to end poverty in the countryside?**

In 1980, about 90 per cent of the PRC's population still lived in the countryside, where radical reform was an economic necessity by the end of the 1970s. Greater agricultural productivity was needed. This was because:

- The PRC relied on grain imports.
- The population was rising.
- The PRC possessed only 0.25 acres of land per capita, compared with 2.1 acres per capita in the USA.

The Third Plenum of the Eleventh Central Committee marked a real turning point. It sanctioned reforms in rural areas and announced that local village markets, which had been prohibited since the 1960s, were necessary. This meant that farmers could grow crops for profit, rather than only to fulfil government production quotas, and sell their produce at local markets. It was evident that the CCP had become less hostile to at least limited capitalism to address certain economic requirements.

Household responsibility system

In 1979, the **household responsibility system** was introduced in order to begin structural reform of agriculture in China. The system of communes and collectivization in agriculture began to be dismantled. Peasants were allowed to lease small plots from the state. The CCP made the ideological point that peasants were merely using land rather than owning it. Initially, peasants negotiated with the communes about what to produce and had to hand over a quota of their crop. As the process of decollectivization advanced, the really important innovation was that farmers could sell any surplus for profit. They could even hire wage labourers. It created a great incentive to produce, but also had limitations (see Source D).

KEY TERM

Household responsibility system From 1980, peasants were allowed to lease land from the state and to generate a profit by selling surpluses.

SOURCE D

Excerpt from *China and the Crisis of Marxism–Leninism*, sixth edition, by Franz Michael, Carl Linden, Jan Prybyla and Jürgen Domes, published by Westview Press, Colorado, USA, 2000, page 65. Michael was a Professor of History at University of Washington and National Chekiang University in Hangchow, China. Linden is a Professor Emeritus of Political Science and International Relations at George Washington University. Prybyla was a Professor of History at Pennsylvania State University. Domes was a Professor of Political Science at the University of Saarland, Germany.

[The] idea that 1 acre per family is socialist but 2 acres is capitalist has not been fully exorcised. Since 1980, however, progress has been made on that front. Consolidation of land parcels and their expansion are now permitted, if still carefully watched for possible capitalist abuses.

> According to Source D, how was capitalism in rural areas defined?

Improvements in output

By 1984, 98 per cent of peasant farmers had adopted this new, more entrepreneurial system. In the southern province of Guangdong, agricultural incomes doubled between 1978 and 1982 and this was not an isolated example. In 1984, China's grain harvest topped 400 million tonnes for the first time, despite the fact that many farmers were now beginning to diversify into other crops.

Improvements in the standard of living

To improve the standard of living, subsidies to food producers became predominant after 1979 in order to keep urban food prices stable as agricultural prices and the cost of producing food increased. Basic industrial goods and urban food tended to be under-priced while non-basic consumer goods were over-priced with profit margins of 30–60 per cent compared with 5 or 10 per cent for the former. An indicator of an improved standard of living after 1976 is the decline in child mortality rates due to the much improved quantity and quality of available food, rising incomes and household consumption, reduced illiteracy and expanded education, child vaccination programmes, improved water supplies and more medication.

Long-term leases

By the end of the decade, the initial restrictions of the household responsibility system had been loosened. From 1987, land could be contracted out or leased for 50 years, encouraging peasants to feel that they owned the land they farmed and could improve it, instead of relying on the state to do so. In fact, the government cut its investment in agriculture from 25 billion yuan to 18 billion yuan from 1981 to 1985. In irrigation, the government went from investing two-thirds of the state agricultural investment in 1980 to one-third in 1986–90. However, these cuts were not replaced by investments on the part of the farmers. Irrigation and drainage systems failed to be replaced or repaired, with predictable results. Without clear land ownership, many peasants were probably less interested in long-term investment than in purchasing consumer goods.

Other reforms

Further reforms included the right of farmers to sub-lease land that they did not wish to farm to others. Also, the Law of Succession in 1985 allowed for contracts to be passed on from generation to generation within a family. Clearly, the Maoist ideal of egalitarian peasant communes in which there was no private enterprise was over. As the historian Edwin E. Moïse has stated: 'collective agriculture was virtually dead'; the family had replaced the commune as the main economic unit in the countryside.

SOURCE E

A Chinese peasant uses a bullock to plough a rice paddy, as his ancestors did, in a village near Xingguo in south China's Jiangxi province, 1993.

? What information is conveyed about the effect of agricultural reforms in the PRC in Source E?

How did the Four Modernizations affect industry?

Industry

Under the Four Modernizations, industry changed:

- Individual enterprises expanded.
- **State-owned enterprises (SOEs)** changed to collective ownership.
- Some enterprises operated under joint ownership (state and individuals, state and foreign companies).
- Some enterprises became privately owned.

Even those that remained SOEs were more exposed to market forces in the 1980s and were now allowed to sell any surpluses, over and above their quota, for a profit on the open market. This was known as the Sichuan Experiment because it was pioneered by the reforming Premier Zhao Ziyang when he was Party Secretary in Sichuan province.

The table in Source F shows the advances in industrial output between 1978 and 1987.

KEY TERM

State-owned enterprises (SOEs) Factories and businesses owned and operated by the government in the PRC.

SOURCE F

A table of the output of major industries from data issued by the Chinese State Statistical Bureau on 23 February 1988. Reprinted in *The Rise of Modern China*, fifth edition, by Immanuel C.Y. Hsü, published by Oxford University Press, UK, 1995, page 857. Hsü was a Professor of History at the University of California, Santa Barbara.

What can be inferred about the Four Modernizations from Source F?

Industry	Annual production (million tonnes)			
	1978	1981	1984	1987
Coal	618	622	789	920
Crude oil	104	101	115	134
Steel	32	36	43	56
Pig iron	35	34	40	54

Sources: *Almanac* 26; State Statistical Bureau, 23 Feb. 1988, *Beijing Review*, 7–13 March 1988; *Monthly Bulletin of Statistics, China*, March 1988.

The labour market

The labour market also became much more flexible. Before 1981, workers were controlled by party bureaucrats, or cadres, who were responsible for each SOE. Workers needed permission from these cadres if they wished to transfer or leave an industry. Rural workers had to obtain a letter of approval from a cadre to even visit a city.

A new labour contract system began in 1981, when urban workers were given more freedom to search for jobs on their own and SOEs were given more freedom to terminate worker contracts. In 1984, Zhao Ziyang advocated further loosening of the restrictions on SOEs. The Central Committee announced that SOEs should be totally responsible for their labour force and have freedom to determine prices of goods produced and worker wages. By September 1986, enterprise managers were allowed to enter into contracts directly with workers instead of accepting workers that had been assigned to the enterprise by government labour bureaus; these had often been contracts for life. Now managers could contract workers for different time spans and dismiss them if the enterprise no longer needed them or if they were inefficient.

Managers were also allowed to use profits to raise wages for more productive workers. All this meant the abolition of the traditional CCP economic principle that had guaranteed permanent employment for state sector workers. The success of **town and village enterprises (TVEs)** created a mass migration from the countryside to urban areas of people searching for non-farm work.

Town and village enterprises (TVEs)

One of the most significant of Deng's economic reforms within the Four Modernizations was the creation of TVEs all over the country. These allowed

 **KEY TERM**

Town and village enterprises (TVEs) Private businesses permitted by the CCP as part of the Four Modernizations policy.

ordinary people to establish small businesses outside the control of the state and the party. Often these were small carpentry shops, grocery stores, lumberyards, ceramics kilns, slaughterhouses, truck and bus systems and more. It was now possible, for what was in effect a new bourgeoisie, to sell goods outside their home districts, as well as to take loans from state banks.

The TVEs were intended to operate on a small scale, but their long-term impact was to initiate an entrepreneurial spirit in China. In 1985, 17 million small businesses were registered, compared with a mere 100,000 in 1978. By 1992, there were 20 million TVEs employing 100 million people. These small businesses generated jobs, soaking up excess rural labour. By the end of the decade, private enterprise was no longer confined to the small business sector and the TVEs were providing real economic competition for SOEs.

Special Economic Zones

In order to further economic reforms, Deng successfully argued the idea of **Special Economic Zones (SEZs)** at a Central Committee conference in April 1979. The first SEZs were established in the same year. The SEZs were designated areas of the country in which it was hoped foreign companies would make significant investments. The positioning of these first SEZs in the prosperous southern coastal belt, near foreign enclaves, was deliberate, so as to make them even more attractive locations for overseas investors. They were:

- Zhuhai, near **Macau**
- Shenzhen, near **Hong Kong**
- Shantou and Xiamen, adjacent to Taiwan.

SEZs functioned as self-contained entities. For example, non-residents needed an internal passport to visit an SEZ. The SEZs did have a significant impact on the rest of the PRC's economy and the experiment was so successful that it was extended to a further 14 cities in 1984. The 24 million migrant workers who arrived in the SEZs between 1978 and 1988 had an economic 'ripple effect' as their **remittances**, often sent back to villages away from the prosperous coastal belt, helped to raise living standards in rural areas. By 1985, PRC exports were worth $25 billion per annum compared with $10 billion in 1978.

Foreign investment

A law on **joint ventures** was passed in 1979 allowing foreign investment in PRC enterprises. Deng went even further in 1982, announcing that he had no objections to 'enterprises wholly owned by foreign businessmen' in the PRC. Tax reductions and devaluation of the yuan, whose value almost halved against the US dollar between 1980 and 1985, also made China attractive to multinational companies.

KEY TERM

Special Economic Zones (SEZs) Designated areas of China, usually on the coast, where foreign investors were encouraged by concessions like tax breaks, to invest and set up businesses.

Macau A colony of Portugal in southern China until 1999.

Hong Kong A colony of Britain from the mid-nineteenth century until 1997.

Remittances Money sent back by a worker to a town or village of origin to support family members.

Joint ventures When two or more parties engage in an economic activity together by sharing control, investment and profits.

SOURCE G

A CCP propaganda poster from 1987 entitled 'Special Economic Zones – The Gateways to China.'

What message is conveyed in Source G and what evidence supports your answer?

Coastal Development Plan

In 1988, the programme was widened as part of the Coastal Development Plan to attract even more foreign investment. The plan called for the development of export-oriented manufacturing industries. This introduced further foreign capital, advanced technology and training into the country.

SOURCE H

Map of China showing the Special Economic Zones.

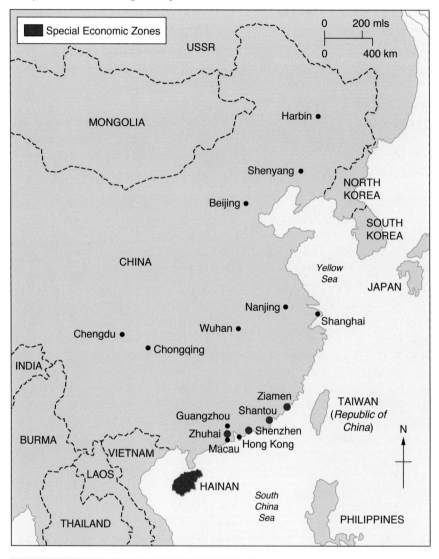

How did the Four
Modernizations affect
science and
technology?

Science and technology

An important part of the Four Modernizations, directed to making the PRC
competitive in the world economy and to improve the standard of living in
China, was science and technology. The changes starting in 1980 were
consistent with the Open Door Policy regarding economic development.
The PRC had to ensure access to world-class technology for economic
development to proceed. To that end, economic incentives to develop and
share technologies were included in the Four Modernizations' reforms. The
state began to sponsor research in technological innovation, in conjunction
with business objectives.

The PRC held a National Science and Technology Conference in 1978, where a serious government commitment to become competitive in the world market was launched. A state science and technology commission was created to this end.

By the mid-1980s, scientists could travel abroad and communicate freely internationally in order to create new technology ventures in the PRC. The state made available the funds required for research institutes and universities and put in place competitive procedures for public funding of research projects. This created an incentive for scientists and technology experts to join the business world by commercializing new knowledge and technology. In 1980, a further incentive was granted with the promulgation of the patent law to protect intellectual property rights.

SOURCE I

Excerpt from 'China's Special Economic Zones' by Xu Dixin, *Beijing Review*, No. 50, published by the China International Publishing Group, 1981. The *Beijing Review* is a national weekly PRC magazine published in English. Xu is Vice-President of the Chinese Academy of Social Sciences and director of its Institute of Economics.

> According to Source I, what was the purpose of the SEZs? **?**

Some people wonder why it is necessary, more than 30 years since the founding of the People's Republic, to set up special economic zones. They also wonder whether the special zones signify that China is seeking help from capitalist countries. Such concerns are understandable, but unwarranted. Since its establishment, New China has scored brilliant achievements in many fields of work, including economic construction. But it has also traversed a tortuous path. Compared with the world's most advanced nations, China's level of production is still rather low. Its funds and technology are incompatible with the requirements of the modernization drive. Furthermore, while implementing its policy of self-reliance in economic construction, China does not exclude co-operation with capitalism. Facts will prove that through developing the economies of the special zones, we will be able to make use of foreign and overseas Chinese capital, as well as state capitalism, to develop China's socialist economy. Economic construction in the special zones will possibly become a special form of supplement to the development of China's socialist economy. The total economies of the special zones will only constitute a very small portion of the national economy. Although the socialist economy will continue to dominate, the role of the special zones must not be overlooked.

Defence

← **How did the Four Modernizations affect defence?**

During the period of border incidents and tension with the USSR in the mid-1970s and the failed invasion of Vietnam in February 1979 (see page 72), it became clear that the army, known as the People's Liberation Army (PLA), had weaknesses that needed addressing. China required a modern, capable army with a hierarchy that supported the other reforms taking place.

By the end of the 1970s, over 70 top-ranking army officers had been dismissed and the army's leadership was restructured. More army officers were appointed to the Central Committee and other administrative positions in the country. The economic reforms as a result of the Four Modernizations contributed to the well-being and efficiency of the army and helped to modernize it and increase its professionalism. For example, salaries increased to be competitive with the civilian world.

In 1989, the army proved its loyalty to the CCP and its leaders by supporting the government against demonstrators in Tiananmen Square (see Chapter 4). It successfully integrated into the economy and defence industries.

To what extent did the Four Modernizations change the PRC?

The impact of the Four Modernizations

By the late 1980s, the PRC had the appearance of a vigorous capitalist economy, presided over by the CCP. This obvious contradiction was the source of discontent within the CCP during the 1980s, especially by its older members. Chen Yun, the architect of the first Five Year Plan in the 1950s (see page 13), felt that Deng's economic reforms were moving too quickly and that the free market should be a 'bird in a cage' – in other words, tightly controlled and regulated at all times. Deng Xiaoping relentlessly referred to the PRC's new policy of modernizations as a new interpretation of Maoist doctrine to end PRC poverty. This view ultimately reigned over opposition in the Politburo and the CCP.

The PRC, in Deng's view, was not meant to become a fully fledged capitalist economy. At the end of the 1980s, for example, it did not possess definitions of property rights, a bankruptcy law or a stock market.

Two economies

In many ways, by the late 1980s, the PRC had two economies. SEZs had helped to create real prosperity along coastal areas and many had become cities in their own right by the end of the decade. Shenzhen, for example, had grown from a fishing village across the border from Hong Kong into a manufacturing hub housing millions of migrant workers. The SEZs were tied into the world economy and had created a new class of managers who were familiar with the workings of global capitalism. There were up to 50,000 PRC managers running factories for foreign investors by the end of the decade. Outside the SEZs and in the PRC's interior, agriculture still dominated the economy and SOEs remained uncompetitive. Rural areas and most cities in the PRC remained poor compared to SEZs.

Inflation

Rapid economic growth created a demand for consumer goods, raw materials and housing that could not be immediately met. Between 1987 and 1989, despite the vigorous reforms in the economy, problems in agriculture, inflation, unemployment, income inequalities, government corruption and worsening urban living standards became apparent. Naturally, the CCP sought to control these market forces by returning to strict price controls and even rationing. Inflation had reached between 18.7 and 30 per cent by 1988. This necessitated strict price controls from the government in order to bring it down.

According to historian Immanuel C.Y. Hsü, those living in urban areas saw their purchasing power decline by 100 per cent between 1983 and 1988. Many workers in SOEs lost their jobs in efforts to make industry more efficient and profitable. As in most **developing economies**, there was a large amount of migration to cities from rural areas across the decade as the average industrial worker earned up to eight times more per month in the early 1980s than the typical peasant. The influx from the countryside created an **urban underclass** of up to one million in Beijing alone by 1989, whose non-urban official residential status meant that they did not qualify for any aid from the state.

KEY TERM

Developing economies
National economies which are in the process of being developed to raise living standards.

Urban underclass The lowest socio-economic group in a city of poor, often unemployed, people.

SOURCE J

Excerpt from *The Rise of Modern China*, sixth edition, by Immanuel C.Y. Hsü, published by Oxford University Press, UK, 2000, pages 843 and 852. Hsü was a Professor Emeritus of History from the University of California, Santa Barbara, California, USA.

On October 1, 1984, on the occasion of the 35th anniversary of the founding of the People's Republic, he [Deng] confidently announced to the nation that the annual economic growth rates of 7.9 percent during the period 1979–83 and of 14.2 percent in 1984, surpassed the 7.2 percent needed to quadruple the GNP to $1 trillion by the year 2000 … Perhaps the most visible result of the economic reforms was the mushrooming of private businesses and free markets in both rural and urban areas. Private businesses grew in number from 100,000 in 1978 to 5.8 million in 1983 and 17 million by 1985, with some making impressive profits in the capitalist fashion … These free markets and private businesses constituted a lively sector in the vast sea of state-owned enterprises … People complained of inflation, which outpaced both wage increases and cost-of-living adjustments. Inflation was officially put at 4 percent in 1979, 6 percent in 1980, 2.4 percent in 1981 and 1.9 percent in 1982, though the unofficial estimates ranged from 15 to 20 percent or more annually … Confusion, fear and disbelief were prevalent. Having experienced the hardships caused by the hyperinflationary period of 1945–49, the Chinese dreaded any sign of its recurrence.

According to Source J, what were the negative economic consequences of the Four Modernizations? **?**

Corruption

Corruption was a major problem during the period of economic development. By the end of the 1980s, the phenomenon of companies operated by the children of senior party officials was commonplace. Deng's own son had a conglomerate with over 100 subsidiaries until it was shut down in 1988 when allegations about non-payment of taxes were made public. Corruption became an established feature of political and economic life in the 1980s. Over 40,000 cases of economic corruption were reported in 1983–4 and in 1987, 150,000 CCP members were punished for corruption or abuse of authority.

What were the economic disadvantages of the 'centralised planning system' described by Roberts in Source K?

SOURCE K

Excerpt from *A History of China*, second edition, by J.A.G. Roberts, published by Palgrave Macmillan, UK, 2006, page 290. Roberts is Principal Lecturer at the University of Huddersfield in 1999, specializing in the history of China and Japan.

China experienced an economic boom and between 1981 and 1986 China's industrial output nearly doubled. Although China's industrial sector had achieved an impressive rate of growth, it was still controlled by a centralised planning system which determined what an enterprise should produce, where it should obtain its raw materials and where and at what price it should sell its products. In 1984, while China was suffering the consequences of an energy crisis, economic policy began to shift away from centralised planning towards the greater use of market forces … Although these reforms freed up the market, they also accelerated inflation and encouraged corrupt practices.

The Four Modernizations

Defence
- PLA became more professionalized

Agriculture
- Local village markets allowed
- Household responsibility system
- TVEs
- 1985: Law of succession
- 1987: Land could be contracted or leased for 50 years

Science and technology
- State funding and incentives for investment in science and technology

Industry
- More flexible labour market
- SEZs
- TVEs

Economic development led to:
- Corruption
- Inflation
- Two economies: SEZs and the rest

SUMMARY DIAGRAM

The Four Modernizations up to 1989

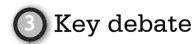 Key debate

---

▶ *Key question: How successful were Deng Xiaoping's economic policies?*

The legacy of Mao Zedong and Hua Guofeng

In order to evaluate the success of Deng Xiaoping's economic policies, many historians have chosen to first evaluate the economic legacy of Mao Zedong and Hua Guofeng. This establishes the exact nature of the economic environment in which Deng Xiaoping operated at the time of the Third Plenum of the Eleventh Central Committee in 1978.

Historian Immanuel C.Y. Hsü writes sternly about Mao in his seminal book *The Rise of Modern China*. Like many historians, he believes that Mao's economic policies had been incoherent and unsuccessful. Hsü argues that economic growth prior to the Four Modernizations was 'erratic' at best and that the standard of living was 'extremely low'.

However, Jack Gray's research, while he was living in China in 1982, has raised the interesting point that the decentralization of the PRC's economy during the Cultural Revolution may have laid the platform for later successes. He has also discovered that some modernizing policies, such as the TVEs, appear to have pre-dated Deng's time as paramount leader. In other words, Deng may have built on foundations that were already in place. Tellingly, Gray argues that despite the Great Leap Forward, 'from 1952 to 1975 China's gross domestic product grew at an average rate of 6.7 per cent per annum'.

Other historians have also argued that Hua Guofeng helped to lay the groundwork for the Four Modernizations. Historian Alan Lawrance makes the important point that it was under Hua that an emphasis was made on educating a more technically knowledgeable class. To that end, universities began to revive and a greater emphasis on academic rigour and scientific accomplishment began to be the norm. This helped to sow the seeds for economic growth in the 1980s.

Deng: a great economic reformer?

As the 1980s continued, it became clear that the PRC had entered a dynamic phase of rapid economic growth. The *Statistical Yearbook for China* for 1986 shows that industrial output nearly doubled between 1981 and 1986. Deng began to be praised in the international press as a Chinese **Colbert** or likened to the leaders of the **Meiji period** in Japan. Deng's powers of persuasion in convincing the Central Committee of the CCP to support his pragmatic approach to end China's lack of economic development was addressed by historian Alan Lawrance: 'it was Deng above all others who

 **KEY TERM**

Colbert A successful French economic reformer in the reign of Louis XIV of France in the late seventeenth and early eighteenth centuries.

Meiji period A time of economic and social reform in Japan from 1868 to 1912 during which Japan successfully industrialized.

masterminded China's remarkable development in the 1980s'. Raw economic data add weight to this argument. World Bank figures show that China attracted $3.393 billion in foreign investment per year by 1989 compared with only $57 million in 1980. Jack Gray believes that Deng's support for TVEs, in particular, was an important catalyst for this rapid economic growth. Hsü agrees, citing the opening of China's economy through policies such as the Coastal Development Plan, as an 'ingenious masterstroke.' It was not just the growth rate that impressed economists and historians but the fact that Deng seemed to have avoided many of the pitfalls that hampered Gorbachev's efforts to liberalize the Soviet economy (see Chapter 6).

Creating inequality and discontent?

 **KEY TERM**

Taizidang A Chinese term used to describe the children of high-ranking officials who used their connections to set up profitable businesses during the 1980s.

Many historians also emphasize the social and economic costs associated with the reform process. Paul J. Bailey points out the corruption associated with the *taizidang*. This term literally means 'princeling's party' and refers to the sons and daughters of party cadres who by virtue of their well-connected relatives have had access to management of TVEs, SOEs, joint ventures and other lucrative businesses. They have come to form a powerful class of their own, with economic means and better education. This nepotism has been perceived by the rest of Chinese society as a negative effect of Deng's liberalizing policies. Corruption, which included embezzlement, theft and extortion, persisted despite anti-corruption campaigns that doled out harsh penalties.

In *The Search for Modern China,* Jonathan Spence also raises the point that despite pragmatic intentions and having gleaned party support, Deng lost control over the reform process due to market economy forces, sometimes linked to global elements and sometimes linked to weaknesses inherent in a mixed economic system like the PRC's. By 1988, the economy was over-heating and weighed down with 'problems of unemployment, inflation and renewed trade deficits'. To support his evaluation, Spence uses sources like the *China Quarterly*, published by Cambridge University Press. Spence paints a convincing portrait of an economy on the verge of crisis in 1988, with food production declining due to the migration of peasants to the cities and the reintroduction of rationing.

Inflation, caused by raw materials shortages, has been identified by several historians as a significant economic problem by 1988, eroding the income of city dwellers in particular, and creating what UCLA Political Science Professor Richard Baum calls an 'urban malaise'. Baum analysed unrest in urban centres in the late 1980s, from work slowdowns to actual strikes by workers and also university student demonstrations. For the first six months of 1988, Baum documented student protests in 77 university campuses in 25 cities.

Although ultimately, the Four Modernizations no doubt modernized some aspects of China's planned agricultural and industrial sectors, the challenges the PRC has had to face have been in the social and political spheres. In the 1980s, socialist and communist economists did not observe this process kindly.

SOURCE L

Excerpt from 'Letter to Novyi Mir' by Larisa Popkova quoted in *China and the Crisis of Marxism–Leninism* by Franz Michael, Carl Linden, Jan Prybyla and Jürgen Domes, published by Westview Press, Colorado, USA, 1990, page 92. Popkova was a Soviet economist. Michael was a Professor of History at the University of Washington and National Chekiang University in Hangchow, China. Linden is a Professor Emeritus of Political Science and International Relations at George Washington University. Prybyla was a Professor of History at Pennsylvania State University. Domes was a Professor of Political Science at the University of Saarland, Germany.

There is no third option. Either planned or market. One cannot be just a little bit pregnant. It is possible to seek and apply something in the middle, but there should be no expectation of successful balancing on two stools. Either a market economy operating according to clear-cut and rigid laws which are identical for each and everyone, with all its advantages (efficiency, for example) and disadvantages (vast inequality of incomes, unemployment …) or a planned socialized economy, also with all its advantages (man's confidence in the future, for example) and disadvantages (shortages, economic mismanagement).

> According to Source L, what does Popkova predict will happen if the two economic systems, socialism and capitalism, are mixed?

How did the Four Modernizations evolve under Deng's leadership?

The economic evidence for the PRC's rapid growth during the 1980s cannot be challenged and as the paramount leader during this pivotal period, Deng had significant responsibility for the PRC's economic expansion. This period, however, has led to significant problems. According to Hsü, the PRC was now more fractured socially and full of 'anxiety, selfishness, resentment and rudeness'. To blame Deng for these developments is perhaps inaccurate, just as it is unconvincing to give him all the credit for the changes taking place in a country as large, complex and difficult to run as the PRC. There were also other key figures in the CCP, such as Zhao Ziyang, who were even more committed supporters of economic reform than Deng himself, and Deng admitted that he failed to foresee all the consequences of his economic policies. Ultimately, the PRC's economy and society changed profoundly in the 1980s, but as is the case with any economic policy, especially in the volatile market economy of an interconnected world, Deng may not have been in total control of the process.

T
O
K

Historians continue to debate the short- and long-term consequences of the Four Modernizations for China. What determines how historians select evidence and describe/interpret or analyse events? (History, Language, Perception and Reason.)

The process originally dubbed the Four Modernizations also underwent some changes under Deng's leadership. At the Twelfth Party Congress in September 1982, according to *China Daily*, there was a change in the sequence of the four components: industrial modernization was given priority over agricultural modernization. The reasoning was that industrialization formed the material basis for the entire modernization programme. After the Thirteenth Party Congress in 1987, the term Four Modernizations was seldom used. Instead, the vocabulary evolved towards the use of such terms as *reform, opening up* and *socialist modernization*, reflecting the move from a planned economy to a mixed planned/market economy.

Chapter summary

China under Deng Xiaoping: economic policies and the Four Modernizations

In 1978, the Third Plenum of the Eleventh Central Committee endorsed Deng Xiaoping's Four Modernizations policies, which were a set of economic policies dealing with national defence, agriculture, industry, and science and technology.

In agriculture, decollectivization took place and the household responsibility system was introduced in the countryside. By 1984, 98 per cent of peasant families were operating under this system. This led to increased crop yields and increased demand for consumer goods by peasant farmers. In addition, town and village enterprises (TVEs) were established, allowing for more goods and services in the countryside as well as a rising standard of living.

In industry, initiatives such as the Open Door Policy and joint ventures encouraged more foreign investment. In 1979, Deng had gained the consent of the Central Committee for Special Economic Zones. The first four were established in coastal regions like Zhuhai and Shenzhen and in 1984, with the rise in joint ventures, a further 14 Special Economic Zones were established.

In addition, science and technology received a huge boost in the Four Modernization reforms, propelling the PRC to become part of the international economy. Seeing the necessity to modernize the army in view of tension with the USSR, the reforms also included the professionalization of the army and its inclusion in the business sector with military-related industries.

Challenges emerged as well, such as corruption and inflation which contributed to political and social discontent, especially in cities. This led the government to introduce price controls while efforts were made to reduce inflation. There remained, however, tensions between the communist and capitalist economic systems which still remain.

Examination advice

Interpreting visual sources

Visual sources are often included in Paper 1 examinations and can be used in any of the questions. Visual sources include cartoons, maps, graphs, charts, tables, photographs, posters and potentially many other types of graphic art. Some visual sources are easier to understand than others.

Graphs, charts and tables

Graphs, charts and tables usually convey very specific information such as economic data, how many people from a particular political party were in parliament or how many leaders a country had over a period of time. However, this type of visual source still needs interpreting.

Example: table

Look at Source F (page 51). This is a table of the output of major industries from data issued by the Chinese State Statistical Bureau on 23 February 1988.

The table shows economic data from China starting with 1978 and ending with 1987.

Industry	Annual production (million tonnes)			
	1978	1981	1984	1987
Coal	618	622	789	920
Crude oil	104	101	115	134
Steel	32	36	43	56
Pig iron	35	34	40	54

There was a spectacular rise in output here.

Clearly states that industrial output in tonnes rose, except crude oil and pig iron in 1981.

This table conveys a tremendous amount of information, although it may appear quite simple. After reading this chapter, you know that in 1978 Deng Xiaoping applied in earnest the Four Modernizations first proposed in 1975 by Zhou Enlai. This meant reforming the PRC economy by adding some elements from capitalist economies, such as private ownership of industries or land, and being able to compete in world markets. The table indicates that coal output increased by a third in the nine years following the reforms. Crude oil, steel and pig iron also showed a rise in output. It would seem that the Four Modernizations did achieve great industrial gains for the PRC, as Deng planned. So:

- How successful were the Four Modernizations reforms in terms of industrial output?
- Was the increase equal among the four industries in the table?
- In general, were the reforms successful?

It is important that you consider this type of question when analysing a table such as Source F.

How to answer

It is likely that you will be asked to analyse one of the visual sources that appear in your Paper 1 examination in Question 1. The questions are usually very straightforward, asking you to indicate what the message of the source is.

Example

This question uses Source F, found on page 51 in this chapter.

> **What can be inferred about the Four Modernizations from Source F?** (3 marks)

The answer indicates which source is being analysed, the type of source and the date.

All major elements depicted in the table are discussed and analysed, including the anomalies in the output figures and the spectacular rise of coal output.

Phrases such as 'it would seem' are used appropriately when presenting a hypothesis based on historical events and probability but where some other interpretation may be possible.

The answer is summarized in the final sentence.

Source F is a table of the output of major industries from data issued by the Chinese State Statistical Bureau on 23 February 1988. The table demonstrates the increase in output of four industries in China between 1978, and when the reforms were instituted, 1987. It shows data from the industries of coal, crude oil, steel and pig iron from Chinese industrial output. The table clearly shows that industrial output in tonnes rose, except crude oil and pig iron in 1981. For coal in 1984 and 1987 there was a spectacular rise in output. The table indicates that coal increased by a third in nine years since the reforms were instituted. Crude oil, steel and pig iron outputs also showed a rise in output, particularly between the years 1978 and 1987. From this source, it would seem that the industrial aspect of the Four Modernizations likely did achieve great gains for the PRC, as Deng had planned.

The answer indicates that the question was understood. There are at least three points made about the table. All points are clear, supported with evidence from the table, and accurate. Good use of analysis and deduction.

Examination practice

Below are some exam-style questions for you to practise. Paper 1 exams are one hour long, not including five minutes of reading time at the exam's start when only reading is permitted. You may wish to only practise specific questions, and if this is the case, allow the following amounts of time per question:

Question 1:	5 minute
Question 2:	10 minutes
Question 3:	10 minutes
Question 4:	35 minutes

These questions relate to Deng Xiaoping's economic reforms from 1978 onwards. The sources used are found within this chapter on the following pages:

- Source A (page 45)
- Source B (page 46)
- Source G (page 53)
- Source J (page 57)
- Source K (page 58)

1 a) Why, according to Source A, did economic reform in the countryside gather pace from 1979 onwards? *(3 marks)*
(For guidance on how to answer this style of question see page 37.)

2 b) What message is conveyed by Source B? *(2 marks)*
(For guidance on how to answer this style of question see page 37.)

3 Compare and contrast the views expressed in Sources J and K about Deng Xiaoping's economic policies. *(6 marks)*
(For guidance on how to answer this style of question see page 91.)

4 With reference to their origin and purpose, discuss the value and limitations of Source J and Source K for historians assessing Deng Xiaoping's economic policies. *(6 marks)*
(For guidance on how to answer this style of question see page 130.)

5 Using these sources (Sources A, B, F, J, K) and your own knowledge, analyse the extent to which Deng Xiaoping's economic reforms were successful. *(8 marks)*
(For guidance on how to answer this style of question see page 160.)

 # Activities

1 Review the following economic reforms that you learned about in this chapter:
- the household responsibility system
- town and village enterprises
- Special Economic Zones
- changes to state-owned enterprises.

Which of these economic reforms was the most significant and which of these economic reforms was the least significant? Justify your decision within the format of a class debate.

2 'Deng Xiaoping was a capitalist in communist clothing.' Work in pairs to construct a 200-word evaluation supporting this statement and a 200-word evaluation challenging this statement. Include as many supporting examples as possible.

3 Based on what you have learned in this chapter, how far do you think that the Four Modernizations succeeded in improving the standard of living for ordinary Chinese people?

CHAPTER 4

China under Deng Xiaoping: political changes 1979–89

This chapter analyses the extent of the political changes initiated by Deng Xiaoping from 1979 and their limits, culminating in the death of protesters in Tiananmen Square in 1989. You need to consider the following questions throughout this chapter:

✪ How far reaching were the political changes between 1979 and 1989?

✪ What caused the protests in Tiananmen Square in 1989?

✪ How close did the 1989 protests come to establishing democracy?

✪ To what extent was Deng Xiaoping responsible for the deaths of the protesters?

 Political changes

> ▶ **Key question:** *How far reaching were the political changes between 1979 and 1989?*

When Deng opened the way for China to resolve its economic problems, he began a crisis of authority as demands for a more democratic, representative system grew. It is true that he thought the political control of the Chinese Communist Party (CCP) would be strong enough to curb any deviation from a communist form of government and, in fact, this form of government continues to exist in the PRC today. Nevertheless, the reforms in the economic realm did begin to spill over into the political realm, in terms of both domestic and foreign policy.

What were the aims of the Democracy Wall movement?

→ The 1978 Democracy Wall movement

In late 1978, pro-democracy posters began to appear on a 200-metre long brick wall along Chang'an Avenue, adjacent to Tiananmen Square in Beijing. Many posters criticized Mao explicitly, but the most memorable was simply entitled 'Democracy – the Fifth Modernization'. Essentially, the message of the poster was that the Four Modernizations were only worthwhile if proper democratic reforms were introduced at the same time. It argued that democracy was a universal right and that the CCP should not deny this right to the people. The poster was the creation of a former Red Guard, Wei Jingsheng, an electrician at Beijing Zoo. He was not a political leader or an intellectual writer, but his impassioned poster was an instant media sensation world-wide, thanks to the many western journalists frequenting the Democracy Wall and the growing numbers of people posting items and reading what was there.

Deng's attitude towards the so-called Democracy Wall was ambivalent. He had consented to the Wall for Red Guards to post their opinions, as a way of criticizing the Cultural Revolution and the Gang of Four, but it soon became more than this. On the one hand, protesters like Wei were supportive of Deng's efforts to modernize China economically and condemnations of Maoism suited Deng's political purposes at the time, as he sought to establish his grip on power. On the other hand, demands for democracy were far too radical for Deng.

The 'four cardinal principles'

In 1979 Deng laid down the **four cardinal principles** of PRC political life. These were:

- socialism
- the dictatorship of the proletariat
- the political leadership of the CCP
- Marxism–Leninism and Mao Zedong Thought.

This doctrine basically argued that key elements of Marxist political thought should not be challenged under any circumstances. Deng at the time was trying to impose economic reform while legitimizing Mao as an important party leader. Although Deng convinced many in the CCP, many citizens were not persuaded. People like Wei objected that the four cardinal principles prevented democratic change.

KEY TERM

Four cardinal principles
Deng Xiaoping's declaration on the nature of the PRC's government that stated that the PRC was a single-party state under the control of the CCP.

SOURCE A

Excerpt from a speech by Deng Xiaoping found in *Legitimating the Chinese Economic Reforms: A Rhetoric of Myth and Orthodoxy* by Alan R. Kluver, published by State University of New York Press, Albany, New York, USA, 1996, page 52. Kluver is Assistant Professor of Speech and Rhetoric and Director of the ASIAN Studies Program at Oklahoma City University in the USA. Deng gave the speech to the drafting committee of the 1981 Resolution on CCP History.

If we don't mention Mao Zedong Thought and don't make an appropriate evaluation of Comrade Mao's merits and demerits, the old workers will not feel satisfied, nor will the poor and lower-middle peasants of the period of land reform, nor the many cadres who have close ties with them. On no account can we discard the banner of Mao Zedong Thought. To do so would, in fact, be to negate the glorious history of our Party.

In Source A, what reasons does Deng give to justify the importance of Mao Zedong Thought?

The end of the movement

The Democracy Wall was pulled down in December 1979 and its most famous demonstrator, Wei, was jailed for 15 years. About 30 others were also arrested and all posters were removed. This crackdown occurred only three months after Deng had said that some criticism was allowed and it effectively quelled pro-democratic protests.

Overall, Deng made it clear he supported economic liberalization, but he also intended for the CCP to continue governing the PRC. Any hopes for democratic reform were ended for the time being.

What power struggles took place in the CCP?

Reformers and conservatives within the CCP

Reformers

Nevertheless, reformers in the CCP, such as Zhao Ziyang and Hu Yaobang, were granted positions of influence by Deng during the 1980s. In many ways, they were his chosen heirs. Zhao succeeded Hua Guofeng as Premier and Hu became General Secretary of the party in 1982. Both men were far more critical of Marxism than Deng had ever been. Zhao was willing to contemplate the privatization of the state-owned enterprises (see page 50), and in a speech given during a visit to the USA, he stated that socialism had failed to deliver economic growth.

Deng was willing to tolerate what in CCP terms were radical economic ideas because they fitted in with the general intention of the 'Four Modernizations'. However, Deng was no democrat and he was determined to ensure that while economic reforms pressed ahead, political reforms did not.

Democratic reforms

Deng did permit direct elections at county level to so-called **people's congresses** in 1980, but this was a long way from multi-party democracy. Even so, they had secret ballots and the candidates were not just party cadres, so this small democratic exercise served the government as it created an atmosphere of liberalization at local level. When the experiment was repeated in 1984, though, campaigning was strictly controlled to prevent candidates from criticizing the government.

In the same way, the **Chinese People's Political Consultative Conference** provided an opportunity for non-CCP members to discuss government policy, but it had no real power.

KEY TERM

People's congresses Legislative assemblies with limited power for political consultation under the leadership of the CCP.

Chinese People's Political Consultative Conference An advisory body to the Chinese government made up of delegates from the CCP and other political groups.

? According to its origin and purpose, assess the value and limitations of Source B.

SOURCE B

Chinese People's Political Consultative Conference, found in www.china.org.cn, accessed 25 June 2012. This open website is the official China Internet Information Centre.

Under the leadership of the CPC [Communist Party of China], the CPPCC [Chinese People's Political Consultative Conference] consists of representatives of the CPC, eight democratic parties, democrats with no party affiliations, various people's organizations, every ethnic group and all walks of life, compatriots from Taiwan, Hong Kong and Macao, and returned overseas Chinese, as well as specially invited individuals, reflecting the interests of various social strata.

However, in 1980, the so-called 'four freedoms' of the PRC's constitution, which had guaranteed certain rights such as freedom of assembly, protest, expression and to go on strike, were removed. This was another instance of showing that Deng was not prepared to allow Zhao and Hu to transform the politics of the country. He was determined to make sure that neither reformers nor the conservative old guard gained dominance within the party.

Leadership and power struggles

In 1987, there was a political crisis which, according to the historian Immanuel Hsü, marked a 'rising tide of conservatism'. Hu Yaobang submitted his resignation on 2 January 1987, having been blamed by Deng for allowing student protests in Hefei (see page 79) to escalate, which were then curtailed. The Politburo also accused Hu of 'a tendency towards complete Westernization'.

Conservatives in the party were glad to see Hu go, as he was viewed by them as an ambitious politician who seemed to have had aspirations to succeed Deng as paramount leader. Zhao, who had failed to support Hu in the Politburo, was named as the new General Secretary. However, it was clear that he faced hostility from within the CCP due to his relatively liberal political and economic ideas.

People's Liberation Army (PLA) generals had made it clear that they did not want Zhao to be in charge of the Military Affairs Commission, a part of the CCP governing body made up of senior generals who often were also senior party members. Deng made sure that there were checks on Zhao's influence. Li Peng, a cautious politician who could be relied on not to upset the CCP balance of power, was appointed Premier in 1987. In addition, a new **Central Advisory Commission** for the oldest generation of party leaders, like Chen Yun (see page 56), was created. According to journalist and author Jonathan Fenby, it acted as a 'solidly anti-progressive bloc'.

 **KEY TERM**

Central Advisory Commission A powerful body of CCP elders, all of whom had been members of the party for at least 40 years. It wielded a lot of political power behind the scenes during the 1980s.

According to Source C, what was the relationship between Deng and the PLA?

SOURCE C

A CCP propaganda poster from 1988 entitled 'Comrade Deng Xiaoping inspects the troops'.

Deng's resignation

In theory, Deng's resignation at the age of 83 from the Central Committee in 1987, after the Thirteenth Party Congress, marked his departure from frontline politics, along with many others from the Long March generation. He was now simply referred to in official pronouncements as Comrade Deng and there was little or no effort to promote a cult of personality similar to that which had surrounded Mao. However, Deng was not willing to give Zhao total independence to rule the PRC; Deng continued to insist that all key policy decisions were referred to him before implementation.

It is telling that one post that Deng did not give up was the chairmanship of the Military Affairs Commission. Of course, this enabled Deng to maintain a firm grip over the PLA, which he had recently modernized, guaranteeing him ultimate political power, as later events would demonstrate.

What did Deng Xiaoping's foreign policy reveal about his political and economic priorities?

Deng's foreign policy

Mao had established China's foreign policy as essentially preserving world peace, and the international *status quo*, in order to concentrate on building a socialist state within China without outside intervention. Deng departed from this route by expanding links with international capitalist economies in order to take China out of its underdeveloped economic state.

The USA and Taiwan

Since 1949, the most serious obstacle to positive relations between the USA and the PRC had always been the issue of Taiwan, also known as the Republic of China. The official policy of the US government had been to recognize Taiwan as the legitimate government of China, therefore denying the communist government of mainland China official diplomatic recognition. The CCP was deeply resentful towards what they regarded as a hostile remnant of the *Guomindang* or Chinese Nationalist Party (see page 18).

In the early 1970s, there was a gradual thawing in relations between the PRC and the USA, culminating in President Nixon visiting Beijing in 1972. Nixon's visit did not lead to the **normalization** of relations between the two countries because the USA continued to support Taiwan, much to the annoyance of the PRC. In May 1978, a compromise was reached and the USA agreed to withdraw its military forces from Taiwan within a year and to deny its government official diplomatic recognition, but to maintain trade links, including the sale of arms. In the end, the USA reduced arms sales to Taiwan and the way was opened for the USA to invest in the PRC.

In 1981, Deng publicly assured the people of Taiwan that he did not plan to take the island by force and were reunification to happen peacefully, the island would retain a high degree of autonomy. As the PRC's economy developed in the early 1980s, trade between Taiwan and the Chinese mainland increased rapidly. However, deep tensions remained in relations

KEY TERM

Guomindang A republican and nationalist political party founded by Sun Yat Sen, which controlled the Chinese government between 1926 and 1949.

Normalization The creation or resumption of regular diplomatic relations usually including an exchange of ambassadors and the establishment of embassies.

between the PRC and an island still perceived by many members of the CCP leadership as little more than a rebel province.

Normalization

What was far more significant than Nixon's visit to China was Deng's visit to the USA in January 1979. Soon the PRC was granted **most favoured nation trading status**. On 1 March 1979, the PRC received full public diplomatic recognition from the USA, as announced by US President Carter. The normalization of relations with the USA enabled Deng to establish closer relations with western nations than any of his predecessors, which of course had clear economic benefits for China.

Ultimately, it was in the interests of both the USA and PRC to have positive relations, as for both of them the USSR remained the main threat. To call the USA and the PRC allies in the 1980s would be an overstatement, but they clearly had a shared interest in opposing what Deng called Soviet **hegemony**. Therefore, by the end of the 1970s, the USA was supplying the PRC with advanced technology, such as electronic surveillance equipment, which could be used to observe Soviet military installations.

KEY TERM

Most favoured nation trading status A term used to describe countries, such as China, granted favourable terms of economic exchange with the USA.

Hegemony A term deriving from ancient Greek used to describe those countries which establish political and military dominance over their neighbours.

SOURCE D

US trade with China, 1970–2007, from 'International trade and US relations with China' by Benjamin O. Fordham and Katja B. Kleinberg in *Foreign Policy Analysis*, Vol. 7, Issue 3, July 2011, page 219. The authors are professors in the Department of Political Science, Binghamton University, State University of New York, USA. *Foreign Policy Analysis* is a journal of the International Studies Association and has been published since 1959 in the USA.

According to Source D, what can be inferred about trade relations between the USA and the PRC from 1985 onwards?

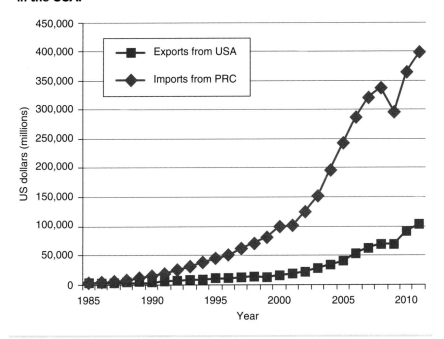

Why did the USSR
pose a threat to the
PRC?

Relations with the USSR

In 1979, one of the key reasons why Deng went to visit US President Carter was to make sure that he would have the support of the USA in any future confrontation with the USSR. Since the 1960s, the USSR and the PRC had had difficult relations and had even fought over territory in 1969. Deng was very open with the US media during his visit about the perceived dangers of Soviet expansionism. However, over the course of the 1980s, there was a gradual thaw in relations with the USSR. In particular, once Mikhail Gorbachev became the leader of the USSR in 1985, there was a gradual improvement in relations. In 1986, the PRC and the USSR signed an agreement over the shared use of rivers on their mutual borders. Gorbachev's 1989 visit to Beijing finally resolved border disputes in central Asia and re-established full economic links between the two states.

The invasion of Vietnam

The PRC's invasion of Vietnam in 1979 was ultimately driven by Deng's hostility to the USSR.

US forces withdrew from Vietnam in 1973 after a failed attempt to prevent South Vietnam from falling to communist guerrillas supported by North Vietnam. Once Vietnam was unified under a communist government 1975, the USSR provided much-needed aid for the state.

🔑 KEY TERM

Vietnam War Part of the
Cold War, this was a conflict
that had started in 1954
between non-communist
South Vietnam, supported by
the USA, and communist
North Vietnam. The USA left
in 1973 and Vietnam was
unified in 1975.

The PRC did not like to see its sphere of influence in eastern Asia threatened. Deng already felt betrayed by Vietnam, as thousands of PRC troops had been sent to help North Vietnam against the USA during the **Vietnam War**. Further, the communist government in Vietnam angered Deng by signing a friendship treaty with the USSR in 1978 and joining COMECON (see page 15), an organization that the PRC had deliberately not joined in order to avoid control by the USSR.

In late 1978, Vietnam invaded neighbouring Cambodia, an ally of the PRC. This invasion, with the assistance of Soviet advisors, was perceived by Deng as a policy of encirclement of the PRC by its enemies: the USSR in the north and now Vietnam in the south. In addition, ethnic Chinese were persecuted in Vietnam and over 100,000 were forced to flee the country.

Deng's intention was to inflict a short, sharp defeat on Vietnam in order to demonstrate the PRC's dominance in south-east Asia. However, the PLA's invasion of Vietnam in February 1979 was not a success and lasted only 21 days. China spent $1.36 billion and suffered 46,000 casualties.

Impact of the invasion on Chinese politics

The brief war with Vietnam revealed that the PLA lacked the modern military equipment of an effective fighting force, especially given the superior forces and equipment of Soviet-backed Vietnam. This had an impact on PRC politics, gradually helping to turn the PLA into the professional armed forces of the country, rather than the standard-bearers of Maoist revolution. By

SOURCE E

Map of the PRC and its neighbouring states in the 1960s.

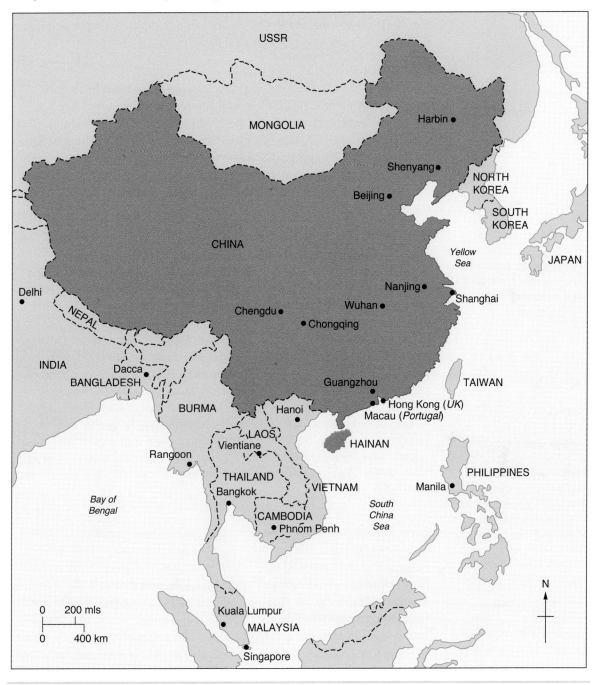

What does Source E reveal about China's geopolitical situation?

1985, the PLA only occupied 15 per cent of seats on the Central Committee, compared to 50 per cent in 1969. In 1986, there were only three PLA generals in the Politburo, compared to 13 in 1969. The PLA's importance diminished over time, as the CCP under Deng became a stronger political body.

Hong Kong

Hong Kong island had been a British colony since 1842 and in 1898 the British government leased further land adjacent to Hong Kong island, known as the New Territories. By the 1980s, the end of the 100-year lease on the New Territories was due to expire. Firms and investors in Hong Kong, both British and Hong Kong Chinese, were worried that their businesses and democratic freedoms would be jeopardized when the port was returned to China in 1997. In 1982, the British Prime Minister Margaret Thatcher visited the PRC.

SOURCE F

Excerpt from *China Daily* online at www.chinadaily.com.cn/china/cpc2011/2010-09/09/content_12481219.htm (9 September 2009). *China Daily* is one of the PRC's five top state news sites. Its purpose is to inform foreign readers in English of the latest news and background about the PRC.

She [Mrs Thatcher] said that if China agrees to continued British administration of Hong Kong after 1997, Britain may consider China's demand for sovereignty over Hong Kong. In response to her views, Deng Xiaoping made important remarks when meeting Mrs. Thatcher. Deng said: 'Our stand on Hong Kong is explicit. Three issues are involved here. First is the issue of sovereignty. The second is that in what way China will administer Hong Kong after 1997 to ensure its prosperity. The third is that the Chinese and British governments should have consultations to ensure that no major disturbances occur in Hong Kong in the 15 years leading to 1997.' Deng pointed out that 'sovereignty is not negotiable'.

There were several years of negotiations regarding the transition of Hong Kong from British to PRC control, reaching an agreement in 1984. Both Deng and Thatcher agreed that in 1997 sovereignty of Hong Kong and the New Territories would be transferred to the PRC and that it would become a **Special Administrative Region** within the PRC. Deng promised to respect Hong Kong's significant degree of political and economic autonomy and British-style educational and legal system. This policy of ensuring the return of Hong Kong by allowing it to retain its free market was known as the **one country–two systems** policy. Sovereignty was transferred to China in 1997.

?

According to Source F, what three issues did Deng point out in his meeting with Thatcher in 1982?

 **KEY TERM**

Special Administrative Region Parts of the PRC, such as Hong Kong, granted a degree of political autonomy in recognition of their colonial past and long history of separation from the rest of China.

One country–two systems A term used to describe Deng's strategy of reunifying China by allowing former colonies such as Hong Kong a measure of political, economic and cultural freedom, within the over-arching framework of the PRC.

Domestic		Foreign
Progressive	**Anti-progressive**	• More conciliatory attitude towards Taiwan
• 1980: direct elections to People's Congresses • 1982: reformers in CCP, such as Hu Yaobang, given positions of influence (economic rather than political reformers)	1979: Four cardinal principles • socialism • dictatorship of the proletariat • political leadership of the CCP • Marxism–Leninism and Mao Zedong Thought 1979: Democracy Wall movement put down – hopes for democratic reform ended 1980: the 'four freedoms' of the Chinese constitution removed 1987: Li Peng appointed premier 1987: Central Advisory Commission created	• Normalization of diplomatic relations with the USA • Late 1970s: tense relations with the USSR which thawed in the mid-1980s • Unsuccessful invasion of Vietnam in 1979 • 1984: 'One country–two systems' agreement on Hong Kong

SUMMARY DIAGRAM

Political changes

The road to Tiananmen Square

> ▶ *Key question: What caused the protests in Tiananmen Square in 1989?*

This section will deal with some of the challenges to authority and political aspirations of some of the Chinese population between 1978 and 1989, which developed with Deng's **market socialism** and led to a violent collision in Beijing's Tiananmen Square in 1989.

PRC society in the 1980s

Students

The social problems associated with economic liberalization described in Chapter 3 led to growing discontent among various groups during the 1980s, especially students. By 1988, many university students were concerned that their study grants from the government were not keeping pace with inflation. They had been subjected to a fiercely competitive school system which allowed only the top five per cent to carry on to university. With economic change sweeping away the old socialist certainties of guaranteed employment (see page 51), there was a lack of jobs for young graduates,

 **KEY TERM**

Market socialism China's blend of a communist command economy with capitalist reforms such as a free price system and a mix of state and privately owned businesses and industries.

← **What sectors of Chinese society were aggrieved by the Chinese government?**

especially if they lacked the patronage of senior cadres. This situation led to corruption as a means of advancement.

Historian Roderick MacFarquhar, Professor of Chinese History at Harvard University, has pointed out that 'One important new source of corruption in the post-reform era was the hybrid nature of China's partially restructured economy ... scattered islands of free-market autonomy floating in a sea of socialist planning.' Government anti-corruption policies were unable to keep up with the inventiveness of new schemes.

? According to Source G, what forms of corruption took place in Hainan Island in 1984?

SOURCE G

Excerpt from 'Reform begins with transgression,' by Wu Xiaobo, from the blog Mind Meters (in Chinese), found in Danwei, 30 May 2006. www.danwei.org/business_and_finance/skirting_the_law_and_the_growth. php. danwei.org is a website about media, advertising and urban life in China. Wu Xiaobo is a financial author and publisher who writes a column in *The Economic Observer*, and contributes to the blog Mind Meters, the source of the following extracts.

The Hainan Island car-trafficking incident erupted in June 1984, and during the course of a year, that region imported and illegally brought to the mainland 89,000 cars. Because of expectations of enormous profit, the entire island went crazy. Even kindergartens made up sales documents ... In this way, graft, bribery, illegal currency exchange, and all sorts of illegal activity took place out in the open ... Apart from cars, 2.86 million televisions and 252,000 video recorders were also imported. During the course of one year, Hainan acquired US$570 million in foreign currency at illegally high prices from 21 provinces and cities as well as 15 central government units. Altogether, companies racked up 4.21 billion RMB [yuan] in loans, more than 1 billion RMB more than the value of Hainan's industry and agriculture in 1984.

Agricultural workers

By the 1980s, as family farming was instituted as part of economic reforms, where before everyone had earned equally low wages, there were now large disparities in incomes, creating resentment. As farming became more efficient and needed less labour, many unemployed peasants flocked to the cities. In the countryside, increasing resentment over Deng's preferential treatment of the coastal regions became manifest. Pollution also became an issue, as lack of environmental regulations led to contaminated reservoirs and health repercussions on people and crops when these waters were used for irrigation and for supplying villages.

Writers and artists

Former city-dwellers who had been forced for re-education to rural areas by the Cultural Revolution (see page 19), began returning to the cities and writing about their experiences and the poor state of the countryside and its workers. Despite the ending of the Democracy Wall movement, various writers and artists continued to express themselves and their concerns.

SOURCE H

Excerpt from 'Who is a feminist? Understanding the ambivalence towards Shanghai Baby, "body writing" and feminism in post-women's liberation China' by Xueping Zhong, in *Gender & History*, Vol. 18, No. 3, November 2006, page 641. Professor Xueping Zhong teaches at Tufts University in Boston, USA. *Gender & History* is a scholarly journal published in the UK that features articles regarding gender identity and relations.

As a whole, together with the general development of literature in China at the time, women's literature in China was to experience a decade of renaissance during the 1980s. Different generations of women writers were writing and publishing at the same time, as they engaged in dialogue with the CCP-led women's liberation legacies, with male intellectuals, with themselves and, either implicitly or explicitly, with feminists outside China. Significantly, open-door reform policies that started in the late 1970s made communication with the outside world increasingly possible.

According to Source H, what was the effect of reforms in the PRC in the late 1970s?

CCP General Secretary Hu Yaobang reversed the anti-intellectual ethos of the Cultural Revolution by calling for writers and artists to become a more valued and respected part of society, while Deng stated that it was possible to be an intellectual and a member of the proletariat. Writer Wang Meng stimulated the budding environment of intellectuals and artists when he became Minister of Culture from 1986 to 1989. Wang was dismissed once it was believed there needed to be more control of intellectuals who were critical of the government and its policies.

One-child policy

Some of the government's social policies were also deeply unpopular. The one-child policy (see page 30) to restrict population growth was severely resented.

SOURCE I

Excerpt from a speech entitled 'Uphold the Four Cardinal Principles' given by Deng Xiaoping on 30 March 1979, taken from *Selected Works of Deng Xiaoping (1975–1982)*, published by Foreign Language Press, Beijing, China, 1984, page 172. Deng Xiaoping gave this speech to a forum on the principles for the party's theoretical work.

… We have a large population but not enough arable land. Of China's population of more than 900 million, 80 per cent are peasants. While there are advantages to having a large population, there are disadvantages as well. When production is insufficiently developed, it poses serious problems with regard to food, education and employment. We must greatly increase our efforts in family planning; but even if the population does not grow for a number of years, we will still have a population problem for a certain period … This is a distinctive characteristic which we must take into account in carrying out our modernization programme.

What arguments does Deng use in Source I to support a strict one-child policy?

This law, implemented in January 1981, was enforced in urban areas and exempted ethnic minorities. It was perceived as a direct challenge to the traditional belief that large families were needed to farm and in order to guarantee a son to continue the ancestral line.

Couples who had a second child often lost economic privileges such as private food plots. On the other hand, the law also gave longer maternity leave and other benefits to couples that postponed childbearing to later years. The policy was severely criticized as encouraging female infanticide, with many couples deciding that if they could only have one child, it must be male. Others, especially in rural areas, simply ignored the policy and in 1981 over 1.5 million children were born into families that already had at least five children. The control of the CCP on such personal decisions as childbearing created increasing tension in the 1980s.

Balance between advances and social discontent

It should be remembered that the PRC under Deng was not as repressive and totalitarian as it had been under Mao. Some intellectual freedom was now permitted. Furthermore, during the 1980s, many in the PRC were economically independent and becoming more socially mobile than in previous decades. A law passed in 1980 confirmed women's legal rights, such as divorce, and it was possible for women to wear modern fashions and make-up in public, without risking the displeasure of the Red Guards as they would have done during the Cultural Revolution. However, despite these advances, social discontent in China by 1989 was significant. Many historians argue that it contributed towards a desire for some sort of political change, especially among the younger generation.

How did grievances and dissent escalate to public protest?

The student movement

Growing unrest

The number of student **dissidents** began to grow in the 1980s, encouraged by a number of factors:

KEY TERM

Dissident A person who challenges the political *status quo* in a single-party state.

- In 1984, US President Reagan had visited China in order to improve its commercial and diplomatic relations with the USA, especially regarding US support of Taiwan, always a sore point with the PRC. While there, he had a made a speech calling for greater political freedom for the Chinese people. Uncensored copies of the speech were soon being circulated, especially on university campuses.
- In 1986, popular demonstrations in the Philippines brought down the Marcos dictatorship, and student demonstrations in Taiwan calling for elections followed later that year, inspiring students in the PRC.
- Many students were also stirred by an academic recently returned from Princeton University in the USA and a world-renowned astrophysicist named Fang Lizhi, who argued in favour of human rights, the gradual

introduction of democracy and total intellectual freedom. Fang had been persecuted in the aftermath of the Hundred Flowers Campaign (see page 18) in 1957 and had emerged as the most famous dissident in China by 1986. Deng dismissed Fang's ideas.

SOURCE J

Excerpts from a speech entitled 'Take a Clear-cut Stand Against Bourgeois Liberalization' of 30 December 1986 by Deng Xiaoping to the Central Committee of the CCP found in the *People's Daily* (in English) at http://english.peopledaily.com.cn/dengxp/vol3/text/c1630.html. This online newspaper is the official organ of the CCP.

I have read Fang Lizhi's speeches. He doesn't sound like a Communist Party member at all. Why do we keep people like him in the Party? He should be expelled, not just persuaded to quit … In developing our democracy, we cannot simply copy bourgeois democracy, or introduce the system of a balance of three powers. I have often criticized people in power in the United States, saying that actually they have three governments. Of course, the American bourgeoisie uses this system in dealing with other countries, but when it comes to internal affairs, the three branches often pull in different directions, and that makes trouble. We cannot adopt such a system. By carrying out the open policy, learning foreign technologies and utilizing foreign capital, we mean to promote socialist construction, not to deviate from the socialist road.

> According to Source J, why is Deng opposed to US-style democracy?

Protests spread

In December 1986, student protests began in Hefei in eastern China, where Fang Lizhi was the Vice-President of the University of Science and Technology. Protests were triggered by alleged manipulation of elections to the People's Congresses, as well as poor boarding conditions for students. What began as a gathering to commemorate an official student event in 1935 became a protest lasting for several hours. Local authorities postponed the People's Congress elections. Since the protests were not crushed, they quickly spread to Shanghai, Wuhan and Beijing, and soon pro-democratic banners were displayed. In Beijing, 4000 students marched on Tiananmen Square and publicly burned copies of communist newspapers. In Shanghai, 30,000 students marched through the centre of the city carrying pro-democracy banners.

CCP repercussions

Initially, the party leadership was surprised, but soon imposed a ban on marches and protest meetings. In January 1987, Fang Lizhi was dismissed from his post but Hu Yaobang (see page 69) was held responsible. He was severely criticized for not having taken a stronger stand from the beginning of the demonstrations and though he remained in the Politburo, Deng made sure he submitted his resignation as General Secretary of the CCP. The PRC government was increasingly concerned about political dissent, despite the fact that the 1986 protests soon died away when demonstrators were threatened with severe punishments. It appeared that protests were quelled for the moment. Deng was so concerned to deny Fang Lizhi publicity that when US President George Bush visited Beijing in February 1989, Fang was prevented from attending a dinner at the US Embassy. Fang was allowed to leave the country in 1990 and to go into exile.

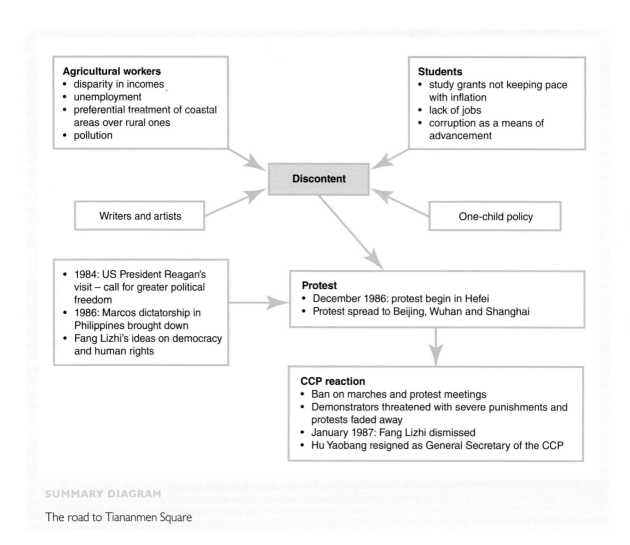

The diagram content:

Agricultural workers
- disparity in incomes
- unemployment
- preferential treatment of coastal areas over rural ones
- pollution

Students
- study grants not keeping pace with inflation
- lack of jobs
- corruption as a means of advancement

Writers and artists

Discontent

One-child policy

- 1984: US President Reagan's visit – call for greater political freedom
- 1986: Marcos dictatorship in Philippines brought down
- Fang Lizhi's ideas on democracy and human rights

Protest
- December 1986: protest begin in Hefei
- Protest spread to Beijing, Wuhan and Shanghai

CCP reaction
- Ban on marches and protest meetings
- Demonstrators threatened with severe punishments and protests faded away
- January 1987: Fang Lizhi dismissed
- Hu Yaobang resigned as General Secretary of the CCP

SUMMARY DIAGRAM

The road to Tiananmen Square

The events of 1989

> ▶ *Key question: How close did the 1989 protests come to establishing democracy?*

After Hu Yaobang was forced to resign, Deng concentrated on strengthening party discipline. Some high-ranking officials were expelled and Zhao Ziyang became General Secretary of the CCP, leading the Thirteenth Party Congress in 1987. The apparent calm was not to last.

April 1989 demonstrations

Hu Yaobang's death

On 15 April 1989, Hu Yaobang died of a heart attack. He had been one of the most committed and popular reformers in the CCP and, in death, he began to be portrayed as a democratic martyr although he was never a committed democrat. Hu's death was the initial catalyst for student protests in Tiananmen Square in much the same way as Zhou Enlai's death had been the pretext for action in 1976 (see page 24). At first, there were few protesters; they marched solemnly paying respects to Hu. But by 17 April, there were up to 10,000 students in Tiananmen Square with some chanting pro-democracy slogans. Specific demands of the students included full disclosure of information by the government regarding the incomes of top CCP leaders and their families. This reflected the widespread public anger at rampant corruption. Relatively few of the demonstrators seem to have wanted the overthrow of the CCP itself.

> **What caused the student demonstrations to begin again?**

CCP reaction

On 20 April, more than 400 student protesters were arrested. However, this failed to prevent the demonstrations from spreading to other large cities like Nanjing and Shanghai, where student boycotts of classes became widespread. In Changsha, posters appeared which read: 'Down with Deng!' Other groups began to join in challenging the government. The Beijing Workers' Autonomous Federation, for example, formed by factory workers, issued a statement blaming corrupt CCP officials for all the ills of the people. Up to 10,000 party cadres joined the demonstrators.

On 22 April, Hu Yaobang's memorial service took place in Beijing. As senior CCP leaders left the ceremony, they were confronted by tens of thousands of students chanting 'dialogue, dialogue, we demand dialogue!' Students tried and failed to pass a petition to Premier Li Peng.

On 23 April, CCP General Secretary Zhao Ziyang departed on a state visit to North Korea. This allowed hard-line elements led by Premier Li Peng to dominate Politburo meetings while he was away. Two days later, a meeting took place at Deng's house at which he declared that the protests were 'a

What, according to Source K, were conditions like in Tiananmen Square on 22 April 1989?

Protesters face to face with the police on the day of Hu Yaobang's memorial service, 22 April 1989.

well-planned plot whose real aim is to reject the CCP and the socialist system'. Deng made clear that in the internal battle between Zhao Ziyang's reformers and Li Peng's hard-liners, he was going to side with the latter. Deng authorized a *People's Daily* editorial that criticized the student demonstrations as an organized plot against the nation. The editorial was also broadcast on the radio so that it would reach the widest possible audience. Zhao sent a telegram from North Korea agreeing with the editorial.

At the end of April, as security forces failed to prevent a protest march through central Beijing, Zhao returned from North Korea. He continued to believe that the protests could be contained without the use of violence and stated that the students' demands were 'reasonable'. Zhao Ziyang and Li Peng clashed; Li was in favour of the immediate restoration of order in Beijing, by force if necessary. In contrast, Zhao stated, 'if the party does not hold up the banner of democracy in our country, someone else will'. In essence, he was arguing that the CCP should begin to take the initiative in terms of political reform.

On 4 May, Fang Lizhi wrote to Deng. In the letter, he asked for the release of political prisoners, including Wei Jingsheng (see page 66). By this stage, there were up to 150,000 students in the square. Zhao made a speech to the Asia Development Bank in which he stated that the government would deal with the crisis peacefully.

Protests intensify

During the second week of May, student leaders like Chai Ling launched a hunger strike in order to put more political pressure on the Politburo. Within a few days, over 300 students were refusing food and posters were put up in English describing their actions for foreign journalists to read. Other student leaders, like Wu'erkaixi from Xinjiang, were openly critical of what he termed the 'corrupt rotten eggs' that ran the country.

On 15 May, Soviet leader Gorbachev arrived in Beijing for the first Sino-Soviet summit in over 20 years. By this stage there were hundreds of thousands of workers and even farmers from the countryside gathered in Tiananmen Square. Some of the placards carried the slogan, 'Zhao Ziyang is China's Gorbachev', referring to Gorbachev's policy of openness to political reform in the USSR (see page 146).

On 17 May, another meeting took place at Deng's house. Deng firmly stated that giving in to student demands would lead to political chaos. His solution was to impose **martial law** and summon troops to Beijing in the hope that this would intimidate students into dispersing. On the same day there was another meeting of the Politburo at which an increasingly isolated and powerless Zhao Ziyang opposed Deng's solution.

Hunger strikes

On 18 May, Li Peng went to Tiananmen Square to meet some student protesters. He delivered a stern lecture, refusing to accept the students'

> ← **Why did the protesters ultimately fail?**

KEY TERM

Martial law The suspension of civil law and the constitution and its replacement by military rule.

SOURCE L

Zhao Ziyang addresses pro-democracy hunger strikers on the morning of 19 May 1989.

> Assess the value and limitation of Source L for discovering the political views of Zhao Ziyang. **?**

definition of their protests as 'patriotic'. By this stage, the student movement itself was divided. More cautious elements believed that the time had come to evacuate Tiananmen Square before the inevitable security crackdown, while radicals like Chai Ling favoured further protests, hopeful that the PLA would not attack its own people. This lack of unified leadership and a clear political strategy was to cost the protesters dearly.

On 19 May, Zhao Ziyang visited a hospital in Beijing and gave a sympathetic hearing to the student hunger strikers; they refused to cease their strike. The Politburo decided to impose martial law.

Martial law

On 20 May, the day after Gorbachev left the PRC, martial law was proclaimed (see Source M).

?

In what ways does Li Peng seek to justify the imposition of martial law in Source M?

SOURCE M

Li Peng's announcement of martial law on 20 May 1989 from *The Search for Modern China: A Documentary Collection* edited by Pei-kai Cheng, Michael Lestz and Jonathan Spence, published by W.W. Norton & Co., New York, USA, 1999, pages 496–9. Cheng is a Professor of History at Pace University in New York, USA. Lestz is Professor of History and Chairman of the History Department at Trinity College, in Connecticut, USA. Spence is a Professor of History at Yale University, USA.

The party and the government have on one hand taken every possible measure to treat and rescue the fasting students. On the other hand, they have held several dialogues with representatives of the fasting students and have earnestly promised to continue listening to their opinions in the future, in the hope that the students would end the hunger strike immediately. But the dialogues did not yield results as expected. Representatives of the hunger-striking students said that they could no longer control the situation in Tiananmen Square, packed with extremely excited crowds who kept shouting demagogic [politically provocative] slogans. If we fail to put an end to such chaos immediately and let it go unchecked, it will very likely lead to a situation which none of us want to see ... It has become more and more clear that the very few people who attempt to create turmoil want to reach their political goals – negating the leadership of the Communist Party of China and the socialist system and violating the Constitution ... They spread rumors and smear party and government leaders. They concentrate their attack on Comrade Deng Xiaoping ... On behalf of the Party Central Committee and the state council, I now call on the whole party, the whole army and the whole nation to make concerted efforts and act immediately at all posts so as to stop the turmoil and stabilize the situation ... All the public security personnel and armed policemen should make greater efforts to maintain traffic and social order, intensify security and resolutely crack down on criminal activities ...

Twenty-three PLA divisions from distant provinces were summoned to the capital. A tense stand-off between student protesters and the PLA took place. The students were helped by workers blocking avenues leading to

Tiananmen Square preventing PLA units from reaching it. The number of protesters staying overnight in Tiananmen Square shrank from hundreds of thousands to tens of thousands.

On 21 May, Deng and other senior figures in the party decided to remove Zhao. He was removed as General Secretary and later replaced by a Deng loyalist, Jiang Zemin.

On 2 June, Deng Xiaoping gave the order that Tiananmen Square should be cleared of protesters within two days. He now had at his disposal 350,000 troops in Beijing. Thousands of protesters still remained in Tiananmen Square, gathered around a replica of the Statue of Liberty, the so-called Goddess of Democracy, erected on 30 May. Some protesters were even explicitly critical of Deng himself. One placard openly mocked the paramount leader's most famous saying: 'it doesn't matter if a cat is black or white, as long as it resigns'. By this stage some leaders, such as the rock singer Hou Dejian, started to realize that a military crackdown was imminent and urged withdrawal. Some wanted a nation-wide hunger strike and for Tiananmen Square to be occupied by the students until at least 20 June.

On the night of 3–4 June, PLA units established control over Beijing by force. Many of the confrontations that took place were relayed live around the world by western television networks. By contrast, on PRC government television, there were simply warnings to citizens to keep off the streets, ominously stating that if they did not, only they were responsible for the consequences. Most fighting actually took place in the western suburbs of Beijing where protesters attacked the PLA with homemade weapons such as petrol bombs. Many of those fighting were not actually students but discontented workers, upset at unemployment and CCP corruption. Historian Jack Gray estimates that up to one million people may have defied martial law that night. At least 1000 civilians died in the clashes. Tiananmen Square was cleared of protesters.

On 9 June, Deng appeared on television to congratulate the security forces for having dealt so effectively with what he termed the 'dregs of society'.

SOURCE N

Excerpt from Deng's address to military commanders on 9 June 1989, reprinted in *The Search for Modern China: A Documentary Collection* edited by Pei-kai Cheng, Michael Lestz and Jonathan Spence, published by W.W. Norton & Co., New York, USA, 1999, pages 501–2. Cheng is a Professor of History at Pace University in New York, USA. Lestz is Professor of History and Chairman of the History Department at Trinity College, in Connecticut, USA. Spence is a Professor of History at Yale University, USA.

First of all, I'd like to express my heartfelt condolences to the comrades in the People's Liberation Army, the armed police, and the police, who died in the struggle ... This storm was bound to happen sooner or later ... It has turned out in our favor for we still have a large group of veterans who have experienced

What message is Deng Xiaoping trying to convey about the Tiananmen Square uprising in Source N?

many storms and have a thorough understanding of things. They were on the side to taking resolute action to counter the turmoil. Although some comrades may not understand this now, they will understand eventually and will support the decision of the Central Committee ... Their [the students'] goal was to establish a bourgeois republic entirely dependent on the West. Of course we accept people's demands for combating corruption. We are even ready to listen to some persons with ulterior motives when they raise the slogan about fighting corruption. However, such slogans were just a front. Their real aim was to overthrow the communist party and topple the socialist system.

To what extent did Deng Xiaoping succeed in maintaining his grip on power after 1989?

The political crackdown after 1989

In the aftermath of the crackdown in Beijing, public discussion of the protests was not permitted. Over 4000 arrests were made and 29 executions of protesters carried out. Some of the arrests included party cadres who had been sympathetic to the demonstrators, who were sentenced to jail for 10–20 years. Deng, with the PLA and the CCP leadership, was actually able to re-establish control relatively easily and show stability, an important element in economic development. In rural areas and many Special Economic Zones (SEZs), there had been little sign of political discontent in 1989.

The main political casualty of the crisis was obviously Zhao Ziyang. However, Deng also blamed Li Peng for having failed to contain the student movement. This perhaps explains why Deng made sure that the mayor of Shanghai, Jiang Zemin, who had controlled demonstrations there, became General Secretary of the Party. Jiang contained protests without using the PLA; he also belonged to the next generation. Several other younger party members were also promoted to the Politburo and continued on Deng's path to uphold the 'four cardinal principles' (see page 67) while at the same supporting economic reform. In August 1989, Deng officially resigned his last remaining post as head of the Central Military Commission and after consultation with the Politburo, Jiang was given that position as well.

On other fronts, Deng did face a backlash from hard-liners in the party, many of whom saw in the events of 1989 the consequences of 'bourgeois liberalization'. A group of 32 senior party members even suggested that the SEZs be abolished altogether. However, Deng and his successors pressed ahead with the PRC's programme of economic liberalization, while carefully avoiding any hint of democratic political reform. Instead, Deng concentrated on convincing disaffected youth to be patriotic and proud of the PRC's advances as a communist country. This was especially important as communism ended in eastern Europe, including the USSR, starting in the late 1980s (see Chapters 6 and 7).

Economic development

One of Deng's last significant political interventions came in 1992, when he felt that his economic reforms were under threat. His visit of four cities, called the 'southern tour', to centres of economic growth like Shenzhen, rallied support for the cause of further economic reform. The path of economic development that Deng had laid down at the end of the 1970s was therefore able to continue into the 1990s. He felt that if more people took part in the PRC's growing economy and obtained a better standard of living, the CCP would have national support to continue to govern. By 1992, the PRC enjoyed an $18.3 billion **trade surplus** with the USA and possessed **foreign currency reserves** of over $40 billion. The foundations of modern economic strength had been laid.

 **KEY TERM**

Trade surplus When a country sells more than it buys from other countries it trades with.

Foreign currency reserves Foreign currencies and precious metals, like gold, that a country holds in its central bank.

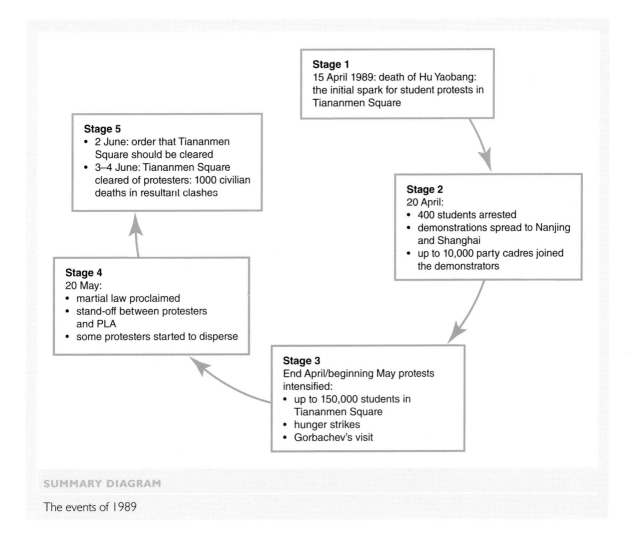

Stage 1
15 April 1989: death of Hu Yaobang: the initial spark for student protests in Tiananmen Square

Stage 2
20 April:
- 400 students arrested
- demonstrations spread to Nanjing and Shanghai
- up to 10,000 party cadres joined the demonstrators

Stage 3
End April/beginning May protests intensified:
- up to 150,000 students in Tiananmen Square
- hunger strikes
- Gorbachev's visit

Stage 4
20 May:
- martial law proclaimed
- stand-off between protesters and PLA
- some protesters started to disperse

Stage 5
- 2 June: order that Tiananmen Square should be cleared
- 3–4 June: Tiananmen Square cleared of protesters: 1000 civilian deaths in resultant clashes

SUMMARY DIAGRAM

The events of 1989

Key debate

> ▶ **Key question:** *To what extent was Deng Xiaoping responsible for the deaths of the protesters?*

Deng Xiaoping: misguided architect of repression?

KEY TERM

Counter-revolutionary
Political action made in opposition to an earlier political change.

Tiananmen Papers
A collection of CCP documents, published in the West in 2001, which include transcripts of key political meetings in 1989 attended by Deng Xiaoping, Zhao Ziyang and Li Peng.

The official CCP interpretation of the events of 3–4 June 1989 is that Deng acted in order to suppress an armed **counter-revolutionary** coup, launched with foreign help. No evidence has been presented that there was foreign involvement.

Nevertheless, it is the view of many historians that the crucial reason for the decisive military crackdown was that Deng was frightened of the political implications of the 1989 protests. Deng undoubtedly had the *power* to act. Following the Thirteenth Party Congress, he still had the formal right to be consulted on crucial decisions of the Politburo and, of course, he also possessed unequalled status as the key architect of the PRC's post-Mao reforms. Having seen the first political cracks beginning to appear in the Soviet bloc, Deng was determined that nothing similar would happen in the PRC.

The **Tiananmen Papers** make it clear that Deng was determined to prevent the sort of anarchy that had occurred during the Cultural Revolution. These papers are also explicit about Deng's determination to impose martial law and bring the PLA into Beijing. It should also be noted that there is a historiographical debate on the true aims of the students. For example, according to historian David Priestland, Deng appears to have misjudged the political views of the protesters. They were not 'counter-revolutionaries' wanting US-style democracy but, rather, anxious to secure a reform of the communist system, as was happening in the USSR at the time (see page 143).

Most recent western scholarship proposes that Deng insisted on taking a firm stance against demonstrators to protect the PRC from disintegrating. Professor Ezra F. Vogel, in *Deng Xiaoping and the Transformation of China*, published in 2011, supports the view that Deng was extremely worried about what was happening at the time in eastern Europe, particularly in Hungary, where concessions had led to further demands. The authority of the CCP had to be emphasized. Deng also pointed out that in Shanghai strong measures had stopped demonstrations and so martial law should be applied in Beijing.

Deng: less powerful than he at first appeared?

Some historians have questioned whether Deng was actually powerful enough to be in a position to take full responsibility for what happened on 3–4 June 1989. He had stepped down from the Politburo after the Thirteenth Party Congress and was less of a frontline political figure than he had been earlier in the decade, albeit still with a major say in key policy decisions. In *Prisoner of the State: The Secret Journal of Chinese Premier Zhao Ziyang*, Zhao portrays Deng as a declining, indecisive figure, and therefore open to manipulation by other politicians. Zhao's memoirs also place a great deal of the blame for what happened on the conservative Li. He is portrayed in this work as a politician actively seeking to break up the political partnership that had previously existed between Deng and Zhao, and the instigator of the crucial *People's Daily* editorial on 26 April (see page 82), which did so much to raise tensions.

Historian Immanuel Hsü goes further and openly questions whether the party elders were actually engaged in what he calls a 'plot' to ensure a military showdown and defeat the cause of political reform once and for all. Hsü identifies Li Peng as the dominant hard-line voice in the Politburo and describes him as issuing the final order on 3 June to clear Tiananmen Square by force.

Conclusion

Whether Deng was the deliberate architect of a brutal crackdown, a shrewd leader or simply an old man in decline, manipulated by forces and politicians beyond his immediate control, few historians dispute the fact that the deaths of hundreds, if not thousands of protesters in Tiananmen Square, left him with what historian J.A.G. Roberts calls a 'tarnished' reputation. Ultimately, it is probably fair to say that the events of 3–4 June 1989 could not have unfolded in the way they did without the political intervention and guidance of a figure who, despite his advanced years, was still the dominant force within the CCP. This is certainly made clear by the most credible evidence that historians have available: the Tiananmen Papers.

Few historians see Deng as a brutal monster, revelling in violence. Instead, their picture is a rather more nuanced one of a politician committed to a one-party state, trying to use martial law and the *threat* of violence as a political tool, to end protests, which endangered the authoritarian system that he believed guaranteed the stability needed for economic development. However, even if Deng acted reluctantly, after exhausting all other political options, it does not alter the fact that he *did* act. He probably did not rejoice at the deaths on 3–4 June 1989 and he almost certainly underestimated the amount of resistance the PLA would face. However, even had he known the death toll, Deng would probably still have pursued the same course of

We know much about the tragic events in Tiananmen Square, but continue to debate its importance. What is it about history that makes continued analysis important? (History, Language, and Reason.)

T
O
K

action, so determined was he to save the PRC from what he perceived as the dangers of political anarchy and a counter-revolution. At the same time, Deng acknowledged that political reform was also necessary to keep up with economic reform, but within the CCP system. Therefore, Deng must almost certainly take ultimate responsibility for the deaths of the protesters in Beijing in 1989. He clearly believed that he was justified in acting as he did in order to safeguard the state, but future generations of historians and commentators may well reach a very different judgement.

Chapter summary

China under Deng Xiaoping: political changes 1979–89

Deng Xiaoping dominated PRC politics between the time of the Third Plenum of the Eleventh Central Committee in 1978 and the 'southern tour' in 1992. During his time as paramount leader, he experienced the humiliation of a short, but disastrous, war with Vietnam. Of much greater significance, in terms of foreign policy, was that Deng established good relations with the USA following his visit there in 1979. Relations with the USA were normalized and agreement with the UK was reached regarding the transfer of Hong Kong to the PRC in 1997.

Deng was a political conservative, who struggled to contain the democratic aspirations of the younger generation as the 1980s unfolded. He ended the Democracy Wall in 1979 and forced the resignation of Hu Yaobang as General Secretary in 1987, after he had struggled to contain student demonstrations. There was some relaxation of the stifling social restrictions of the Mao era, but nevertheless, by 1989, there were deep tensions in the PRC's society. Inflation, rampant corruption among CCP cadres and the loss of employment guarantees created a sense of unease, and the failure of dissidents like Wei Jingsheng and Fang Lizhi to secure political change frustrated many.

The death of Hu Yaobang from a heart attack in 1989 was the catalyst for a student movement, demanding political reform and an end to corruption. General Secretary Zhao Ziyang favoured negotiating with the protesters in order to secure a peaceful outcome. However, more hard-line elements in the Politburo, led by Li Peng, saw in the protests a danger to the CCP's monopoly of political power. Deng Xiaoping intervened in the crisis by supporting the imposition of martial law and on the night of 3–4 June 1989, protesters were removed by force. In the aftermath of the crisis, even though he was now in advanced old age, Deng remained the dominant force in PRC politics until 1992. He dismissed the 1989 protesters as 'counter-revolutionary' and promoted the cause of economic reform through his 1992 'southern tour'.

✔ Examination advice

Paper 1 Question 2: comparing and contrasting sources

Question 2 on the IB History Diploma examination requires you to compare and contrast two sources. This means you will discuss the similarities and differences between them. The most commonly used form of the question will ask you to compare and contrast two sources and how they view a certain historical event, document or person. Usually the similarities and differences are fairly clear and can be easily answered in a few minutes.

Question 2 requires no own knowledge, just the ability to read and understand the sources. It is possible that one of the sources will have been used in Question 1. If this is the case, read the source again.

Question 2 is worth 6 marks out of the 25 total for Paper 1. This means it is worth 24 per cent of the overall mark. Answering Question 2 should take 10 minutes or less of your examination time.

How to answer

Read Question 2 carefully. Determine which sources you need to read and what exactly you are being asked to compare and contrast. You will be asked to compare and contrast not just the two sources, but the two sources' view on something specific. Do not discuss the origins or purpose of the sources; focus only on the demands of the question. You should make notes on your paper from the source regarding the question's focus. Do this for both sources. There is no need to record or utilize any information which does not specifically address the question. Once you have completed answering your question, you should draw a line through any notes you made so they will not be reviewed by the examiner.

- First paragraph: explain how the sources compare, or are similar, on whatever is being asked in the question.
- Second paragraph: explain how the sources contrast, or are different, on whatever is being asked in the question.

You should not treat each source separately, but integrate them in the same sentences as much as possible. Use quotes from the sources to strengthen your answer and help you to obtain more marks, but you should also paraphrase and summarize the sources.

Remember, the total mark available for this question is 6. A general rule to follow would be to have at least three points of comparison and three of contrast. This is not always possible, so in certain circumstances it may be possible to have four compares or contrasts and two of the other. Again, this is a general rule and it is always better to have as many of each as possible, making sure that all points are completely relevant and focused on the question. There may be minor similarities and differences between the sources. Do not let these take the place of the more significant points.

Example

This question uses Sources J and N, found in this chapter on pages 79 and 85.

> Compare and contrast Deng Xiaoping's changing views on criticism of the CCP and demonstrations for democratic reforms, as expressed in Sources J and N.

You will immediately make a note on your examination paper, 'Deng's views on criticism and democratic reforms' and then 'Source J'. You will go to Source J and start reading it, making notes on Deng's views on criticism of the party democratic reforms so that they can be compared and contrasted easily. You will repeat this for Source N. Use these notes to determine how the sources are similar and different regarding Deng's views, to eventually determine any changes in Deng's views. Your notes may appear something like this, in order to be able to see at a glance what the similarities and differences are:

Source J	Source N
Those who engage in criticism, or 'People like Fang Lizhi should be expelled' from the CCP	'The outbreak of the rebellion is worth thinking about'
China can't simply copy bourgeois democracy China cannot introduce a system of a balance of three powers	'Goal was to establish a bourgeois republic entirely dependent on the West' Deng thinks protesters want to overthrow the socialist system
Criticism of US democracy where the three powers 'pull in different directions'	Evidence of change or moderation in Deng's views. 'accept people's demands for combating corruption' 'we are even ready to listen'
China will not 'deviate from the socialist road' but will carry on an 'open policy' China will 'learn foreign technologies' China will 'use foreign capital'	No political reform towards democracy, but stronger economic reform: 'go ahead with reform and the open-door policy at a more steady, better and even faster pace'

A sample answer is given below.

Both Sources J and N agree that China will not change from its socialist government to a democratic one. Sources J and N both agree that China will not have a 'bourgeois' or 'US' style democracy. Both Sources J and N indicate that economic reforms will nonetheless proceed. In Source J, Deng mentions an 'open policy', that China will 'learn foreign technologies' and will 'use foreign capital.' Source N also points to economic reform and an 'open-door policy at a more steady, better and even faster pace.'

Sources J and N contrast strikingly in tone, denoting a change in Deng's attitude after the Tiananmen Square clashes. In Source J, Deng will not tolerate criticism of the CCP and wants to expel protesters like Fang Lizhi from the party. In Source N, however, Deng indicates that his views have changed or become more moderate when he is willing to 'accept people's demands for combating corruption'. In sharp contrast with his intransigent tone in Source J, in Source N he is even open to considering others' opinions by saying that 'We are even ready to listen'. This shows that Deng's views have changed and become somewhat more open to criticism.

There is running comparison in both paragraphs, with both sources usually mentioned together in the same sentence.

There is an appropriate use of quotations as supporting evidence.

Comparisons and contrasts have been separated into two paragraphs.

The comparisons and contrasts are the most significant ones. Minor points have not been used, keeping the paragraphs focused and strong.

There is an appropriate use of language, especially in connecting sources or points. Examples of words that help build linkage include 'both' and 'however'.

The answer indicates that the question was understood. There are at least three comparisons and three contrasts between the two sources. There is running comparison and contrast in each paragraph with both sources treated in the same sentence. Appropriate quotations used from the sources to reinforce the answer. The answer addresses all criteria.

Examination practice

Below are some exam-style questions for you to practise. Paper 1 exams are one hour long, not including five minutes of reading time at the exam's start when only reading is permitted. You may wish to only practise specific questions, and if this is the case, allow the following amounts of time per question:

Question 1:	5 minute
Question 2:	10 minutes
Question 3:	10 minutes
Question 4:	35 minutes

These questions relate to the Tiananmen Square Protest in 1989. The sources used are found within this chapter on the following pages:

- Source K (page 82)
- Source L (page 83)
- Source M (page 84)
- Source N (page 85)

1 **a)** What, according to Source M, was the justification for the imposition of martial law in 1989? *(3 marks)*
    (For guidance on how to answer this style of question see page 37.)

2 **b)** What message is conveyed by Source K? *(2 marks)*
    (For guidance on how to answer this style of question see page 41.)

3 Compare and contrast the views expressed in Sources K and M about the nature of the student protests which took place in 1989. *(6 marks)*
    (For guidance on how to answer this style of question see page 91.)

4 With reference to their origin and purpose, discuss the value and limitations of Source L and Source N for historians analysing the 1989 Tiananmen Square protests. *(6 marks)*
    (For guidance on how to answer this style of question see page 130.)

5 Using Sources K, L, M, N and your own knowledge, analyse the extent to which Deng Xiaoping and Li Peng can be blamed for the violent crackdown which took place on 3–4 June 1989. *(8 marks)*
    (For guidance on how to answer this style of question see page 160.)

 # Activities

1 Stage an imaginary debate between Deng Xiaoping and Zhao Zhiyang, in which both justify their actions during the 1989 student protests. You will need to explore the motivations, objectives and actions of both men during April, May and June 1989.

2 All historical arguments are simply assertions unless they are backed up by evidence. Look at the statements below and decide how far you agree or disagree with them. You may wish to use a 10-point scale with 10 equating to strong agreement with the statement and 1 equating to total disagreement with the statement. Then make a list of evidence to support your point of view on each statement.

- The positive aspects of Deng Xiaoping's rule outweigh the negative.

- The causes of the 1989 student protests were primarily economic.

- The events of 3 and 4 June 1989 revealed that the PRC was a totalitarian regime.

3 Write an obituary for Deng Xiaoping summing up his impact on the PRC. If you are working in pairs one of you could write the piece from a western perspective, such as the *New York Times*, and another could write the kind of obituary that might have appeared in the *People's Daily*. How and why might these obituaries differ?

CHAPTER 5

Domestic and foreign problems of the Brezhnev era

This chapter analyses Leonid Brezhnev's rule of the USSR until his death in 1982. The extent to which this was an era of political, economic and social stagnation is fully explored. Soviet foreign policy in the 1970s is also discussed, in particular the reasons for the Soviet intervention in Afghanistan and its consequences.

You need to consider the following questions throughout this chapter:

✪ What were the key features of the USSR's politics, society and economy under Brezhnev?

✪ Was Brezhnev's leadership to blame for Soviet stagnation from 1964 to 1982?

✪ What challenges did Soviet foreign policy face in the Brezhnev era?

✪ To what extent were the USSR's aims achieved in Afghanistan?

✪ Why did the USSR invade Afghanistan?

✪ How serious were the socio-economic and political problems confronting the USSR by the time of Brezhnev's death?

 ## Politics, economy and society under Brezhnev

> ▶ *Key question: What were the key features of the USSR's politics, society and economy under Brezhnev?*

By 1964, Nikita Khrushchev, the First Secretary of the Communist Party of the Soviet Union (CPSU), was viewed by senior party members as increasingly unable to exercise the necessary leadership and stability required for the USSR to uphold its world position.

Khrushchev was removed from party leadership following a plot by members of the **Presidium**, in which Leonid Brezhnev played a leading part. Brezhnev was installed as First Secretary and gradually consolidated his power until by the late 1970s, he had amassed as much political power as almost any of his predecessors. Brezhnev's era saw political, economic and social **stagnation** within the USSR and among its satellites in eastern Europe.

 **KEY TERM**

Presidium Dominant, policy-making body within the CPSU formed by the Council of Ministers, renamed the Politburo in 1966.

Stagnation A state of inactivity or low economic growth.

What was the
significance of the
changes made to the
USSR's constitution
in 1977?

Political stagnation

In 1977, a new constitution replaced the one created by Stalin in 1936. What justified this change was the argument that the USSR had reached an advanced stage in its socialist development towards full-scale communism, the ideal espoused by Karl Marx (see page 10). Brezhnev wanted stability and to avoid social discontent by creating satisfaction with the achievements of the USSR, such as public health and education and military parity with the West, and by underplaying the lack of material and technological development. No timeframe was given in the constitution about when or if the USSR might progress beyond this advanced stage, providing an excuse for preserving the political *status quo*.

What does Source A say
about the central political
role of the CPSU?

SOURCE A

Article 6 of the USSR constitution of 1977 from *The Soviet Union: A Documentary History: Volume 2, 1939–1991* by Edward Acton and Tom Stableford, published by the University of Exeter Press, Exeter, UK, 2007, page 324. Professor Acton of the University of East Anglia, UK, and Assistant Librarian Stableford at the Bodleian Library, Oxford, UK, compiled documents from newly available archival material on the former USSR. Their purpose was to provide non-Russian speakers with documents from the Cold War USSR.

Article 6. The leading and guiding force of the Soviet society and the nucleus of its political system, of all state organisations and public organisations, is the Communist Party of the Soviet Union. The CPSU exists for the people and serves the people.

The Communist Party, armed with Marxism-Leninism, determines the general perspectives of the development of society and the course of the home and foreign policy of the USSR, directs the great constructive work of the Soviet people, and imparts a planned, systematic and theoretically substantiated character to their struggle for the victory of communism.

All party organisations shall function within the framework of the Constitution of the USSR.

The new constitution reaffirmed the one-party state nature of the USSR. Brezhnev believed that by stating this in more appealing terms, he could limit its criticism.

According to Source B, what
freedoms are guaranteed to
Soviet citizens?

SOURCE B

An extract from a report by Brezhnev to the Central Committee entitled 'On the Draft Constitution of the USSR', 24 May 1977 from *A Documentary History of Communism in Russia: From Lenin to Gorbachev* edited by Robert Vincent Daniels, published by the University Press of New England, Lebanon, NH, USA, 1993, page 314. Daniels was Professor Emeritus of History at the University of Vermont, USA.

The draft gives significantly fuller formulation to the political rights and liberties of USSR citizens … Freedom of speech, of the press, of assembly, of mass meetings, and of street processions and demonstrations, which are included in the Constitution now in effect, are re-stated in full … Needless to say, comrades, the draft Constitution proceeds from the premise that the rights and liberties of citizens cannot and must not be used against our social system or to the detriment of the Soviet people's interests. Therefore, the draft clearly states, for example, that the exercise by citizens of their rights and liberties must not injure the interests of society and the state … and that political liberties are granted in accordance with the working people's interests and for the purpose of strengthening the socialist system.

SOURCE C

A CPSU propaganda poster with the slogan 'the unity of the party and the people – unbreakable'. Brezhnev is shown in the foreground leading the people.

What is the message of Source C and what is the significance of the image of Lenin?

The Soviet economy in the Brezhnev era

Once Brezhnev's power base was secure within the party, he aimed to improve the lives of the people of the USSR by trying to solve the problems of agriculture through increasing state subsidies. This, along with military expenditure, was the major focus of the economy during this period and other areas suffered.

Agriculture

One of the major problems facing Soviet agriculture was that not enough food was being produced as the population grew and consumption of food rose. In the event of a poor harvest, as in 1972 and 1975, the USSR had to rely on grain imports from the USA, Argentina and Canada. The grain imports dealt a damaging blow to the economic credibility of the socialist system, as well as being expensive for a system already under severe financial pressure.

State subsidies of agriculture

By 1973, the most important forms of agricultural production were the *kolkhozy* and *sovkhozy*, massive collective agricultural enterprises which had to be subsidized heavily by the state. By 1980, subsidies had increased to 20.3 per cent of the state budget from 19.5 per cent in 1972. This placed a huge strain on other sectors of the economy that were starved of investment, such as consumer goods.

This diversion of the state's resources to agriculture had an impact on food production, as the table in Source D shows.

KEY TERM

Kolkhozy Collective farms made up of different families who farmed on state land according to centrally planned production directives and quotas, although production surpluses could be sold on the open market.

Sovkhozy Groups of collective farms converted into huge agricultural enterprises run on an industrial model.

? What does Source D indicate about agricultural production in the Brezhnev era?

SOURCE D

Agricultural output from *An Economic History of the USSR, 1917–1991* by Alec Nove, published by Penguin, London, 1992, page 379. Nove was Professor Emeritus of Economics at the University of Glasgow, UK. He was born in Russia as Alexander Novakovsky. He compiled this table from original Soviet yearly statistical handbooks.

Agricultural product (millions of tonnes)	Annual averages			
	1961–5	1966–70	1971–5	1976–80
Grain harvest	130.3	167.6	181.6	205.0
Cotton	4.9	6.1	7.7	8.9
Sugar beet	59.2	81.1	76.0	88.4
Potatoes	81.6	94.8	89.6	84
Meat	9.3	11.6	14.0	14.8
Milk	64.7	80.6	87.4	92.6

In the long run, it proved impossible to sustain low consumer prices for food and agricultural products through state subsidies. According to agricultural economist Karl-Eugen Wädekin, the problem was that massive subsidies during the Brezhnev era did not focus on the real problem of Soviet agriculture. This had to do the structure of the farming system with its large bureaucracy and awkward organization, as well as not allowing demand to decide on distribution, rather than the state.

Industry

Soviet industry also stagnated during the Brezhnev era. Brezhnev showed no real interest in economic reform. Factory managers were discouraged from risk-taking by the requirements issued by the State Planning Committee, or **GOSPLAN**. Factory managers continued to produce no more than the quota assigned with little regard for costs or quality of production. Factories, mines and transport industries operated with antiquated machinery. By the 1970s, the industrial sector was slowing down, as Source E indicates.

 **KEY TERM**

GOSPLAN A government committee set up in 1921 which was responsible for centralized economic planning.

SOURCE E

'Basic indices of social and economic development in the USSR – average annual percentage rates of growth over Five-Year Plan periods, 1966–1985,' from *The Soviet Union: A Documentary History, Volume 2, 1939–1991* by Edward Acton and Tom Stableford, published by the University of Exeter Press, Exeter, UK, 2007, page 285. Professor Acton of the University of East Anglia, UK, and Assistant Librarian Stableford at the Bodleian Library, Oxford, UK, compiled documents from newly available archival material on the former USSR. Their purpose was to provide non-Russian speakers with documents from the Cold War USSR. This table was compiled by Soviet economists in 1988.

What evidence can you find in Source E that average annual percentage rates of growth in the USSR slowed down in the Brezhnev era?

Index	Average annual percentage growth per five-year period			
	1966–70	1971–5	1976–80	1981–5
National income	7.2	5.1	3.8	3.1
Industrial production	8.5	7.4	4.4	3.7
Average annual agricultural production	3.9	2.5	1.7	1.1
Social sector labour productivity	6.8	4.5	3.3	3.1

There were other serious problems such as shortages of raw materials. If a factory produced its quota, but had materials remaining, these were hoarded for future use instead of being sent to other factories that needed them.

Compare and contrast Sources E (page 99) and F. To what extent do these sources agree?

SOURCE F

A table of industrial output from *An Economic History of the USSR 1917–1991* by Alec Nove, published by Penguin, London, UK, 1992, page 387. Nove was Professor Emeritus of Economics at the University of Glasgow, UK. He was born in Russia as Alexander Novakovsky. He compiled this table from original Soviet yearly statistical handbooks.

Output	1980	1985
Oil (millions of tonnes)	603	595
Coal (millions of tonnes)	716	726
Steel (millions of tonnes)	103	108
Tractors (thousands)	555	585
Cement (millions of tonnes)	125	131
Fabric (millions of square metres)	10,746	12,052

KEY TERM

Tolkachi Helpers or facilitators who had the contacts to procure commodities needed by industrial managers.

Sovnarkhozes New economic planning institutions, often translated as regional economic councils, set up by Khrushchev in 1957 that tried and failed to improve the Soviet economy by giving more autonomy to regions with regard to economic policy.

GDP Gross domestic product, or what a country makes in selling the goods and services it produces in a year.

Akademgorodok 'Academy Town' in Russian; also known as the Novosibirsk Scientific Centre, built to house scientists and innovators in a pleasant atmosphere to foster creativity.

Corruption

The Brezhnev era also saw the rise of unofficial deal-makers called *tolkachi*, known for their ability to obtain raw materials through personal connections in GOSPLAN, which led to corruption and criminal networks. An example of the extent of corruption was the establishment of fictitious factories that the state then supplied with raw materials. The state-owned raw materials would then be sold to state factories or to other participants in the black market. All this was possible since government officials could be bribed to grant licences to establish the factories in the first place and have them supplied by the government itself. Between 1980 and 1985, at least two million Soviet citizens were arrested on charges of embezzling state property.

Industrial successes

There were some economic successes during the Brezhnev era:

- **Sovnarkhozes** were abolished in 1966 as they caused competition between regions within the USSR.
- There was a return to a Stalinist model of industrial development (see page 13) that used targets established by Five Year Plans and co-ordinated by GOSPLAN. The tenth Five Year Plan from 1976 to 1980 delivered some economic growth and **GDP** increased by 2.7 per cent annually in the late 1970s.
- An area of exceptional growth was in the sphere of military, aeronautical and space technology. There, Soviet industry managed to keep up with the West during the Brezhnev era as 220 million roubles were invested in **Akademgorodok**, which housed many of the USSR's most eminent nuclear scientists.

However, there were also a number of disastrous investments in prestige projects that had little or no positive economic impact. The most notorious example of this was the construction of the 3200-km (2000-mile) long Baikal–Amur railway which was completed only in 1989.

Oil

Oil production increased significantly during the Brezhnev era. Newly discovered oil deposits in Siberia produced 31 million tonnes of oil in 1970 but over 300 million tonnes annually 10 years later. In an era of high international oil prices, this significantly affected the Soviet economy. Increased oil production fostered a growing dependence on the export of oil and gas, rather than manufactured goods, as a source of hard currency that could be used to purchase imports such as grain. This postponed the need for painful but necessary economic reforms.

Foreign relations

As the Brezhnev era drew to a close, partnerships with foreign firms like Fiat, which built a factory in the USSR, became more commonplace. This had the side-effect of making contact between ordinary Soviet citizens and people from non-communist countries more frequent. They could compare experiences and, in this comparison, the standard of living in socialist countries did not fare well.

Soviet society in the Brezhnev era

> **How was quality of life affected by Soviet policies in the Brezhnev era?**

Birth rate

In the Brezhnev era, a declining birth rate in some republics of the USSR, such as Ukraine, caused a fall in population. This was largely caused by the fact that the living space available to families in urban areas was cramped, amounting to just 13.4 square metres per person in 1980. In addition, women were under huge pressure to remain in the labour force, especially in rural areas. Women, faced with the double burden of being in the workforce and also bearing children, increasingly practised birth control and legal abortions. On the other hand, the fact that the birth rate rose in the central Asian republics of the USSR, such as Uzbekistan and Tajikistan, raised the possibility of Russians eventually becoming a minority within the USSR. This was an unwelcome prospect to most members of the Politburo, despite the rhetoric of socialist brotherhood and a multinational USSR.

Life expectancy and infant mortality

Life expectancy remained at 68 years, unchanging in the Brezhnev years. This was at least partly due to rising levels of alcohol consumption. By 1982, the USSR had 28 million alcoholics, or 10 per cent of the population, as compared to four per cent of the US population at that time. Death by alcohol poisoning in the USSR in 1976 was the highest in the world: 25.7 per 100,000 people. By comparison, the USA had a rate of 2.94 the same year.

In addition, the routine dumping of industrial waste and pesticides into water supplies ruined the health of many Soviet citizens. These developments also had an impact on the infant mortality rate, which grew worse during the Brezhnev era and by 1981, Soviet infant mortality was triple that of West Germany.

Education

Educational standards during the Brezhnev era were on the rise and, by 1979, approximately 10 per cent of the population entered university. This compares with only one per cent of the population doing so in 1939. The number of graduates produced by Soviet universities amounted to nearly one million in 1980, compared with only 343,000 in 1960.

Standard of living

Living standards were also rising, albeit modestly, and the average Soviet household's standard of living approximately doubled between 1945 and 1970. One reason for this was the rise in wages that increased savings for the purchase of consumer goods. The difficulty was that consumer goods were in short supply.

The Soviet diet improved during this era and per capita consumption of meat rose by 40.5 per cent between 1965 and 1980. It became commonplace for Soviet workers to holiday on the Baltic or Black Sea coast at trade union-run holiday centres. By the time of Brezhnev's death, 86 per cent of Soviet families owned a television and a refrigerator, so some basic consumer goods were available. Despite this progress, the standard of living in the USSR lagged behind the West.

SOURCE G

?
According to Source G, what were conditions like in the USSR in the Brezhnev era?

Excerpt on the standard of living in the 1970s in the USSR from _A History of Twentieth-century Russia_ by Robert Service, published by Harvard University Press, Cambridge, MA, USA, 1998, page 417. Professor Service teaches History at Oxford University, UK. He wrote this after being allowed access to newly opened Soviet archives in the 1990s.

The Politburo was given no credit for the material improvements secured in the 1970s, and the cheap provision of food, shelter, clothing, sanitation, health care and transport was taken for granted. Brezhnev's successes were noted more for their limitations than their progress beyond the performance before 1964. He earned neither affection nor respect … Consequently, Soviet citizens, while remaining resolutely slack at work, had to be indefatigable in obtaining alleviation of their living conditions … Each looked after himself or herself and relatives and close friends. On the inside, this collectivistic society fostered extreme individualism.

Culture within the USSR

As long as criticisms of the government were not overt, artists and writers had freedom to discuss alternative ways of life and to analyse what it was like to live in the USSR. Kyrgyz novelist Chingiz Aitmatov, for example, wrote about how both the ecology and culture of central Asia were being wrecked by the CPSU. Also, the guitar poet Vladimir Vysotski, a very popular singer, wrote songs about life in the USSR in the 1970s, although rock concerts were strictly controlled by the state. The arts were freed of constraints to deal with socialist and realistic themes, thereby widening avenues of creativity. One example is the emergence of sots art, a term meaning socialist pop art, as a parody of the forced socialist realism of the 1950s and 1960s.

Emergence of dissidents

Nevertheless, the USSR was a totalitarian state and the **KGB** devoted most of its efforts to dealing with internal opposition rather than **counter-espionage**. It was forbidden to question the doctrine of Marxism–Leninism in print and the gulag, or corrective labour prison system, remained fully operational with approximately one million imprisoned during the Brezhnev era. Gulags achieved notoriety for those political prisoners imprisoned for criticizing the government, but the figures also included common criminals.

One prominent critic of the regime was the scientist Andrei Sakharov, who established a human rights committee in 1970 to defend freedom of opinion and self-expression. In 1980, he was confined to the city of Gorki, where non-Soviet citizens were not allowed. It is likely that he was not imprisoned because in 1975 Sakharov was awarded the Nobel Peace Prize; the Soviet government did not wish to draw further attention to its human rights record.

 **KEY TERM**

KGB State Security Committee or Soviet secret police, founded in 1954, from the Russian *Komitet Gosudarstvennoi Bezopasnosti*.

Counter-espionage Efforts to prevent spying.

SOURCE H

An extract from an open letter dated 19 March 1970, to Soviet leaders by the dissidents, physicists Andrei Sakaharov and Valentin Turchin, and historian Roy Medvedev, from *The Rise and Fall of the Soviet Union 1917–1991* by Richard Sakwa, published by Routledge Sources in History, London, UK, 1999, page 364. Sakwa is Professor of Russian and European Politics at the University of Kent, UK. He compiled this book of primary sources for student use. The three dissidents wanted to work with their government on economic and political reforms for the USSR.

… The source of our difficulties does not lie in the socialist system, but on the contrary, it lies in those peculiarities and conditions of our life which run contrary to socialism and are hostile to it. The source lies in the antidemocratic traditions and norms of public life established in the Stalin era, which have not been decisively eliminated to this day …

What can be learned from Source H about the views of Sakharov, Turchin and Medvedev? **?**

Politics	Society	Economy
• 1977: new constitution preserved the *status quo* • Dissidents like Sakharov emerged	• Birth rate declined in some areas in USSR and rose in others • Life expectancy remained unchanged • Infant mortality got worse • Improvements in education • Improvements in diet	• Increase in state subsidies of agriculture • *Kolkhozy* remained inefficient and unproductive • Large military expenditure • Industry stagnated and corruption restricted growth • Oil production increased

SUMMARY DIAGRAM

Politics, economy and society under Brezhnev

② Key debate

▶ **Key question:** *Was Brezhnev's leadership to blame for Soviet stagnation from 1964 to 1982?*

Was Brezhnev merely a 'consensus politician'?

Brezhnev's rise to power was marked by what historian Robert Service calls the 'guiding aim … to avoid getting himself into trouble with higher authority'. Many other historians such as Martin McCauley have found it difficult to hide their low opinion of him. Robert Service describes Brezhnev as 'very limited intellectually'. He is especially dismissive of Brezhnev's grip on political affairs at the end of his life, describing him as 'a dreadfully ill old man', whose diary reveals little apart from an inability to spell and a liking for ice hockey. He was also vain, nepotistic and corrupt enough to profit from office by having a large fleet of foreign cars, as well as appointing his son and son-in-law deputy foreign minister and deputy interior minister, respectively. Historian Roy Medvedev described Brezhnev as 'cynical … vain [and] stupid'. In essence, Brezhnev favoured building consensuses, not questioning the fundamentals of the political system that he had inherited. This made him popular with powerful vested interests, such as the ***nomenklatura*** élite who had a clear stake in the *status quo*.

On the other hand, to simply dismiss Brezhnev as an uninspiring ***apparatchik*** is perhaps a little harsh. This interpretation also does little to explain how Brezhnev was able to remain at the very apex of Soviet politics for almost 20 years. He certainly had a talent for ensuring consensus within the Presidium and the Politburo, which was welcomed by many after the volatile Khrushchev. He was skilful at maintaining political contacts and

KEY TERM

Nomenklatura The powerful class of officials and bureaucrats that emerged during the Brezhnev era.

Apparatchik Usually used in a pejorative sense to describe faceless administrators and bureaucrats.

shrewdly built a political power base in the party by recruiting old colleagues from his days as a provincial party secretary in Ukraine. Even so, when Brezhnev died in 1982, fewer than half of the Politburo could legitimately be described as close political allies. The fact that Brezhnev was also the leading conspirator in the overthrow of Khrushchev suggests that he was much more than a mere political nonentity. His rivals consistently underestimated him so they failed to act to forestall his rise to supreme power. It should also be remembered that Brezhnev avoided the excesses of Stalinism and capable contemporaries were permitted long and influential careers. For instance, Andrei Gromyko remained the most influential voice in foreign affairs, having run this ministry since 1957, and he outlived Brezhnev.

What was the cause of stagnation?

Ultimately, Brezhnev's caution and conservatism were both a root cause of the USSR's stagnation between 1964 and 1982, and his greatest political strengths, paving the way for a period of stability after the chaos of Stalinism and the **Great Patriotic War** and the hyperactive Khrushchev years. However, most historians argue that any positive aspects of Brezhnev's rule were outweighed by the negative. By 1982, what had started as Brezhnev's widely welcomed embrace of political stability had turned into a stultifying and damaging refusal to consider political reform.

> **KEY TERM**
>
> **Great Patriotic War** What the Second World War was known as in the USSR.

> With reference to origin and purpose, assess the value and limitation of Source I for reaching a final judgement about the political career of Leonid Brezhnev.

SOURCE I

Excerpt on the death of Brezhnev from *A History of Twentieth-century Russia* by Robert Service, published by Harvard University Press, Cambridge, MA, USA, 1998, pages 426–7. Professor Service teaches History at Oxford University in the UK. He wrote this book after being allowed access to newly opened Soviet archives in the 1990s.

The Politburo instructed that he [Brezhnev] should be buried outside the Kremlin Wall on Red Square. Statesmen from all over the world attended. His wife and family were accompanied to the funeral by the central party leadership – and daughter Galina outraged spectators by refraining from wearing sombre garb. Brezhnev had been dressed in his Marshal's uniform with all his medals. But the careless way the coffin was dropped into his grave was taken as a sign that not all Politburo leaders wished to be seen to regret that at last he had left the political stage. In truth it was hard to feel very sorry for Brezhnev. When he had succeeded Khrushchev, he was still a vigorous politician who expected to make the party and the government work more effectively. He had not been inactive; he had not been entirely inflexible. But his General Secretaryship had turned into a ceremonial reign that had brought communism into its deepest contempt since 1917.

Other historians have pointed to Brezhnev's leadership style in trying to make sense of Soviet stagnation between 1964 and 1982.

According to Source J, what were the reasons for political and economic stagnation in the Brezhnev era?

Excerpt on Brezhnev's long reign in *From Brezhnev to Gorbachev: Infighting in the Kremlin* by Baruch A. Hazan, published by Westview Press, Boulder, CO, USA, 1987, pages 9–10. Hazan teaches at the Institute of European Studies in Vienna, Austria.

The various stages of Brezhnev's long tenure (1964–1982) demonstrate the gradual development of the power struggle. During this period he expanded his power and then ingeniously protected it by sharing part of it with lower-level officials. Brezhnev was a pragmatic leader who quickly perceived the importance of institutionalized and regularized methods of government. A possible reason for Brezhnev's approach apart from his personal character, is that his crucial role in organizing Khrushchev's overthrow would naturally make him very wary upon taking office himself and anxious to prevent the same fate. Brezhnev protected his power by delegating some of the decision-making to lower officials in the party pyramid …

The outcomes of this policy were twofold. First, the system devised by Brezhnev guaranteed his own power and security by granting similar power and security to his supporters … This naturally led to the development of the Brezhnev personality cult, which in its latter stages reached preposterous proportions. Second, the CPSU apparatus and the local party and state officials who benefitted most from this situation became paragons of conservatism, acting only to preserve the established order … Thanks to the efforts of his Politburo faction and the support of the nomenklatura, Brezhnev was able to protect his power to the very end, although the conservatism thus generated developed into a debilitating stagnation in all areas of Soviet political and economic life.

Historians use evidence to make arguments. What gives evidence value and makes it convincing? Does national origin always affect historical writing? Why or why not? (History, Ethics, Language, Emotion, Reason.)

③ Soviet foreign relations under Brezhnev

▶ *Key question: What challenges did Soviet foreign policy face in the Brezhnev era?*

In general, Brezhnev's foreign policy was relatively simple: maintain the international *status quo*, including retention of power in areas of the world under Soviet influence. The USSR, however, had strained relations with the People's Republic of China (PRC), Warsaw Pact nations were dominated and tensions with the USA and other countries varied, alternating between agreements and stress, especially over Afghanistan after 1979.

Soviet relations with the PRC

What caused tensions between the USSR and PRC from 1964 to 1979?

Relations between the USSR and the PRC deteriorated after Stalin's death and a fierce rivalry emerged for the ideological leadership of communist states. Once the PRC became a nuclear power in 1964, the traditional strategic rivalry in central Asia between these powers revived and intensified and relations between the USSR and China worsened as border conflicts escalated. By 1969, the Soviet Red Army had 25 divisions and 1200 aircraft stationed along its long border with the PRC and a major border clash between the two states along the Ussuri River almost erupted into a war. There was serious discussion at a high level in the Soviet government about whether to attack Chinese nuclear installations. In the end, a full-scale war between the two most powerful socialist states did not take place but a sense of simmering hostility defined Sino-Soviet relations in the 1970s.

Sino-Soviet relations were complicated by the fact that each power sponsored rival states in south-east Asia. The USSR established close ties with Vietnam and the PRC supported the Khmer Rouge regime in Cambodia. The PRC's invasion of Vietnam in 1979 (see page 72), although short-lived, also raised tensions.

SOURCE K

Excerpt from Brezhnev's speech given 2 March 1979 called 'For the Happiness of the Soviet People,' in *Peace Détente Cooperation* by Leonid I. Brezhnev, published by Consultants Bureau, New York, USA, 1981, pages 133–4. Brezhnev states in the book's foreword that the purpose of the book is to explain to US citizens the aims of Soviet foreign policy.

The position of the Chinese leaders is increasingly converging [coming together] with this policy of imperialism. By their unprecedently [unusual] brazen bandit-like attack on a small neighboring country – socialist Vietnam – the present Peking [Beijing] rulers revealed before the eyes of the whole world the perfidious [disloyal] and aggressive essence of the great power hegemony-seeking policy that they are pursuing. Everyone sees that it is precisely this policy that at the present time constitutes the gravest threat to world peace … The Soviet people, together with all peace-loving peoples of the world demand an immediate end to Chinese aggression against Vietnam and the withdrawal of all interventionist troops, down to the very last soldier, from the territory of Vietnam.

According to Source K, why should the PRC remove its troops from Vietnam? **?**

 **KEY TERM**

Brezhnev Doctrine
Brezhnev's assertion that if any Warsaw Pact member threatened socialism, it was the right and duty of the rest of the members to engage in military intervention.

There was a gradual improvement in relations during the early 1980s, although the only visible sign of a thaw was the fact that the PRC sent its foreign minister, Huang Ha, to attend Brezhnev's funeral in 1982.

Relations with Warsaw Pact countries

Brezhnev was determined to maintain Soviet hegemony in central and eastern Europe (see page 14). Some dissent from Soviet policy was permitted, but Brezhnev's foreign policy ultimately sought to maintain and strengthen Soviet control. This became known as the **Brezhnev Doctrine**, a policy that if socialism in Warsaw Pact nations was threatened, all the other members of the pact had to militarily intervene. Pact members included the USSR, East Germany, Poland, Czechoslovakia, Hungary, Romania, Bulgaria and Albania.

In what ways did the **Brezhnev Doctrine** affect the USSR's relations with eastern Europe?

KEY TERM

Socialism with a human face A term used to describe the less repressive and more liberal political and social system developed by Alexander Dubček in Czechoslovakia.

Prague Spring Name given to the 1968 attempt by Czechoslovakia's Communist Party leader Alexander Dubček to liberalize socialism by allowing freedom of the press, expression and political reforms. The Warsaw Pact nations under the leadership of the USSR invaded the country and deposed Dubček.

Solidarity Movement Non-communist trade union movement in Poland that used civil resistance to demand economic, social and other changes.

Coup An abrupt seizure of power, or takeover of a country, by the military or another armed group.

Czechoslovakia

When Brezhnev became concerned that the new leader of the Communist Party of Czechoslovakia, Alexander Dubček, was implementing liberal ideas too quickly by abandoning censorship and trying to build 'socialism with a human face', Brezhnev exerted a great deal of political pressure, meeting Dubček six times between January and August 1968, in order to persuade him to abandon this reform programme. In August 1968, having failed to coerce Dubček through diplomacy, Brezhnev ordered Warsaw Pact troops to occupy Czechoslovakia, ending the so-called the **Prague Spring**. Dubček was replaced by the more conservative and pragmatic Gustáv Husák, who remained in power until 1989.

Romania

In the late 1960s, Romania was permitted to adopt a neutral stance in the Sino-USSR dispute and even to seek economic aid from the West. However, this can be explained in part by the fact that Romania possessed a relatively small population and did not occupy a strategically important location. Still, Romania voiced opposition to the Brezhnev Doctrine after 1968 at world conferences of communist parties.

Hungary

In Hungary, some economic reforms were permitted within the socialist, planned economy system. These were implemented under party leader János Kádár by 1968. Kádár tried to convince neighbouring Czechoslovakia's Dubček to limit reforms in order to avoid conflict with the USSR, to no avail. Historian Robert Service relates that at a Moscow meeting with Brezhnev, Kádár warned Dubček: 'Don't you understand what kind of people you are dealing with?'

Poland

In Poland, rising inflation and a scarcity of consumer goods despite price controls and a planned economy were creating serious worker opposition in 1970. Workers at the Gdańsk shipyards began to strike and demonstrate and many were killed when the military police were sent to control them. Repression worked for a while, but by 1976 the strikes continued and a strong union developed, led by worker Lech Wałęsa. Students and other workers unions joined in by 1980. It was known as the **Solidarity Movement** and soon became emblematic of the struggle against Soviet control and eventually against communist control in Poland.

Soviet intervention in Poland was prevented in 1981 when General Wojciech Jaruzelski's Military Council of National Salvation staged a successful **coup** against the ineffective government of Edward Gierek. This helped to contain the threat posed by Solidarity and, for the moment, maintain the unity of the Warsaw Pact, two of the fundamental aims of Soviet foreign policy in the early 1980s.

Relations with the USA: the spirit of *détente*

How did relations between the USA and USSR develop in the early 1970s?

Starting in the early 1970s, Brezhnev's foreign policy proclaimed interest in developing a better relationship with the USA. He met with US presidents both in the USSR and in the USA. The increasingly warmer connection was branded *razryadka* in the USSR and ***détente*** in the West.

Ostpolitik

One of the first examples of *détente* was in August 1970, when the USSR and the Federal Republic of Germany (FRG), or West Germany, signed the Moscow Treaty that confirmed the division of Germany into two states after the Second World War (see page 15). Germany also lost land held prior to 1939 to Poland and the USSR. This meant that the frontier between the GDR, or East Germany, and Poland was now formally recognized. Historian John Mason describes this treaty as a victory for Brezhnev because it won western acceptance for the Soviet position of keeping Germany weak and divided. It also opened an era of *détente* in Europe.

The negotiations and treaties also vindicated Willy Brandt, West German Chancellor from 1969, and his ***Ostpolitik*** policy, which he described as 'easing the relationship between the two parts of Germany out of its present rigid state'. The object of *Ostpolitik* was to take steps, however small, in the direction of German reunification. The Treaty of Moscow was followed in 1972 by a Basic Treaty between the FRG and the GDR which led to the exchange of permanent diplomatic missions between the two countries and to both countries joining the United Nations (UN). Harry Gelman, a former senior analyst of Soviet affairs in the **CIA**, contends that Brezhnev supported Brandt's *Ostpolitik* as a model for improving relations with the USA. Being involved in negotiations and treaties regarding East and West Germany afforded the USSR a chance to increase its influence in Europe, thereby reducing US influence.

Détente in the 1970s

The next crucial stage in *détente* came when US President Richard Nixon was invited to the USSR in May 1972. Nixon believed that nuclear parity with the USSR was sufficient to secure the USA's strategic interests. At the 1972 meeting, both leaders promised not to pursue **proxy wars** in the **Third World**. Two further meetings took place between Brezhnev and Nixon: New York in 1973 and Moscow in 1974.

The Middle East

Despite Soviet military, financial and technical support, Soviet **client states** like Egypt were defeated in the Six Day War with Israel in 1967. The Soviet presence was increased in the Middle East after this, as Brezhnev boosted arms sales to Egypt and Syria and acquired naval rights in some ports. The USSR backed Egypt once again in the 1973 October War with Israel, a key US ally in the Middle East. However, the Soviets were betrayed when Egypt,

🔑 **KEY TERM**

Détente A French word meaning relaxing or loosening; refers to the relaxing of tensions in the Cold War.

Ostpolitik A German term meaning eastern policy; a West German effort to improve diplomatic relations with East Germany, eastern Europe and the USSR.

CIA Central Intelligence Agency, a US government espionage organization.

Proxy wars Name given to military conflicts during the Cold War in which the USA and the USSR participated only indirectly, avoiding direct confrontation.

Third World Cold War term for countries not in the First World (developed, capitalist countries) or the Second World (socialist and communist countries). The Third World included developing countries in Africa, Asia and Latin America.

Client state A country that depends on economic, military and/or political support from a more powerful one.

KEY TERM

Camp David Accords
Series of agreements
regarding borders and
military considerations
between Egypt and Israel that
were signed at US
Presidential retreat Camp
David in 1978.

ICBM Intercontinental
nuclear ballistic missile.

SLBM Ballistic missile
launched from a submarine
with a nuclear warhead.

MIRV Multiple
independently targetable
re-entry vehicle: a nuclear
missile equipped with
multiple warheads, therefore
capable of hitting more than
one target.

having been a client of the USSR, entered the US political orbit, signing the
Camp David Accords in 1978 and an Israeli–Egyptian peace treaty in
March 1979.

Despite tensions in the Middle East, relations improved between the USA
and the USSR in the negotiations about nuclear weapons.

SALT

In the spirit of conferences and negotiations during *détente*, the USSR and
the USA signed the first Strategic Arms Limitation Treaty (SALT I) in 1972.
This ended construction of new **ICBM**s and **SLBM**s, maintaining the
narrow Soviet lead in these types of nuclear weapon delivery systems.

No agreement was reached on the deployment of long-range bombers or of
MIRVs. SALT I established an important diplomatic precedent: negotiations
between the superpowers over their nuclear stockpiles could be both
productive and worthwhile, but they could only advance so far. As Soviet
foreign policy in the Brezhnev era proceeded in negotiations with the West,
the USSR broadened its military capacity, both in nuclear and in
conventional armaments. This added leverage to Soviet relations with both
the communist and the capitalist world.

SOURCE L

**Nuclear warhead stockpiles of the USA and the USSR 1945–2006 from
'Global nuclear stockpiles, 1945–2006' by Robert S. Norris and
Hans M. Kristensen in *Bulletin of the Atomic Scientists* Vol. 62, No. 4,
July/August 2006, pages 64–6. Kristensen is Director of the Nuclear
Information Project at the Federation of American Scientists in the USA.
Norris is a senior research associate with the Natural Resources Defense
Council in Washington, DC, USA. The high for the USA is 32,040 in 1966;
the high for the USSR is 45,000 in 1986.**

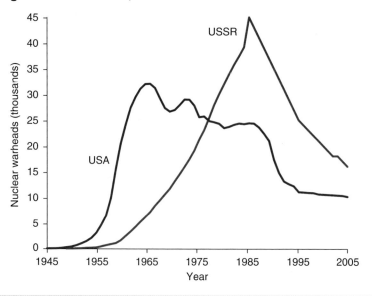

What are the limitations of
Source L?

The Helsinki Accords 1975

The high point of the partial thaw in superpower relations was the **Helsinki Accords** in 1975. The Accords, signed by 33 European statesmen as well as the leaders of the USA and Canada, confirmed international borders as of 1945. This satisfied Soviet security concerns in Europe.

A clause regarding respect for human rights and a commitment to non-intervention in the affairs of other states was difficult to reconcile with the Brezhnev Doctrine. Economic assistance was also part of the document, so Brezhnev agreed to this human rights clause. It would be, after all, very difficult for the West to enforce, short of outright war. Foreign Minister Andrei Gromyko was able to reassure Brezhnev that they could decide what to implement and what to ignore from the Accords.

The number of dissidents began to multiply throughout the Warsaw Pact nations and by 1976 a Public Group to Promote Observance of the Helsinki Accords was operating in Moscow. They operated as a watch group, monitoring and publishing reports on human rights violations, and others soon worked in Ukraine, Lithuania, Georgia and so on, creating increasing pressure on the Soviet government.

Relations with the USA: cracks in *détente*

In the mid 1970s, cracks in diplomatic relations between the USA and USSR began to reappear, especially following the resignation of Nixon in 1974 after the **Watergate Scandal**. After Nixon's departure, the US Congress passed restrictions on presidential powers to act at home and abroad. At first there was some sense of political continuity as Henry Kissinger continued as Secretary of State, but gradually *détente* lost the political momentum that had sustained it in the first half of the decade. Significant sources of tension remained.

East/West relations after 1975

According to historian John Dunbabin, SALT I only mildly curbed the nuclear arms race and had not responded to the build-up of **conventional arms**, especially Soviet tank forces, in eastern Europe. Soviet negotiators remained frustrated by the fact that British and French nuclear arsenals were not covered by the SALT talks. Sino-Soviet relations were not going well and in the SALT talks Brezhnev made every effort to downplay this split so that the USA could not gain leverage and get closer to the PRC.

On the US side, the new President Jimmy Carter in 1977 felt optimistic that *détente* could proceed and even asked the USSR to consider mutual reductions in conventional weapons. At the same time, he angered Brezhnev by establishing contact with Soviet dissident Andrei Sakharov in an effort to promote human rights. Carter became frustrated at the cynical Soviet interpretation of the Helsinki Accords such as the treatment of Soviet Anatole Sharansky, a computer scientist who led the dissident movement,

 **KEY TERM**

Helsinki Accords An agreement between the Soviet bloc and the West for acceptance of existing boundaries and for economic, commercial and scientific collaboration. The final clause included respect for human rights.

Why did tensions between the USSR and USA increase again from the mid-1970s?

 **KEY TERM**

Watergate Scandal A general term used to portray an intricate web of political scandals by President Richard Nixon between 1972 and 1974, including the wire-tapping of the Democratic National Committee housed in the Watergate building in Washington, DC.

Conventional arms These include small arms and light weapons, sea and land mines, (non-nuclear) bombs, shells, rockets and missiles. They are not biological, chemical or nuclear, but are explosive.

and was held under house arrest and then sent to jail for 11 years until he was able to emigrate to Israel. Another example was Soviet intervention in Angola and Ethiopia, strongly censured by Carter, as well.

It could be argued that Carter's attitude to the USSR was somewhat contradictory. On the one hand his Secretary of State, Cyrus Vance, favoured a conciliatory approach to dealing with Brezhnev through negotiations in the SALT talks, while his National Security adviser, Zbigniew Brzezinski, a **hawk**, remained suspicious of Soviet intentions. In 1977, Brzezinski felt threatened by the Soviet stationing of **SS-20** mobile missile launchers, each with three nuclear warheads, in eastern Europe. This seemed to provide the USSR with the capability of waging a limited nuclear war in Europe and Brzezinski advised Carter to take a strong opposing stand. President Carter responded in June 1977 by approving the development of a cruise missile programme that provided for the development of new nuclear missiles. In addition, by 1979, the UK, West Germany, Italy, Belgium and the Netherlands had all agreed to station 108 **Pershing II** nuclear missiles, heightening Soviet fears of a US **first strike**.

Proxy wars

Proxy wars in Angola, Ethiopia and Cuba continued to damage chances of genuine reconciliation.

Angola

The bitter civil war in Angola was a proxy war in which the USSR supported Agostinho Neto's left-wing Popular Movement for the Liberation of Angola (MPLA). On the other hand, CIA support was directed towards Holden Roberto's National Front for the Liberation of Angola (FNLA) and Jonas Savimbi's Union for the Total Liberation of Angola (UNITA). By the end of the decade the MPLA appeared to have triumphed, with the help of soldiers from Soviet client-state Cuba.

Ethiopia

In its conflict with neighbouring Somalia, Ethiopia's communist regime, led by Colonel Mengistu, was backed by 16,000 Cuban troops and Soviet munitions. The clash was over the disputed Ogaden region, yet it reflected wider tensions between the USA and USSR. By March 1978, the Ethiopian army, backed by Soviet and Cuban military aid, had expelled the Somali troops from the Ogaden. Once again, a proxy war had served to sour superpower relations.

Cuba

The status of Cuba also remained a source of dispute. In 1970, the USSR had begun constructing a port at Cienfuegos to maintain nuclear-powered submarines. From 1979, Brezhnev stationed aircraft and submarines there. Strong warnings from the USA caused the USSR to curtail its military presence, but Cuba remained the Soviet stronghold in the Americas.

 **KEY TERM**

Hawk Refers to a person likely to react strongly and even use military force in world conflicts.

SS-20 Soviet intermediate-range nuclear missiles.

Pershing II US intermediate-range nuclear missiles.

First strike A term used to describe a pre-emptive nuclear attack by one superpower on another.

The failure of SALT II

Negotiations between the USSR and the USA enabled the signing of the
SALT II treaty in Vienna in June 1979. This treaty had taken many years,
during which nuclear technology and missiles had advanced, especially in
the USSR (see Source L, page 110). This formalized the agreement that was
reached between Brezhnev and US President Ford in 1974, with both
superpowers agreeing to reduce their nuclear weapons to 2250 by 1981.
Nevertheless, meaningful efforts towards nuclear disarmament remained a
distant dream. In 1977, US President Carter linked advances in negotiations
to improvements in rights in the USSR, infuriating Brezhnev and stalling
talks. In an atmosphere of growing distrust, Carter and an ageing Brezhnev
signed SALT II but it failed to deal with the issue of new weapons like MIRVs
and the Pershing II missiles in western Europe. Crucially, the US Senate
refused to ratify SALT II, and one of the last political acts of Carter was to
increase the US defence budget to a mammoth total of $165 billion in 1981.
This was a sign that *détente* was at an end.

SOURCE M

**Excerpts from the treaty between the USA and the USSR on the limitation
of strategic offensive arms, together with agreed statements and common
understandings regarding the treaty (SALT II), from the website of the US
Department of State at www.state.gov/www/global/arms/treaties/salt2-2.
html. This is an official US government website and provides the full text of
the treaty and its protocols.**

*Upon entry into force of this Treaty, each Party undertakes to limit ICBM
launchers, SLBM launchers, heavy bombers and ASBMs [anti-ship ballistic
missiles] to an aggregate number not to exceed 2,400 … Each Party undertakes
not to start construction of additional fixed ICBM launchers … each Party
undertakes to limit launchers of ICBMs and SLBMs equipped with MIRVs … to
an aggregate number not to exceed 1,200.*

What can be inferred about
the aims of Brezhnev's
foreign policy from
Source M?

Détente

1970 • Moscow Treaty: confirmed the division of Germany
1972 • Basic Treaty between FRG and GDR
     • US President Nixon's visit to Moscow
     • SALT I
1973 • Brezhnev met Nixon in New York
1975 • Helsinki Accords: confirmed international borders as of 1945

Cracks in détente

1974 • Nixon resigned following Watergate Scandal
     • Start of Angolan Civil War
1977 • Start of Ethiopian–Somali War
1979 • Brezhnev stationed aircraft and submarines in Cuba
     • SALT II not ratified
     • USSR's invasion of Afghanistan
     • Pershing II nuclear missiles stationed in western Europe

End of détente

SUMMARY DIAGRAM

Soviet foreign relations under Brezhnev

The invasion of Afghanistan

> ▶ *Key question:* To what extent were the USSR's aims achieved in Afghanistan?

Since the 1950s, the USSR had sent military advisers to Afghanistan and trained Afghan Army officers in the Soviet Union. Following an uprising against the ruling party in March 1979, the USSR invaded the country later that year, unleashing enormous consequences for itself and the rest of the world.

Why did the Soviets invade Afghanistan in 1979?

→ Reasons for the Soviet invasion of Afghanistan

In 1973, the King of Afghanistan, Mohammed Zahir Shah, was overthrown by his cousin Mohammed Daoud Khan. Daoud formed a republic to be ruled by his National Revolutionary Party. He appointed himself as both President and Prime Minister. In a spirit of Afghan nationalism, Daoud dismissed Soviet advisers and technicians and banned communists from his government. Instead, he sought foreign aid from Middle Eastern states, made a new constitution in 1977 and became increasingly autocratic.

The April Revolution and its aftermath

In April 1978, after a communist leader was murdered, Daoud was killed in a coup known as the April Revolution. This was led by Soviet-trained Afghan army officers with links to the People's Democratic Party of Afghanistan (PDPA), a pro-Soviet group.

The new government was led by President Nur Mohammed Taraki and it was much more pro-Soviet in its outlook. Taraki was a member of the **Khalq**, a faction of the main Afghan Marxist Party, the PDPA. This faction was strongest in the rural parts of the country and, in contrast to the rival **Parcham** faction, which it energetically persecuted while in power, it believed that there could be no compromises when it came to the implementation of Marxist ideas. The USSR was the first to recognize the new government and sign a treaty of co-operation and assistance.

As President and Prime Minister, the radical Taraki took steps to implement land and social reforms, such as encouraging women to join literacy classes, and all Afghans to abandon the habit of deference to *mullahs* and landowners. Taraki, taking the hard-line Marxist view of religion, began a strong anti-Islamic campaign, which included arresting religious leaders and burning the Qu'ran in public. He also persecuted the Kabul Jewish community. When 130 men from a **Shi'ite** clan were massacred, rebellion grew.

🔑 KEY TERM

Khalq A faction of the People's Democratic Party of Afghanistan strongly influenced by Stalinist ideas.

Parcham A moderate faction of the People's Democratic Party of Afghanistan.

Mullah A religiously educated leader of a mosque or an Islamic cleric.

Shi'ite A Muslim who follows the Shia version of Islam.

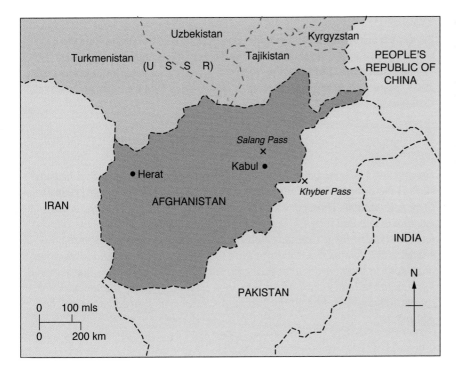

A map of Afghanistan and neighbouring states in 1979. The mountainous geography of the country meant that transportation was difficult. The Salang Pass was the main route north to the USSR. The Khyber Pass was the route to the south and to Pakistan and the coastal port of Karachi.

An armed uprising against the Taraki regime began in Herat, near the border with Iran, in March 1979. This was spearheaded by *mujaheddin*, who were especially angry at girls being educated. During these disturbances in Herat, several Soviet officials and their families were killed. This led to Taraki issuing an urgent appeal to the USSR for troops and aircraft to help him to crush the uprising. The country was hurtling towards a civil war.

The initial Soviet response

The Soviet Politburo was initially reluctant to respond, having witnessed the USA's humiliation in Vietnam, and understood the limited nature of support for the PDPA. There was the issue of the burden on an ailing economy, as well as the reaction of Third World nations, notably India. Brezhnev allowed his colleagues input into deciding the Soviet response to the PDPA's plea for assistance.

Soviet Foreign Minister Gromyko was aware that military intervention in Afghanistan by the USSR would weaken *détente*. Yuri Andropov, Chairman of the Committee for State Security, was equally pessimistic and questioned whether Afghanistan was ready for a full socialist revolution. At this stage, all that the USSR was prepared to offer in terms of military aid to the PDPA was 500 military advisers to help train the Afghan government's armed forces which were struggling to cope as military resistance to the PDPA spread to other parts of the country.

 **KEY TERM**

Mujaheddin Islamic warriors, usually guerrilla fighters.

?

Assess the origin, purpose, value and limitations of Source N in determining why the USSR did not intervene in Afghanistan in March 1979.

SOURCE N

Excerpt from statements by Andropov and Gromyko at the Politburo meeting on 17–18 March 1979 in *The Soviet Union under Brezhnev* by William Tompson, published by Pearson/Longman Education, London, UK, 2003, page 132. Tompson teaches in the Politics Department at Birkbeck College, University of London, UK.

Andropov – 'we know Lenin's teaching about a revolutionary situation. Whatever type of situation we are talking about in Afghanistan, it is not that type of situation …'

Gromyko – 'I fully support Comrade Andropov's proposal to exclude a measure such as the introduction of our troops into Afghanistan. The [Afghan] Army there is unreliable. Thus, our army if it enters Afghanistan will be the aggressor. Against whom will it fight? Against the [Afghan] people first of all and it will have to shoot at them. Comrade Andropov correctly noted that indeed the situation in Afghanistan is not ripe for a [socialist] revolution. And all that we have done in recent years with such effort in terms of a détente in international tensions, arms reductions and much more – all that would be thrown back. Of course, this will be a nice gift for China. All the non-aligned countries will be against us …'

The overthrow of Taraki

Taraki was overthrown and murdered in September 1979 by Foreign Minister Hafizulla Amin, a rival from within his own government and another leader from the Khalq faction of the PDPA. Amin was assisted by his son-in-law, Colonel Yakub, the Army Chief of Staff.

SOURCE O

?

What does Source O suggest about Soviet attempts to control Amin?

An excerpt from a coded telegram to Soviet representatives in Kabul on 15 September 1979 by Gromyko, from *The Soviet Union: A Documentary History, Volume 2, 1939–1991* by Edward Acton and Tom Stableford, published by the University of Exeter Press, Exeter, UK, 2007, page 245. Professor Acton of the University of East Anglia, UK, and Assistant Librarian Stableford at the Bodleian Library, Oxford, UK, compiled documents from newly available archival material on the former USSR. Their purpose was to provide non-Russian speakers with documents from the Cold War USSR.

It is considered expedient in view of the real situation which is developing in Afghanistan, not to refuse to deal with Amin and his government. At the same time it is essential to restrain Amin by all means possible from taking repressive measures against Taraki's supporters … Moreover, it is vital to use contacts with Amin to ascertain further his political colours and intentions. It is also considered expedient for our military advisers in the Afghan forces and for our advisers on state security and internal affairs to stay put … They must of course not take part in repressive measures against persons out of favour with Amin, if units and subunits containing our advisers are drawn into such actions.

From Brezhnev's point of view, Amin now began to show signs of trying to end Soviet influence. The KGB reported the growing influence of the CIA in Kabul, as well as developing diplomatic contacts between Amin and Pakistan, an ally of the USA. According to British diplomat Rodric Braithwaite, on 27 September, Amin told Bruce Amstutz, the US *charge d'affaires* in Kabul, that he hoped for improved relations with the USA. From a Soviet point of view, this opened the frightening prospect of Afghanistan becoming a pro-western state in which nuclear missiles targeted at Soviet territory might be stationed. In addition, the recent radical Islamic revolution in Iran posed a possible danger to the USSR if Islamic fundamentalism spread to the USSR's republics in central Asia. The Soviets decided to topple Amin.

KEY TERM

Charge d'affaires An interim diplomat who substitutes for a missing ambassador or minister.

NATO North Atlantic Treaty Organization, a military alliance of the USA, Canada, and much of western Europe.

The reasons for Soviet intervention

Ever since the nineteenth century, influence in Afghanistan had been regarded as a vital means of projecting Russian and later Soviet power into central Asia. Within the Politburo, Andropov now believed that firm action was needed not only to preserve Soviet influence in the region, but also to stop the rise of Islamic fundamentalism. Andropov was also well aware that two of the major ethnic groups in Afghanistan, the Uzbeks and Tajiks, were also significant national minorities within the USSR, making the internal politics of Afghanistan of direct relevance to the Soviet state.

Many figures in the Politburo, Andropov included, could see the potential political and military dangers of sending Red Army troops into Afghanistan and knew that any invasion would sour relations with the USA. However, without Soviet military support against the *mujaheddin*, it appeared likely that the PDPA regime would collapse. Amin only controlled 20 per cent of the country and his policy of ruthless repression alienated what little support he still had. What really tipped the balance within the Politburo in favour of intervention was Amin himself. His motives were not trusted. He was also perceived as being unable or unwilling to construct a stable, broad-based regime and the KGB in particular had much closer ties to members of the Parcham faction of the Afghan communists.

The Politburo meeting, December 1979

The crucial Politburo meeting that made the decision to send Red Army troops to Kabul took place on 12 December 1979, which was the same day that **NATO** announced the introduction of Pershing II nuclear missiles into western Europe. This was taken as further proof that *détente* was dead and with the SALT II treaty not ratified by the US Congress (see page 113), it was felt that in terms of superpower relations, the USSR had little more to lose. It was also hoped that President Carter's reluctance to arm Somalia during its conflict with Ethiopia (see page 112) was a sign of the likelihood of a weak diplomatic response to an invasion of Afghanistan from the USA. Andropov seems to have accepted that no viable alternative existed if Soviet credibility, as well as strategic and political interests, were to be upheld. He was particularly concerned about the alleged links between Amin and the CIA and the danger of Afghanistan becoming a pro-western client state. Gromyko summed up the mood of the meeting when he stated in his memoirs that they were all upset by the murder of Taraki, especially Brezhnev. The Politburo decided to introduce a limited contingent of Soviet forces into Afghanistan.

To what extent was Soviet military intervention in Afghanistan successful?

Soviet military intervention in Afghanistan

On 25 December 1979, Soviet troops entered Afghanistan. This took place with the knowledge and backing of Amin, who believed that the influx of Red Army troops would support his regime.

The overthrow of Amin

On 27 December 1979, the presidential palace in Kabul was stormed by Red Army and KGB special forces, killing Amin and his son. A new pro-Soviet leader, Babrak Karmal, the leader of the Parcham faction of the PDPA, was now installed in Kabul. One of his first actions was to authorize a purge against the remnants of the Khalq faction.

? What, according Source P, was the impact of the Soviet invasion of Afghanistan?

SOURCE P

Excerpt from Andrei Sakharov's open letter to Brezhnev regarding the invasion of Afghanistan, 1980, from *The Soviet Union: A Documentary History, Volume 2* by Edward Acton and Tom Stableford, published by the University of Exeter Press, Exeter, UK, 2007, page 365–7. Professor Acton of the University of East Anglia, UK, and Assistant Librarian Stableford at the Bodleian Library, Oxford, UK, compiled documents from newly available archival material on the former USSR. Their purpose was to provide non-Russian speakers with documents from the Cold War USSR.

I am writing to you on a matter of extreme importance – Afghanistan … Military actions in Afghanistan have been going on for seven months now. Thousands of Soviet people and tens of thousands of Afghans have been maimed or killed; the latter are not only partisans [mujaheddin] but mainly civilians … Reports about the bombing of villages aiding and abetting the partisans and the mining of mountain roads, thereby threatening hunger to whole regions, are particularly ominous … Nor is there any doubt that events in Afghanistan have changed the political world. They have struck a blow against détente and have created a direct threat to peace, not only in this region but everywhere … Soviet actions have contributed to (and how could it be otherwise!) increased defence budgets and the adoption of new weapons programmes by all the major powers, which will have repercussions for years to come and increase the danger from the arms race. At the UN General Assembly, Soviet actions have been condemned by 104 states, including many which hitherto unequivocally supported any actions by the USSR.

Guerrilla warfare and its impact

This Soviet-backed coup had little effect on the wider insurrection of the *mujaheddin*, which developed under the guidance of skilful and charismatic commanders like Ahmad Shah Massoud, who successfully used **guerrilla warfare** tactics.

By the end of 1980, 125,000 Red Army troops were involved in a country whose language, culture and history they did not really understand, fighting a guerrilla war for which they had not been trained, and receiving little support from the Afghan government forces that consisted of reluctant conscripts. The mechanized nature of the Red Army forces, well suited to mobile, armoured conventional warfare against an equally mobile and armoured army, was actually a disadvantage in Afghanistan as it confined Soviet troops to the country's basic road network. Here, they became easy targets for *mujaheddin* ambushes. Facing a non-uniformed enemy, numbering up to 250,000, often indistinguishable from the civilian population, increased the likelihood of atrocities against civilians.

> 🔑 **KEY TERM**
>
> **Guerrilla warfare** Use of the military technique of ambush and the avoidance of open battle, usually in order to avoid defeat against a technologically more sophisticated opponent.

SOURCE Q

Leonid Brezhnev greets Babrak Karmal in Moscow in 1981.

> How does Source Q portray the relations between Brezhnev and Karmal? ❓

By the end of 1982, nearly 5000 Soviet troops had died in Afghanistan. Increasingly, the Red Army made use of its special forces, the Spetznaz, to conduct aggressive raids and reprisals. Soviet citizens were ambivalent about the conflict. Some, such as Andrei Sakharov and his wife, publicly opposed the invasion. However, many veterans returned home to find that their families knew little about the nature of the fighting, beyond propaganda platitudes about international socialist solidarity.

SOURCE R

A Soviet supply column in the Salang Pass in Afghanistan in 1988.

SOURCE S

Mujaheddin fighters in the hills of Afghanistan in 1988.

The increasingly brutal nature of the fighting forced many Afghan civilians to flee the country. Over three million Afghans moved to refugee camps in Pakistan, which became recruiting centres for the *mujaheddin*. A turning point in the conflict came in 1986 when the *mujaheddin* began receiving US supplies of highly portable Stinger anti-aircraft missiles. This made Soviet helicopters, a crucial part of Red Army operations in such a mountainous country, vulnerable to ground fire. Soviet aircraft were also now forced to bomb targets from higher altitudes, lessening their accuracy and increasing the likelihood of civilian casualties, making already poor relations with the civilian population even worse.

Morale among the Soviet forces declined as the war continued. Ordinary soldiers were poorly paid, which acted as a catalyst for corruption. There was a case of members of the Soviet military mission in Kabul selling weapons directly to the *mujaheddin* and laundering the proceeds abroad.

The response of the USA and its allies

US President Carter was deeply angered by the Soviet invasion of Afghanistan. He denounced the invasion in 1980 as the most severe danger to peace since the Second World War. The USA suspended grain sales to the USSR and a US boycott was announced of the 1980 Olympic Games in Moscow. Carter also announced the Carter Doctrine, which stated that any attempt by an 'outside force' to imposed its authority on the Persian Gulf region, which held vast oil reserves, would be perceived as a challenge to vital US strategic interests and be repelled by any means necessary, including military force. Carter's National Security Adviser, Zbigniew Brzezinski, also saw an opportunity to tie down the Red Army in a costly guerrilla war. Sending US troops to Afghanistan was strategically impractical and would have risked the outbreak of a larger war between the USA and the USSR. Instead, large shipments of US weapons and munitions were sent to Pakistan, whose military dictator, General Zia ul-Haq, agreed to act as a conduit for weapons ultimately intended for the *mujaheddin*. Support for the *mujaheddin* was increased when Ronald Reagan became the US president in 1981. As the decade went on, Saudi Arabia funded the *mujaheddin*. By the time the Red Army withdrew in 1988, over $9 billion had been funnelled to the *mujahheddin* via Pakistan.

The withdrawal of the Red Army

As early as 1980, the USSR was keen to find a face-saving exit strategy, which would leave a pro-Soviet regime in control. Discussions between the Soviet ambassador to Pakistan and General Zia ul-Haq and talks between Pakistan, Iran and Afghanistan were brokered by the UN. What emerged from these talks was that key figures in the Politburo such as Andropov were more than willing to agree to the Red Army's withdrawal provided that Pakistan's aid to the *mujaheddin* ceased. US President Reagan agreed, and in 1985 he wrote to the new Soviet General Secretary Mikhail Gorbachev that he understood Soviet security concerns and would work to address them as the Red Army withdrew from Afghanistan.

The Geneva Agreement

Gorbachev informed President Karmal that Red Army troops would be withdrawn in 1985. From 1986, he continued to look for a way to end Soviet involvement in Afghanistan, with little success since the Soviets continued to have security concerns. In 1987, Gorbachev told Reagan that it was no longer necessary for Afghanistan to be a socialist state but that it needed to have a government friendly to the USSR. Talks in Geneva continued until 14 April 1988 when a UN-supported peace agreement was signed. The USSR agreed to withdraw its forces over a 10-month period but remained committed to maintaining its political and economic support for the pro-Soviet regime in Kabul. Afghanistan and Pakistan also agreed not to interfere in each other's internal affairs. Crucially, none of the *mujaheddin* factions signed the **Geneva Agreement**, thus guaranteeing a continued internal struggle against the Soviet-supported government led by Mohamed Najibullah after 1986.

What was the lasting impact of Soviet intervention in Afghanistan?

The impact of the war

By the time the last Red Army troops returned home in 1989, many were embittered and traumatized by their experiences; 15,000 Soviet military personnel had lost their lives in the conflict.

The impact on Afghanistan was far reaching: up to two million killed and five million refugees out of a total pre-war population of 15.5 million. In addition, there were two million internal refugees displaced from their villages by war.

After Soviet troops had withdrawn, the vicious civil war between President Najibullah's supporters, backed by the USSR, and *mujaheddin* forces, backed by the USA, continued. The USA started to rein in the guerrillas that it had once encouraged, but it was too little too late; efforts to buy back the Stinger missile launchers for $100,000 each were unsuccessful.

The overall impact of the conflict on Afghanistan was to create a large body of well-armed fighters, motivated by conservative religious and cultural beliefs and strong enough to impose their own form of government. Within the *mujaheddin* movement there were at least seven major factions, with some being relatively moderate. Nevertheless, when President Najibullah was finally toppled in 1992, it did serve to pave the way for the establishment of the **Taliban** regime, which ran the country until the US-led offensive against Kabul in 2001.

🔑 KEY TERM

Geneva Agreement
Signed in April 1988 in Geneva by Afghanistan and Pakistan to agree on non-interference and non-intervention, return of refugees and Soviet withdrawal from Afghanistan, with international guarantees by the USA and the USSR.

Taliban Ultra-conservative Islamic militants who took over a large part of Afghanistan in 1995, and in 1996 overran the capital of Kabul and declared an Islamic state.

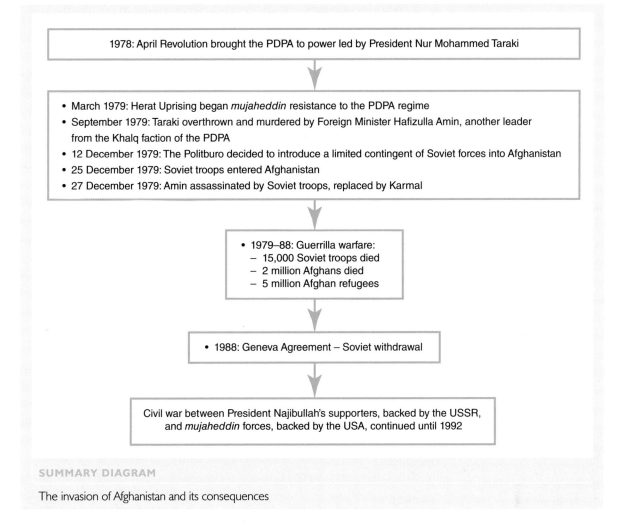

1978: April Revolution brought the PDPA to power led by President Nur Mohammed Taraki

- March 1979: Herat Uprising began *mujaheddin* resistance to the PDPA regime
- September 1979: Taraki overthrown and murdered by Foreign Minister Hafizulla Amin, another leader from the Khalq faction of the PDPA
- 12 December 1979: The Politburo decided to introduce a limited contingent of Soviet forces into Afghanistan
- 25 December 1979: Soviet troops entered Afghanistan
- 27 December 1979: Amin assassinated by Soviet troops, replaced by Karmal

- 1979–88: Guerrilla warfare:
  - 15,000 Soviet troops died
  - 2 million Afghans died
  - 5 million Afghan refugees

- 1988: Geneva Agreement – Soviet withdrawal

Civil war between President Najibullah's supporters, backed by the USSR, and *mujaheddin* forces, backed by the USA, continued until 1992

SUMMARY DIAGRAM

The invasion of Afghanistan and its consequences

 Key debate

> ▶ **Key question:** *Why did the USSR invade Afghanistan?*

Historians continue to debate the reasons for the Soviet incursion into Afghanistan in 1979.

Was the war provoked by the USA?

One of the most controversial explanations is that it was deliberately provoked by hawks in the USA such as National Security Adviser Zbigniew Brzezinksi and the CIA. This is the thesis of Nigel Hamilton, Professor of Biography at De Montfort University in the UK. He argues that Brzezinski's formative years, during which he saw his Polish homeland under German and then Soviet occupation, made him inherently suspicious of totalitarian states and dubious about the benefits of *détente*. For Brzezinski, whose world-view was dominated by the need to confront and defeat Soviet communism, the USSR's success in proxy wars in Africa demanded a response. In an interview with *Le Nouvel Observateur* in 1998, Brzezinski explained that on 3 July 1979, over five months before the Soviet invasion of Afghanistan, US President Carter signed a directive authorizing $500,000 worth of aid to the *mujaheddin*. This became known as Operation Cyclone and was allegedly a plot to destabilize the PDPA regime in Afghanistan, thus forcing the Red Army to intervene in order to prop it up; it was then intended to involve Soviet forces in a Vietnam-style military quagmire.

This interpretation relies on the testimony of a Cold War hawk, perhaps anxious to highlight his own role, and that of the CIA, in the eventual collapse of the USSR. Also, the level of funding provided to the CIA in order to support the *mujaheddin* was minimal and before December 1979 only three Soviet citizens had been killed by the *mujaheddin* in the Herat insurgency (see page 115). Furthermore, until early December the Politburo remained deeply reluctant to even consider military intervention, repeatedly ignoring requests from the Afghan government for military support.

Ultimately, Operation Cyclone may have played a role in pushing the Politburo to commit troops, most likely by reinforcing pre-existing Soviet fears of growing US influence in the region, which then led to the fateful decision to unseat President Amin. However, it is probable that Soviet intervention would still have occurred, even without the actions of Brzezinski and the CIA. Historian and former US Secretary of State Henry Kissinger takes a wider view of Soviet reasons to act, within the Cold War context of the early 1980s (see Source T).

SOURCE T

According to Source T, what were the goals of the USSR in Afghanistan?

Excerpt from 'Reflections on a partnership: British and American attitudes to postwar foreign policy' by Henry A. Kissinger, *International Affairs*, Vol. 58, No. 4, Autumn 1982, published by Blackwell Publishing, Oxford, UK, page 585. Kissinger was a History Professor at Harvard University, USA, and the US Secretary of State from 1973 to 1977.

… today's [crisis], I am afraid, is more genuinely, objectively, serious than ever. It comes after decades of a relentless Soviet military buildup, when the West, for a decade, is edging in some areas toward a dangerous dependency on economic ties with the East; while in Poland the Soviet Union enforces the unity of its empire, its clients press on to undermine the security interests of the West from South-east Asia to the Middle East to Africa to Central America. Not all our difficulties are caused by the Soviet Union, but the Soviet Union has shown little restraint in exploiting them, and their solution – whatever their cause – has been impeded by the lack of a unified Western response.

The USSR's geo-political ambition to secure a warm water port in the Persian Gulf and therefore direct access to the Middle East's oil supplies was seen at the time, in the western media, as one of the main factors driving the Soviet invasion of Afghanistan. President Carter described it as 'a stepping stone to their [the Soviets'] possible control over much of the world's oil supplies.' However, no Machiavellian master plan to this end existed, unless one takes into account vague strategic aspirations allegedly expressed by Defence Minister Ustinov, according to the testimony of Alexander Maiorov, the chief Soviet military adviser in Afghanistan in 1980–1. In the main, the inner core of the Politburo consisting of Brezhnev himself, Andropov and Gromyko, were concerned with preserving existing Soviet influence in Afghanistan, rather than expanding it southwards.

A pragmatic response to events?

The Soviet invasion of Afghanistan is perhaps better understood as a pragmatic and reluctant response to events on the ground in Afghanistan. This is certainly the view of former British Ambassador Rodric Braithwaite who depicts Soviet politicians as 'driven step by step, mostly against their will'. The Politburo was affected by the perception of growing US influence in the region that threatened Afghanistan's traditional status as a friendly buffer state. Developments such as US financial grants to the Daoud regime and the openness of President Amin to western diplomatic overtures must be seen in this wider historical context, and seemed in Soviet eyes to threaten its relationship with Afghanistan.

It would be wrong to over-state the direct impact of the US government in shaping the Politburo's thinking. After all, US President Carter's decision to

SOURCE U

Excerpt from 'Decision-making and the Soviet War in Afghanistan from intervention to withdrawal' by Artemy Kalinovsky in *Journal of Cold War Studies*, Fall 2009, Vol. 11, Issue 4, pages 49–50. Kalinovsky teaches Eastern European Studies at the Universiteit van Amsterdam, The Netherlands.

The decision to invade was an example of how Andropov, Gromyko, and Ustinov dominated Soviet foreign policymaking. By this point Brezhnev … had become more amenable to the idea of intervention … The failure of the U.S. Congress to consent to ratification of the Strategic Arms Limitation Treaty (SALT II) in the summer of 1979, heralding a turn away from détente *on the part of the United States, was one reason. The anticipated decision to deploy Pershing II intermediate-range missiles in Europe (a decision formally approved on the same day that the Soviet authorities decided to invade Afghanistan) was another. The murder of … Taraki by his rival … Amin, despite Brezhnev's pledge of support, helped convince Brezhnev that Amin had to be removed from power. Growing suspicion that Amin might be considering a turn toward the United States contributed to this belief. When Andropov and Ustinov pressed for intervention in December, they cited the above arguments, pointing out that a Western-oriented Afghanistan could become a base for short-range nuclear missiles targeted at the USSR. Brezhnev no longer objected to intervention.*

According to Source U, why did the USSR invade Afghanistan?

TOK Historians continue to debate Soviet reasons for the war in Afghanistan. To what extent are some questions about history unanswerable? (History, Language, and Reason.)

install Pershing II nuclear missiles in Europe, on the same day as the decisive Politburo meeting, which has been seen as one of the key 'sparks' pushing the USSR into a disastrous invasion, was actually nothing of the sort. Braithwaite makes a compelling case from an insider's perspective that 'given the complex and confused way in which decisions are taken by most governments, it is unlikely that the news would have affected the Politburo, even had it reached them in time'.

It seems that the Soviet invasion of Afghanistan is an event that lacks a neat and straightforward explanation. Certainly no strategic master plan for Soviet domination of the region existed and instead the Politburo acted because the perceived alternatives – such as the *mujaheddin* dislodging the PDPA, Afghanistan becoming a US client state or President Amin becoming a close ally of Pakistan – seemed too awful to contemplate, given the Politburo's ideological and world outlook. As Braithwaite succinctly states, 'the Russians [*sic.*] slithered towards a military intervention because they could not think of a better alternative'.

 # The USSR in 1982

> ▶ *Key question: How serious were the socio-economic and political problems confronting the USSR by the time of Brezhnev's death?*

As with any long-term leader, Brezhnev's personality made an impact on USSR. He strove to reach consensus in decision-making and avoided direct conflict with colleagues or countries whenever possible. By 1982, his health was failing. By the time Brezhnev died on 10 November 1982, there was serious social and economic malaise in the USSR. World opinion of the USSR and the Soviet–Afghan War was low.

→ ## Social tensions

What inequalities existed in Soviet society?

Soviet society was far from being a Marxist utopia for most of the USSR's citizens at the time of Brezhnev's death:

- There was anti-Jewish prejudice.
- Urban workers received more consumer goods and services than collective farm workers.
- Emigration out of the USSR was hindered.

Senior members of the *nomenklatura* élite received privileges such as access to special shops in which prices were heavily subsidized. Brezhnev promoted the 'stability of cadres' which meant that high-level government officials retained their positions for great lengths of time especially after term-limits for offices were ended. The *nomenklatura* remained a self-perpetuating élite.

Officials used their influence to ensure that their children attended the best schools and universities. Nepotism and corruption prevented a truly socialist way of life.

The best that can be said of Soviet society at the time of Brezhnev's death is that its brand of socialism ensured that workers and their families received sufficient welfare benefits to secure an adequate standard of living. However, modest rises in living standards that had taken place in 1945 were threatened by inflation. Khrushchev's hope that Soviet living standards would overtake those of western capitalist countries proved to be wildly optimistic.

Economy

The Soviets found it increasingly difficult to sustain the expenditure necessary to maintain superpower status. Costly conflicts in Angola and Afghanistan (see page 112) provided evidence of the 'burden of empire' hypothesis. This means that the USSR started to stagger under the economic weight of maintaining strategic and military parity with the USA. By the time of Brezhnev's death, the defence budget may have consumed as much as 30 per cent of gross national product, making it even less likely that there would ever be adequate investment in other sectors of the economy. It should also be remembered that for ideological and foreign policy reasons, the USSR subsidized communist governments in eastern Europe and Cuba. The annual discount on Soviet oil for Warsaw Pact members alone amounted to $3 billion.

This meant that under Brezhnev there had been relatively little investment in new industries such as information technology and in 1982 the USSR possessed only one per cent of the amount of computers that existed in the USA.

Politics

On the surface, the Soviet political system appeared relatively stable at the time of Brezhnev's death. However, the senior echelons of the party had become a **gerontocracy**, resistant to change and innovation. By 1980, the average age of Politburo members was 69 years. Many key figures had been politically active since the 1930s. Of the members of the CPSU in 1981, 75 per cent had joined the party before 1950 and most had joined the party in the era of Stalin.

This élite appeared increasingly removed from the concerns and aspirations of ordinary Soviet citizens by the time of Brezhnev's death. Within this élite, relatively few seemed able or willing to challenge the prevailing economic and political *status quo*. When the Deputy Prime Minister Vladimir Kirillin made a speech in 1979 stating that the USSR was on the verge of a financial crisis and that the West was establishing an unbeatable technological lead, he was dismissed and his speech was banned from circulation.

> Why was the USSR on the brink of an economic crisis?

> How stable was the Soviet political system?

KEY TERM

Gerontocracy A state whose political élite is almost exclusively comprised of a narrow circle of elderly men.

Nationalism within the Soviet republics

Brezhnev appeared to have little or no sympathy with the concerns of the non-Russian inhabitants of Soviet republics. Many felt that the USSR served the needs of Russians first while non-Russians were disregarded. By 1981, 10 out of the 14 members of the Politburo were Russian. Protests in Soviet republics, with nationalist overtones, such as that in Armenia in 1965, were invariably crushed by force. This provoked violence; the Moscow Metro was bombed by Armenian nationalists in 1977. Riots erupted in Tashkent, Uzbekistan, in 1969, and several Russian officials were killed.

In 1972, a student set himself on fire in Kaunas, Lithuania, demanding freedom from the USSR. His death set off anti-government riots in the city. Discontent in the Baltic states of the USSR was due to the legacy of Soviet actions during the Second World War, when Lithuania, Latvia and Estonia had been annexed. In addition, the Baltic states' geographical proximity to democratic states, such as Sweden and Finland, meant that it was more feasible for citizens in this part of the USSR to familiarize themselves with events there. For instance, many people in Estonia were able to watch Finnish television stations.

Despite signs of acute political tension, nothing had been done by 1982 to address the political aspirations of non-Russians or the associated problem of how Russian minorities in various republics should be treated. Central Asian republics with large Muslim populations were restless as a result of the Soviet–Afghan war and the revolution in Iran in 1979 which led to the creation of a religious state. According to historian Robert Service, under Brezhnev the problems of a multinational and multicultural state were concealed rather than faced and resolved. Furthermore, regional party bosses such as Sharif Rashidov in Uzbekistan started to cement their hold on power by tacitly encouraging nationalist sentiment. It all added to an increasingly tense political scene and rising ethnic tensions lacked an easy solution.

Politics	Society	Economy

• Gerontocracy, resistant to change and innovation
• Nationalist protests cause of tension
	• Anti-Jewish prejudice
	• Urban workers received more consumer goods and services than collective farm workers
	• Emigration out of the USSR was hindered
	• *Nomenklatura* élite received privileges
	• Nepotism and corruption
		• Burden of empire:
		  – costly conflicts in Angola and Afghanistan
		  – subsidies to Warsaw Pact countries
		  – defence budget 30% of GNP
		• Little investment in new industries

SUMMARY DIAGRAM

The USSR in 1982

Chapter summary

Domestic and foreign problems of the Brezhnev era

Leonid Brezhnev came to power in 1964 following the overthrow of Nikita Khrushchev. As First Secretary of the CPSU, he gradually emerged as the dominant force in Soviet politics. In 1977, a new constitution further cemented Brezhnev's political position and that of the CPSU.

There is some evidence that the standard of living for ordinary Soviet citizens improved during the Brezhnev era and by the time of his death, 86 per cent of Soviet citizens possessed a television or a refrigerator. However, a static level of life expectancy and rising infant mortality suggest that there were deep-seated social problems. Rising oil exports failed to mask the growing economic problems facing the Soviet state. Despite huge state subsidies, the *kolkhozy* were inefficient and unproductive and the USSR became increasingly reliant on food imports from the West. Soviet industry was also beset by problems, such as widespread corruption and an obsession with quantitative targets to the exclusion of other economic goals. The work of GOSPLAN did little or nothing to ameliorate these problems.

One significant reaction to the socio-economic and political stagnation of the Brezhnev era was the emergence of a dissident movement. Individuals like Andrei Sakharov became more vocal in their criticisms of the regime, especially in the aftermath of the Helsinki Accords. By the time Brezhnev died in 1982, the USSR was in a state of crisis. The economy was failing to bear the burden of the USSR's imperial commitments and the Politburo was increasingly a gerontocracy and out of touch with the aspirations and needs of ordinary citizens.

Soviet foreign policy up to the late 1970s was characterized by poor relations with China. Brezhnev was also determined to maintain the Soviet grip on eastern Europe, as shown by the Red Army's invasion of Czechoslovakia in 1968 in response to Dubček's Prague Spring. Crucially, the US Presidents Nixon and Ford worked towards *détente* with the Brezhnev regime, creating the SALT I treaty that placed limits on nuclear arsenals and the Helsinki Accords, which acted as a catalyst for the development of human rights movements in the Eastern Bloc.

With proxy wars continuing in the Third World, especially in Africa, and with US Pershing missiles and Soviet SS-20 missiles reigniting the arms race, the period of *détente* came to an end. Crucial to this shift away from *détente* was the Soviet invasion of Afghanistan in 1979, driven by Soviet concerns about the growth of US and conservative Islamic influence in the region. This military intervention was a disaster for the USSR, leading to the Red Army being embroiled in a bloody guerrilla war that cost the lives of over 15,000 Soviet soldiers and up to two million Afghans. The Soviet military intervention was brought to an end by the 1988 Geneva Agreement, which, by withdrawing Soviet troops, paved the way for the collapse of President Najibullah's PDPA client regime.

Inside the USSR there were serious challenges as well. The make-up of the Politburo and other top governing bodies included increasingly elderly members, creating a gerontocracy. This hindered the development of a dynamic system for dealing with political, social and economic issues that required urgent attention. One very volatile issue was nationalism in some of the Soviet republics. Mounting anti-Russian resentment flared up in the Baltic republics and spread to central Asia. The seemingly monolithic USSR was about to crack.

✅ Examination advice

Paper 1 Question 3: OPVL

Question 3 on the IB History Diploma examination requires to you to discuss the origin and purpose of two sources and then to use that information to determine each source's potential value and limitations (OPVL). The question always asks you to refer to the origin and purpose of two named sources to assess their value and limitations for historians. Unlike Questions 1 and 2, some knowledge of the topic, value of types of sources, or authors can be useful, although this is not required. Question 3 is worth 6 marks out of the 25 total for Paper 1. This means it is worth 24 per cent of your overall mark. Answering Question 3 should take approximately 10 minutes of your examination time.

How to answer

Read Question 3 carefully. You will notice that it is asking you to discuss the origins and purpose of two different sources and then to determine the value and limitations for these two sources for historians. This question is not like Question 2; you must treat each source separately. The first source mentioned in the question should be the one you start with and it should be in its own paragraph, with the second source treated in the second paragraph. At no point should you compare or contrast the sources or discuss them in the same paragraph.

Structure will help you in answering the question. Incorporate the words origin, purpose, value and limitation into your answer. 'The origin of Source B is … ', 'the purpose of Source B is … ', 'the value of this source is … ' and 'a limitation of this source may be … '. This keeps you focused on the task, making sure you covered all the required elements, but also helps the examiner understand your answers by providing a framework that they can follow. It is important to remember that you are to use the origins and purpose to determine the value and limitations. The actual text of the source is not to be used as it is just an excerpt from a much larger work.

Origin

The origin of a source is the author, the type of publication, the year it was published and sometimes the country it originates from. If there is biographical information included as part of the source's introduction, this also may be used in addressing the source's origin.

Purpose

The purpose of a source is usually indicated by the source's title, the type of source, the writer or speaker, if it is a speech, or the location of the source, such as in a newspaper, an academic book or a journal article. Purposes can range from speeches that try to convince certain groups or nations that what the speaker is saying is the truth or should be heeded, to explaining the history of a certain time period.

- If a journal article's title is 'Decision-making and the Soviet War in Afghanistan from intervention to withdrawal' the purpose of this particular source is likely to explain the decision-making process of the Soviet War in Afghanistan.
- If the author of this source is Russian, it may be that the purpose is to explain Soviet policy in Afghanistan, to convince the reader that the Soviet government's policies in Afghanistan were the best it could manage in a tough situation, and so forth.
- If the source's author is a US academic, then the purpose could very well be to convince the reader that this proxy war worsened the Cold War or perhaps something else.

Since this is a hypothesis on your part, be sure to include the words 'perhaps' or 'possibly'. In order to determine the purpose or purposes of a source, be sure to read the title, the date of publication, the name of the author, and any biographical information given.

Value

The value of a source flows naturally from the origins and purpose.

Perhaps a book exists that is entitled *The Soviet War in Afghanistan* and was written by an Afghan leader during the 1980s. The value will be that this leader probably witnessed or participated in certain events, perhaps experienced the effects of Soviet troops in the region, and may have even met prominent Soviet officials. This would give the author first-hand knowledge of the Soviet War in Afghanistan.

If the author lived 20 years after the war ended, a value could be that the writer has access to Soviet and Afghan sources, may be less connected and therefore less emotional about the subject and therefore more objective, or perhaps is able to better determine the long-term impact of the war on international relations during the Cold War.

Your answer will have to be determined by the origin and purpose of the source you are asked to discuss. Do not state that primary sources have more value than secondary sources; this is not necessarily true.

Limitation

The limitation of a source is determined in much the same way that you determined the source's value. If the writer of *The Soviet War in Afghanistan* is Russian, the writer is likely to have more access to Soviet sources than Afghan ones. This would be a limitation in that the author is *possibly* unable to present a truly balanced view. Other than the author's nationality, there may be other ways to determine possible limitations:

- The title of the source may be of a limited nature or too broad for the topic.

- The date of publication may be limiting if it is too close to or far from the historical events.
- A source that is political in nature may be trying to advocate a certain view or policy instead of being objective.

Do not state that sources are limited because they are secondary sources; this may not be true and often is not.

Visual images

Visual sources will have information explaining to you their origin. Remember that photographs can capture a single moment in time so that they can show exactly what happened, but they can also be staged to send a particular message. A photograph of smiling *mujaheddin* in the hills of Afghanistan captures a moment when they were either genuinely happy or told to smile, perhaps not knowing even what they were smiling about. Cartoons, posters and even photographs often have a political message. The purpose of any of these could potentially be to convince the viewer of a certain point of view. Another purpose could be to make fun of a particular idea or person for some other reason. Apply analytical skills from Chapters 2 and 3 if appropriate.

Example

This question uses Sources O and U, found on pages 116 and 125.

> With reference to their origins and purpose, discuss the value and limitations of Sources O and U for historians studying the reasons for Soviet military intervention in Afghanistan.

There is no need to brainstorm or outline for this question, so go to your examination paper and start writing. A sample answer is given below.

The title of each source and its author are clearly stated, as is the year of publication.

The terms origin, purpose, value and limitation are used throughout both paragraphs.

The origin of Source O is a coded telegram to Soviet representatives in Kabul on 15 September 1979 by Soviet Minister of Foreign Affairs Andrei Gromyko, found in **The Soviet Union: A Documentary History, Volume 2**. *It is included by British academic historians who have compiled new archival material on the former USSR.*

The purpose of the telegram is to give official instructions to the Soviet representative in Kabul regarding how to deal with the Afghan political situation, as well as the military one.

A value of this source is that it is a primary source written by Gromyko, an official member of the Soviet government in 1979 on the eve of the Soviet war in Afghanistan. It is valuable as an official government document which was written just at the time prior to Soviet military intervention, so it provides a unique view of Soviet reasons for military intervention in Afghanistan. The author,

Gromyko, was Minister of Foreign Affairs, so he was privy to government decisions at the highest spheres in the USSR and had ample power to affect decisions abroad. It is also coded, to prevent reading by non-official eyes, so it is less likely to have been manipulated or changed.

A limitation of Source O could be that, as it is official Soviet policy, it views the Soviet military intervention strictly from the Soviet viewpoint, discounting the Afghan perceptions at the time. A historian would need to look at alternative views. Another limitation may be that since the telegram was giving specific instructions to the Soviet representatives in Kabul in dealing with Amin, it does not fully address all the reasons for the Soviet War in Afghanistan.

*The origin of Source U is an excerpt from the article 'Decision-making and the Soviet War in Afghanistan From Intervention to Withdrawal' by Artemy Kalinovsky in **Journal of Cold War Studies**, fall 2009. Kalinovsky teaches Eastern European Studies at the Universiteit van Amsterdam, The Netherlands. He is an academic and Russian, so has probably had access to Russian-language sources to write his article.*

*The purpose of Professor Kalinovsky in writing this article is to discuss decision-making and the Soviet War in Afghanistan from Intervention to Withdrawal and to publish his findings in a respected academic journal, the **Journal of Cold War Studies**.*

A value of Source U is that Kalinovsky is an established professor of Eastern European Studies at the Universiteit van Amsterdam, The Netherlands. He is an academic and Russian, so has probably had access to Russian-language sources to write his article, indicating that he is an expert in his field. Another value of Source U may be that since it was written 20 years after the end of the Soviet war in Afghanistan, Kalinovsky has had access to newly opened Soviet archives since the early 1990s and the work of other researchers, and can assess the reasons for Soviet military intervention within the larger context of the end of the Cold War.

*A limitation of Source U **may be** that since the author is Russian, he may be primarily interested in the Soviet perspective or just official internal Soviet reasons for the decision to invade Afghanistan. It is possible that a larger context of the Cold War may not be present in the article.*

> Each source is discussed in its own paragraph and nowhere is there comparison or contrasting of the two sources.

> More than one value or limitation was found for each of the sources based on the origin and purpose.

> Terms such as 'may be' are appropriately used since the value and limitations are based on hypotheses.

> The answer indicates that the demands of the question were understood. Both sources assessed. There is clear discussion of the origins, purpose, value and limitations of both sources, often with multiple examples.

Examination practice

Question 1:   5 minute
Question 2:   10 minutes
Question 3:   10 minutes
Question 4:   35 minutes

Below are some exam-style questions for you to practise. Paper 1 exams are one hour long, not including five minutes of reading time at the exam's start when only reading is permitted. You may wish to only practise specific questions, and if this is the case, allow the following amounts of time per question:

These questions relate to the domestic policies of Leonid Brezhnev. The sources used are found within this chapter on the following pages:

- Source A (page 96)
- Source B (page 96)
- Source D (page 98)
- Source F (page 99)
- Source G (page 102)
- Source J (page 106).

1 a) How did Soviet citizens feel about Brezhnev, according to Source G?   *(3 marks)*
(For guidance on how to answer this style of question see page 37.)

2 b) What can be inferred from Source D about Brezhnev's focus on agriculture?   *(2 marks)*
(For guidance on how to answer this style of question see page 63.)

3 Compare and contrast the views expressed in Sources A and B about the Soviet constitution. *(6 marks)*
(For guidance on how to answer this style of question see page 91.)

4 With reference to their origin and purpose, discuss the value and limitations of Source E and
Source J for historians studying Brezhnev's domestic policies.   *(6 marks)*
(For guidance on how to answer this style of question see page 130.)

5 Using these sources (Sources A, B, G, E and J) and your own knowledge, analyse the extent
to which the Brezhnev era can be seen as a period of failure and stagnation.   *(8 marks)*
(For guidance on how to answer this style of question see page 160.)

 Activities

1 Write an obituary for Leonid Brezhnev summing up his impact. If you are working in
pairs one of you could write the piece from a western perspective, such as the *New
York Times*, and another could write the kind of obituary that might have appeared in
the *Pravda*. How and why might these obituaries differ?

2 What's in a name? In conjunction with what you have learned about Language in
TOK and what you know about Cold War terminology, visit the site of Nations
Online at http://www.nationsonline.org/oneworld/third_world_countries.htm and
explain why the term Third World was coined. Why is it a misnomer?

3 Listen to the music of Vladimir Vysotski on YouTube and find the lyrics of his songs.
To what extent do you think he posed a threat to the Soviet government?

CHAPTER 6

Gorbachev's reforms and the consequences for the Soviet state

Mikhail Gorbachev faced a huge array of social, political and economic challenges when he became the General Secretary of the Communist Party of the Soviet Union in 1985. This chapter analyses his attempts to deal with the domestic problems bequeathed to him by his predecessors, in particular looking at the aims of his policies of *glasnost* and *perestroika*. It examines the following key questions that you need to consider:

✪ What was the purpose of Gorbachev's domestic reforms?

✪ What was the impact of *perestroika* and *glasnost* on the Soviet state?

✪ To what extent did Gorbachev precipitate the USSR's downfall?

 ## Gorbachev's domestic reforms

▶ *Key question: What was the purpose of Gorbachev's domestic reforms?*

Brezhnev was succeeded as General Secretary in 1982 by Yuri Andropov. Andropov's health declined steadily and he delegated much of his work to Konstantin Chernenko. On 9 February 1984, Andropov died. Chernenko succeeded him but died in March 1985. Mikhail Gorbachev was the unanimous choice within the Politburo to become the next General Secretary. He was the youngest member of the Politburo, at 54 years of age, ending the period of gerontocracy.

Gorbachev, a strong believer in the strength of the Communist Party of the Soviet Union (CPSU) and communism as a way of governing the USSR, recognized that reform was needed for economic and political development. He believed that his reforms would succeed; he was mistaken.

> **KEY TERM**
>
> **Perestroika** Russian for 'reconstruction' or 'restructuring'. Gorbachev's policy of economic and political reform within the socialist system, to improve the standard of living and society in the USSR.

Perestroika

Perestroika was the economic and political 'restructuring' embarked on by Gorbachev from 1985. It was a deliberately vague term, so as to avoid any connotations of reform or political change that might alarm the *nomenklatura*. The policy was intended to strengthen the USSR by revitalizing the stagnant Soviet economy and reversing the disastrous trends of the Brezhnev era.

 > **How successful was Gorbachev's policy of *perestroika*?**

Gorbachev was not the only advocate of *perestroika*. Its architect, according to historian Martin McCauley, was one of Gorbachev's close advisers, Alexander Yakovlev. He wanted to close the technological gap with the USA and quickly; he advocated rapid action to do so. Gorbachev and Yakovlev hoped to maintain the best features of socialism, while making the system more productive and efficient through a small dose of free-market economics.

The aims of *perestroika*

Gorbachev embarked on his ambitious reform programme with a set of vague aspirations, such as to reduce the amount of central planning and to allow managers greater autonomy. He made his proposal known to the CPSU Central Committee in April 1985.

? According to Source A, how could the Soviet economy be improved?

SOURCE A

Excerpt from Mikhail Gorbachev's report to a CPSU Central Committee plenary meeting, 23 April 1985 from *The Soviet Union: A Documentary History, Volume 2, 1939–1991* by Edward Acton and Tom Stableford, published by the University of Exeter Press, Exeter, UK, 2007, page 385. Professor Acton of the University of East Anglia, UK, and Assistant Librarian Stableford at the Bodleian Library, Oxford, UK, compiled documents from newly available archival material on the former USSR. Their purpose was to provide non-Russian speakers with documents from the Cold War USSR. This excerpt is from the political journal of the Central Committee of the CPSU, *Kommunist*.

We must follow this Leninist tradition unswervingly, enriching and developing our Party policy and our general line for social improvement under advanced socialism.

The main question is how, and with what, the country can speed up its economic development. When looking into this problem in the Politburo, we unanimously came to the conclusion that real possibilities for this do exist. The task of speeding up growth rates substantially is definitely feasible, if at the centre of all our work we put economic intensification, the acceleration of scientific and technological progress, the restructuring of management, planning, and structural and investment policy, lightening up organization and discipline all round and fundamentally improving the way we do things.

Gorbachev convinced enough key members of the Politburo to forge ahead with *perestroika*.

Economic restructuring in the industrial sector

Gorbachev's first significant piece of economic legislation was the Law on Individual Labour Activity in November 1986, which legalized certain kinds of small business, such as taxi services and private tuition. Gorbachev then passed the Law on State Enterprise in January 1988. This gave greater autonomy for state-operated businesses and factories:

SOURCE B

Gorbachev (centre right, wearing a hat), with his wife Raisa (to the right of Gorbachev), conversing with car factory workers in Tolyatti on 8 April 1986.

What is the message conveyed by Source B about the Gorbachevs? ?

- Managers were elected by ordinary workers.
- Managers were given control over what they produced, budgets, prices and wages.
- Businesses were required to be self-financing and to make a profit, as government orders and contracts would no longer absorb the entire productive capacity of industry.

A major change also occurred in how the USSR conducted its foreign trade, which had previously been under the sole jurisdiction of the Ministry of Foreign Trade. This changed in 1987 and other ministries and enterprises were henceforth allowed to engage in foreign trade directly.

Another major law liberalizing the economy was the Law on Co-operatives in January 1988. This legalized co-operatives and enterprises of the type that had long flourished in the **second economy**, allowing them to set prices and export goods. They could employ workers who were not part of the co-operative; in practice this made them hard to distinguish from private companies in capitalist countries. By 1990, this sector of the economy, outside the direct control of the state, employed 6.2 million people, mainly in the service and retail sectors. State ownership of enterprises, however, remained predominant.

Taken together, these reforms and laws amounted to the greatest change to the Soviet economy since the introduction of the NEP in 1921 (see page 12), which, indeed, Gorbachev often invoked as inspiration and justification for allowing some market additions to improve socialist economic practice.

 **KEY TERM**

Second economy An underground economy of small-scale capitalists and merchants that existed within the USSR.

According to Source C, what is Gorbachev's attitude to Marxism–Leninism?

SOURCE C

Excerpt from a speech by Gorbachev to the Central Committee plenum on 18 February 1988 from *The Rise and Fall of the Soviet Union 1917–1991* by Richard Sakwa, published by Routledge, London, UK, 1999, page 439. Sakwa is Professor of Russian and European Politics at the University of Kent, UK.

Over 70 years our party and people have been inspired by the ideas of socialism and have been building it. But because of external and internal causes we have been unable fully to realise the Leninist principles of the new social system. This was seriously hampered by the cult of personality; the system of management by command and administration that formed in the '30s, bureaucratic, dogmatic and voluntarist aberration and arbitrariness; and the late '70s early '80s lack of initiative, and hindrances, that have led to stagnation ... No, we do not retreat even a step from socialism, from Marxism-Leninism, from everything that has been gained and created by the people. But we decisively reject a dogmatic bureaucratic and voluntarist legacy, as it has nothing in common either with Marxism-Leninism or with genuine socialism.

The human factor

Other important reforms related to what Gorbachev called the human factor. Quality control inspectors monitored products and services for safety and other factors. Corruption was targeted and a new government agency was established to root it out, along with new punishments and public humiliation.

There was an anti-alcohol campaign from 1985 to 1988. This was designed to restrict the sale of liquor and raise prices to pay for the health costs and address the negative impact on labour productivity caused by alcohol abuse. It has been estimated that alcohol consumption reduced labour productivity by about 10 per cent in the early 1970s, but four times as much in the 1980s. This campaign led to reductions in alcohol consumption and had some health benefits, but led to tax yields from liquor falling, which in 1985 had provided 14 per cent of government revenues.

According to Source D, why was Gorbachev's alcohol policy not particularly successful?

SOURCE D

Excerpt from 'The success of a failure: Gorbachev's alcohol policy, 1985–88' by Daniel Tarschys, from *Europe–Asia Studies*, January 1993, Vol. 45, Issue 1. Tarschys teaches Political Science at the University of Stockholm, Sweden.

Thus, in spite of the widespread contempt for Gorbachev's alcohol policy, it seems undeniable that it did yield some substantial results. Then why did it collapse? Bestuzhev-Lada, a sociologist who participated in the analytical work preparing the new line [the new anti-alcohol campaign], argues that the recommendations got lost in the bureaucratic labyrinths of the administrative-command system. Perhaps so. But it can also be contended that the policy was a product of late centralism, launched in the last years of the empire when civic and regional resistance to the established authority structure had already begun to undermine the legitimacy of leadership. With the whole fabric of Soviet society loosening up and with citizens beginning to assert their own integrity and individual autonomy, mobilising the old command system against such a deeply rooted habit as the taste for vodka stood little chance of succeeding.

Economic restructuring in agriculture

In the agricultural sector, Gorbachev had all aspects of production centralized under Gosagroprom, the State Committee for the Agro-Industrial Complex, supposedly to streamline planning. As during the times of Khrushchev and Brezhnev, the committee was plagued by inefficient layers of bureaucracy in a complicated system of collective farming. In 1989, Gorbachev dissolved Gosagroprom, creating a small food commission instead and allowing a mix of market and socialist agribusiness.

Other economic mistakes of the past were also continued, such as the massive introduction of expensive mechanical cotton-harvesters in the central Asian Soviet Republics. Since labour was plentiful and wages were low, *kolkhoz* managers accepted them, but did not use them, preferring manual harvesting, which also gathered more cotton.

Gorbachev did try to reform the system of collective farming. The programme called for peasants to lease land from the *kolkhoz* that they could then farm as they desired. Farm managers discouraged peasants from accepting this offer as it threatened their positions. Since these managers controlled farm equipment and supplies, their efforts were largely successful and the USSR continued to import grain and food.

SOURCE E

Excerpt from 'Can Gorbachev feed Russia?' by Mark Kramer in the *New York Times Magazine*, 9 April 1989, page 2. Kramer was a writer in residence at Smith College in Massachusetts, USA, who was invited to tour Soviet state farms. The *New York Times Magazine* is a division of The New York Times which has been published since 1851 in New York, USA, and has one of the largest circulations of any newspaper in the world for over 100 years.

*I had accepted a rare invitation to make a post-*perestroika *tour of Soviet farms … Harvesting damages more than 80 percent of potatoes,* **Isvestia** *tattled – a high figure by Western standards. An additional 50 percent, spoils in storage. A farm-equipment procurer discovered new irrigation pumps rusting out-of-doors in an obscure storage yard, proclaimed* Pravda. *Another* Pravda *journalist found tubercular cattle kept in Kazakhstani herds …*

'Agriculture is the most painful spot in the Soviet system,' Mikhail Gorbachev said last month in a nationally televised speech to the plenary session of the Central Committee. Here was the chief of all bureaucrats, speaking as candidly as anyone ever has about the failure of the Soviet Union's 50,000 state and collective farms, its rudimentary food processing, transport, storage and sales systems.

According to Source E, what problems did Soviet agriculture face?

KEY TERM

Isvestia A leading, official newspaper in the USSR.

The impact of economic restructuring

The reforms associated with *perestroika* were ambitious. However, they did not amount to a successful economic revolution and the system as a whole remained plagued by shortages, corruption and other long-standing problems dating back to the Brezhnev era. Most factories continued to function in an inefficient and unproductive way. Industrial production actually fell by six per cent in 1987. Living standards did not rise as Gorbachev had promised and by the end of the decade, the USSR's **credit rating** had plunged as foreign companies were no longer confident that contracts would be honoured or even who would actually pay them. Defence spending, not addressed by *perestroika*, continued to consume 40 per cent of the government's budget.

KEY TERM

Credit rating A judgement on the ability of a nation to pay back loans.

? What are the origin, purpose, value and limitations of Source F for a historian studying the economic impact of *perestroika*?

SOURCE F

Table of industrial output from *An Economic History of the USSR, 1917–1991* by Alec Nove, published by Penguin, London, UK, 1992, page 400. Nove was Professor Emeritus of Economics at the University of Glasgow, UK. He was born in Russia as Alexander Novakovsky. He compiled this table from official Soviet sources.

Industrial output	1985	1988	1990
Electricity (billions of kilowatt-hours)	1545	1705	1728
Oil (millions of tons)	595	624	570
Gas (billions of cubic metres)	643	770	815
Coal (millions of tons)	726	772	709
Rolled steel (millions of tons)	108	116	112
Chemical fibres (thousands of tons)	1394	1535	1500

Discontent

Gorbachev's economic reforms gave enterprises the freedom to set prices, but this created an inflationary spiral which affected consumers. Workers who had benefited from low prices for basic commodities and patronage networks during the Brezhnev era now felt more insecure about obtaining goods needed to live. This caused more discontent, leading to an increasing number of strikes. In 1989 alone, 7.3 million working days were lost to strike action, such as that of Siberian miners who resented rationing, queues and being denied basic consumer items such as soap.

The demands of strikers were not always purely economic; many wanted greater political freedom and to establish independent trade unions. There was also deep resentment of official corruption. This was certainly the case with coalminers in the Kuz and Don Basin regions who started a strike in July 1989. Their efforts were co-ordinated by independent strike committees that threatened to develop a Soviet version of Solidarity (see page 192). The number of protests and demonstrations increased and in the summer of

1989, up to 350,000 people protested, complaining about the growing economic and political crisis. By October 1989, strikes had been legalized and the government gave in to the strikers' demands.

SOURCE G

Excerpt from *A History of Twentieth-century Russia* by Robert Service published by Harvard University Press, Cambridge, MA, USA, 1998, page 472. Professor Service teaches History at Oxford University in the UK. He wrote this book after being allowed access to newly opened Soviet archives.

A further strike occurred in November in the mines around Norilsk in the Siberian far north. All these strikes were settled in favour of the strikers, who demanded higher wages and improved living conditions; and in contrast with Soviet political practice since the Civil War [1918–21] no repressive sanctions were applied against the strike leaders …

But the Soviet authorities weathered the storm. The strikers lived in far-flung areas, and [Soviet Premier] Ryzhkov and his fellow ministers managed to isolate them from the rest of society by quickly offering them higher wages. Yet the government was faced by a society embittered against it.

According to Source G, how did the Soviet government handle the strikes?

Political restructuring

The difficulty with enacting major economic reform was that it also meant major political reform, which would be politically dangerous and difficult. Gorbachev realized that if his economic reforms were to succeed, he would need to break the power of conservatives in the *nomenklatura*. Gorbachev began to promote reform-minded politicians that would support his policies:

- Thirty-nine government ministers were discharged within a year of Gorbachev becoming General Secretary.
- A new generation of provincial party leaders were appointed who supported him.
- Politburo members who opposed reform were replaced.
- Andrei Gromyko, who had nominated Gorbachev to the position of General Secretary, was elevated to the ceremonial role of President of the Supreme Soviet Presidium.

The Politburo

Controlling the Politburo was a key task for Gorbachev. With the old guard having largely been swept out of the way, Yegor Ligachev, organization and agriculture specialist, and Nikolai Ryzhkov, an industrial specialist, became key members of the Politburo, as they had supported Gorbachev for General Secretary. Ligachev was given the crucial role of running the Secretariat, a group which in the Brezhnev era had emerged as a key decision-making body at the apex of the CPSU. Rzyhkov became Prime Minister, or Premier. In addition, Eduard Shevardnadze, the reformist leader of the Georgian Communist Party, was appointed as Minister of Foreign Affairs. The cumulative effect was to reduce the average age of the Politburo from 69 at the end of 1980 to 64 by the end of 1985. Gorbachev also called for more political participation of young people and women at the local level of the party and increased ethnic diversity at the highest levels of the CPSU. He applauded the election of the first woman to the Politburo: Galina Semyonova.

These new appointments did not always support Gorbachev wholeheartedly, a reflection of his political miscalculation. In 1987, for example, Ligachev opposed the creation of a commission to investigate the rehabilitation of the victims of Stalinist repression. He also took the lead in attacking one of leading reformers in the Politburo, the Moscow Communist Party Secretary Boris Yeltsin, who had been one of Gorbachev's new appointments. When put in charge of agriculture, Ligachev refused to increase the size of private plots. Ryzhkov, for his part, was very cautious and at a Politburo meeting in February 1987, he insisted that Gorbachev's reforms should not go beyond the framework of socialism.

Gorbachev still lacked reliable allies in the Politburo who shared his aims. Sometimes these allies attracted too much attention, like Boris Yeltsin, who dismissed Moscow party personnel and replaced them with inexperienced cadres, mixed with workers in factories and took a public bus instead of party limousines on occasion. Yeltsin came into conflict with Gorbachev when he proposed removing privileges accorded to the office of the General Secretary. This, and Yeltsin's mounting political enmity with Ligachev, resulted in Yeltsin's removal from the Politburo in 1987. This has been described by the former US Ambassador Jack Matlock as Gorbachev's first major political mistake. Gorbachev chose to maintain the support of Yegor Ligachev, who became increasingly wary of Gorbachev's reforms.

SOURCE H

According to Source H, why is capitalism not to be adopted by the USSR?

Excerpt from a speech given by Yegor Ligachev at Gorki on 5 August 1988 quoted in *The USSR 1945–1990* by John Laver, published by Hodder Arnold, London, UK, 1991.

Our Party is a ruling party. And, although increasing the sovereignty of the Soviets, the Party is not going to renounce its leading role … Notions that the economy in our socialist society can develop exclusively on the basis of market laws are unfounded … The market is not a panacea for all ills … Copying the western model of a market based on private ownership is fundamentally unacceptable to a socialist system of economic management founded on social ownership.

In 1987, Gorbachev ousted the Azeri politician Geidar Aliev, charging him with corruption and nepotism; Aliev opposed Gorbachev's reforms. Once Aliev was removed from the Politburo, all its members were ethnic Russians, with the exception of Georgian Eduard Shevardnadze. In a purported Union of Soviet Socialist Republics that included many non-Russian nationalities and ethnic groups, this state of affairs rankled non-Russians. This would have serious repercussions on the fragile unity of the USSR, as will be explored later in this chapter.

The Congress of People's Deputies

The idea of creating the Congress of People's Deputies evolved in 1987, at a CPSU Central Committee plenum. Gorbachev announced that members of local Soviets would be directly elected and that there would be a choice of candidates for the first time. The process of change was slow at first; in the elections to local Soviets in June 1987, there was only one name on the ballot paper in 96 per cent of districts.

The crucial political shift came in 1988, at the nineteenth party conference. Here, despite the opposition of Ligachev, Gorbachev announced that the first multi-candidate elections since 1917 for a new Congress of People's Deputies would take place in 1989. It was intended that this Congress would then select 450 of their members to constitute the Supreme Soviet. The Supreme Soviet would then be responsible for checking and scrutinizing the actions of the government, have the power to veto policies or legislation, and have the ability to confirm or reject ministerial appointments.

The 1989 election

The elections in 1989 certainly had the appearance of a democratic process. Even so, 33 per cent of the seats in the Congress were reserved for members nominated by communist organizations like **Komsomol**. When the first elections took place, the majority of those elected were conservative, anti-reform *nomenklatura*. Diversity of opinion was tolerated, but only within the overall framework of socialism. In addition, Gorbachev was elected unopposed as Chairman of the Supreme Soviet, a post which he held until his elevation to the new post of President of the USSR in 1990.

Emerging factions

Even though the vast majority of those elected to the Congress of People's Deputies professed to be Marxists, they were not a unified body. Instead, deputies immediately began to group together in different ideological factions. For instance, the Soyuz (Union) Group wanted to call a halt to further reform and viewed Gorbachev's policies as a major threat to the USSR. On the other hand, the **Inter-Regional Group**, to whom dissident Andrei Sakharov (see page 103) belonged, wanted the pace of reform to quicken. Another stated aim of this group was a full transition from totalitarianism to democracy. In parts of the USSR, like the Baltic republics of Latvia, Estonia and Lithuania, more independent-minded, non-communist candidates were elected to the Congress of People's Deputies. The unity of the CPSU was beginning to fracture.

Across the USSR as a whole, 38 province-level party secretaries were defeated. In Moscow, Boris Yeltsin won 90 per cent of the vote. This enabled him to defeat the *nomenklatura* candidate and become Mayor of Moscow.

KEY TERM

Komsomol CPSU youth organization which at its peak in the 1970s had tens of millions of members.

Inter-Regional Group Opposition party emerging from the Congress of People's Deputies.

Yeltsin had become a well-known and popular Soviet politician even outside Moscow.

According to Source I, what are Yeltsin's political qualities?

SOURCE I

Excerpt from 'Boris Yeltsin: ups and downs in the eyes of the world' by Marina Darmaros from *Rossiyskaya Gazeta*, 2 February 2011. Darmaros is a Brazilian journalist and sub-editor of *Rossiyskaya Gazeta*, a Russian government daily newspaper founded in 1990.

Yeltsin's popularity increased as he responded to the frustration over plans Gorbachev proposed but wasn't able to accomplish. 'People in the then Soviet Union used to say: "We open the fridge and don't see perestroika *inside it," because the goods started to be scarce and the crisis was becoming deeper and deeper, creating opportunities for an audacious, ambitious and daring alternative, such as Yeltsin was at that time,' said Aarao. [Daniel Aarao, a Professor of History at Fluminense Federal University in Rio de Janeiro, Brazil.]*

SOURCE J

According to Source J, what was the role of Gorbachev in creating the Congress of People's Deputies?

A cartoon by Nicholas Garland that appeared in a British newspaper, *The Independent*, 26 May 1989. Garland is a British cartoonist who has worked for many major British publications. *The Independent* is a daily British newspaper in publication since 1986.

Impact of reforms

The proceedings and debates of the Congress of the People's Deputies were televised, giving many Soviet citizens their first taste of genuine political debate. While many citizens were excited by the prospect of a genuine voice in the political process, many members of the *nomenklatura* became increasingly disillusioned, as their political and social privileges were eroded and others were held responsible for corruption and so forth. The end result was that in 1989 alone, 136,000 party members chose to leave the CPSU. Gorbachev's political reforms began to break the stranglehold of the CPSU on the political life of the USSR.

The presidency

In February 1990, in a further round of constitutional reform, the Supreme Soviet endorsed Gorbachev's plan to create a new post of President of the USSR. Rather than gaining an electoral mandate, the President would be named by the Congress of People's Deputies and serve for five years; Gorbachev now became President of the USSR. His expanded authority included command of the armed forces and the ability to dismiss ministers; Gorbachev retained his post as General Secretary of the CPSU.

Gorbachev appointed Gennadi Ianev, a conservative communist and former head of KGB, as Vice-President, probably to maintain the support of anti-reform members in the CPSU. However, this new concentration of power alienated key reformers like Yakovlev and Shevardnadze, who felt that the USSR was in danger of becoming a dictatorship. Shevardnadze resigned in protest in December 1990.

SOURCE K

A cartoon by Nicholas Garland that appeared in a British newspaper, *The Independent*, 9 January 1990. Garland is a British cartoonist who has worked for many major British publications. *The Independent* is a daily British newspaper in publication since 1986.

According to Source K, what was Gorbachev attempting to do to the Soviet political system?

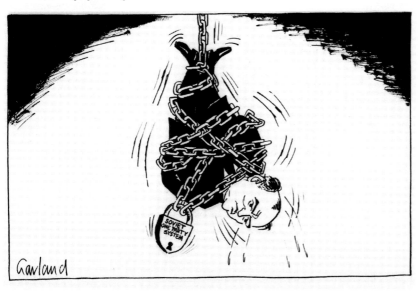

How successful was
Gorbachev's policy of
glasnost?

KEY TERM

Glasnost Russian for
'openness'. Gorbachev's
policy of government
transparency, where citizens
were encouraged to point
out ineffectiveness in industry
and the economy, in order to
work toward solutions and
improvements.

According to Source L, what
was the importance of
'pressure from below'?

Glasnost

The aims of *Glasnost*

Gorbachev believed that only by giving ordinary citizens greater freedom of
information could his reforms acquire the support needed to bring about the
change required to make the country work efficiently. Gorbachev called this
policy *glasnost*, which is commonly translated from the Russian as a policy
of 'frankness' or 'openness'. Gorbachev also intended the policy to permit a
thorough analysis of what he believed to be the catastrophic impact of
Stalin's rule, which would in turn lead to discussion on solutions for Soviet
issues.

SOURCE L

**Excerpt from 'Reform in the political system: limits and possibilities' by
Wolfgang Leonhard from *From Brezhnev to Gorbachev: Domestic Affairs
and Soviet Foreign Policy* edited by Hans-Joachim Veen, published by Berg
Publishers, Leamington Spa, UK, and Hamburg, Germany, 1984,
page 346. Leonhard is a German historian who lived in the USSR and
participated in the formation of East Germany.**

*Political reform of the [Soviet] system depends not only on the extent of
contradictions within it and the presence of social and political forces which
support the liberalisation and 'opening' of Soviet society ... In this respect the
coincidence of 'pressure from below' and serious disagreements in the leadership
has proved to be an important precondition ... The history of Soviet Communism
has shown repeatedly that relaxation of control, concessions to the population,
reforms and liberalisation are as a rule granted only as a result of economic
necessities and in the face of growing political dissatisfaction among the masses
(pressure from below).*

What *glasnost* did not involve was allowing Soviet citizens absolute freedom
of action. After all, Gorbachev came to power determined not to dismantle
the existing Soviet political system, but to preserve many elements of it.
Therefore, it was inevitable that there would be limitations to how much
glasnost there could actually be in practice. In April of 1986, Gorbachev's
glasnost policy was tested.

Glasnost in action

One of the first examples of *glasnost* in action was Gorbachev's willingness to
meet ordinary workers and discuss government reforms with them, albeit in
carefully managed encounters. He was also much more willing to meet
western journalists than his predecessors and he gave what was, by the
standards of his predecessors, a very frank interview to US magazine *Time* in
1985. More significantly, the aftermath of the explosion at the Chernobyl
nuclear plant in the Ukraine in April 1986 showed how *glasnost* was
beginning to impact Soviet politics. It was no longer possible to keep
national problems hidden.

Chernobyl

The Chernobyl catastrophe was caused when a reactor exploded at a nuclear power station, releasing large amounts of radiation into the atmosphere. The official response was initially a mixture of inertia and ineptitude, such as not evacuating local inhabitants until after they had been exposed to radiation for 72 hours. After an initial cover-up and denial more typical of the Brezhnev era, Gorbachev sent an investigative team to the region led by Premier Ryzhkov.

Gorbachev then acknowledged what had happened. In many ways, he had no choice as radioactive clouds now drifted over central and western Europe and radiation detectors at a nuclear power station in Sweden, over 1000 kilometres away, were activated.

SOURCE M

A statement from the Council of Ministers of the USSR published in *Pravda*, 2 May 1986 from *The Collapse of the Soviet Union* by David Marples, published by Pearson Education, Harlow, UK, 2004, page 117. Marples is a Professor of History at the University of Alberta, Canada. This statement was published in *Pravda* one week after the explosion. *Pravda* was the main government-sponsored newspaper of the USSR from 1921 to 1991.

Throughout the day on 30 April at the Chernobyl atomic power station, work has continued to realize complex technical measures. Radioactivity on the territory of the station and in the immediate vicinity has been reduced by 1.5–2 times. Work is being introduced to decontaminate polluted areas adjacent to the territory of the atomic power station. Aid to the injured is continuing, including the 18 people who are in a serious condition. There are no foreign citizens among the injured.

> With reference to its origin and purpose, assess the value and limitations of Source M for historians studying the impact of *glasnost* up to May 1986.

The disaster, more than anything else, opened the possibility of much greater freedom of expression, although it should be noted that it took until 1989 for authorities to releaze accurate maps to the media, revealing the full geographical extent of the areas affected by radiation from Chernobyl. However, events at Chernobyl did mark a shift in the political culture of the USSR. Subsequent disasters were not hidden, but fully disclosed to the outside world.

The relaxation of censorship

From June 1986 onwards, censorship rules were relaxed. Works of literature such as Boris Pasternak's novel *Doctor Zhivago* and Alexander Solzhenitsyn's *Gulag Archipelago* were published in the USSR for the first time. Furthermore, the jamming of BBC radio broadcasts was ended in 1987, giving ordinary Soviet citizens greater freedom to access western media outlets. Independent media began to develop, spearheaded by weekly newspapers such as *Moscow News*. For Gorbachev, this was a crucial development as it placed pressure on CPSU members who opposed reforms.

Dissidents

Treatment of dissidents by the government changed as well. Gorbachev personally telephoned Andrei Sakharov (see page 103) in 1986 to invite him back to Moscow as a tangible demonstration of *glasnost*. No doubt this helped Gorbachev to legitimize his reforms, but Sakharov and other dissidents took him at his word. Sakharov joined the Congress of People's Deputies in 1989 and supported a multi-party system in the USSR.

The Orthodox Church

The relaxation of censorship also benefited the Russian Orthodox Church. Although the Russian Orthodox Church had been marginalized and made illegal in the atheist, communist state, it had managed to survive by keeping a low profile, maintaining three seminaries and a few convents and monasteries. In 1988, Gorbachev met publicly with the **Patriarch** to co-opt another segment of Soviet society to support his reforms. Nevertheless, the Church continued to be regulated by the Council for Religious Affairs and monitored by the KGB. The thaw, however, did lead to a revival of religion and Soviet citizens began to attend services, marry in churches and baptize their children. Religious texts could now be sold and purchased openly.

Re-examination of Stalin

Gorbachev used this new, more open political culture to re-examine Stalinist policies. Stalinist crimes such as the massacre of Polish officers in 1940 at Katyn were admitted for the first time and victims of Stalinist purges, such as **Nicolai Bukharin**, were officially rehabilitated. Gorbachev had his aide, Yakovlev, publish articles about Bukharin as a positive Soviet leader and as a victim of Stalin's excesses. The message of *glasnost* and being held accountable was not lost on party members.

KEY TERM

Patriarch The head of the Russian Orthodox Church.

Nicolai Bukharin A prominent Politburo member in the 1920s who supported Lenin's NEP and was executed in 1938 during one of Stalin's purges.

What image of Soviet society is conveyed by the photograph in Source N?

SOURCE N

Soviet youth in Leningrad (St Petersburg) in 1987.

Perestroika
- Aim: economic restructuring to make system more productive and efficient

Glasnost
- Aim: openness and freedom of information

Policies
- Consultation
- Relaxation of censorship
- Dissenters allowed
- Better relations with Church
- Re-examination of Stalin's policies

Policies

Industry
- Law on Individual Labour Activity, November 1986
- Law on State Enterprise, January 1988
- Law on Co-operatives, January 1988
- Quality control inspectors
- Government agency to root out corruption
- Anti-alcohol campaign, 1985–8

Agriculture
- All aspects of production centralized under Gosagroprom (dissolved 1989)
- Introduction of expensive mechanical cotton-harvesters
- Attempts to reform collective farming through land-leasing scheme

Political restructuring
- New generation of provincial party leaders and Politburo members appointed – gerontocracy replaced
- Congress of People's Deputies – first elections 1989
- 1990: Presidency established

Impact
- Inefficiencies remained
- Living standards did not rise
- Inflation
- Discontent and strikes

Impact
- 1989: first taste of political debate for many Soviet citizens
- *Nomenklatura* disillusioned
- CPSU began to have less stranglehold on politics

SUMMARY DIAGRAM

Gorbachev's domestic reforms

The consequences of *perestroika* and *glasnost* for the USSR

▶ **Key question:** *What was the impact of* perestroika *and* glasnost *on the Soviet state?*

Perestroika and *glasnost* produced results different from those that were intended. There was an increase in nationalism and tension within the country's political and economic systems as well.

Why did Gorbachev's policies lead to demands for secession in many Soviet republics?

→ # Nationalism

Political reforms initiated by Gorbachev, long-standing historical grievances and greater freedom of expression as a result of *glasnost,* all acted as catalysts for the development of separatist political movements in many republics of the USSR.

KEY TERM

SSR An acronym for Soviet Socialist Republic, of which there were 15 within the USSR.

Kazakh Soviet Socialist Republic

The first major sign of tension was in Kazakh **SSR** in December 1986, when the party's First Secretary, Dinmukhamed Konayev, a Kazakh, was removed. He was replaced by an ethnic Russian, Gennady Kolbin, leading to demonstrations in the capital, Alma-Ata (now Almaty). The demonstration

The republics of the USSR

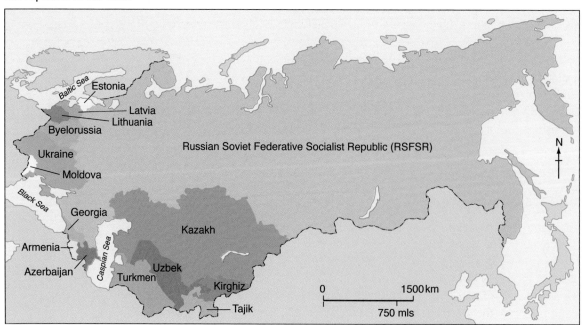

was ended with armed force, killing some people and injuring over 1200 others.

Georgian Soviet Socialist Republic

In 1989, demonstrations by Georgian nationalists were suppressed by state security forces, killing at least 19 people. Hundreds more were injured. Many in Georgia, including many communists, began to believe it would be better to be independent than remain part of the USSR.

SOURCE O

Excerpt from *The Gorbachev Factor* by Archie Brown, published by Oxford University Press, Oxford, UK, 1996, page 265. Brown is Professor Emeritus of Politics at Oxford University, UK, and an expert in Russian and Eurasian Studies.

The massacre of the young demonstrators outraged public opinion in Georgia and gave an enormous stimulus to the movement for complete independence from the Soviet Union.

… The events of Tbilisi of April 1989 thus demonstrated that the harsh use of force could, in the new climate of raised expectations and aroused civic courage, produce the opposite effect from that intended by the Soviet authorities. They also were to become a prime example of misinformation, whether deliberate or through ignorance, on the part of Gorbachev's enemies at home and abroad who held him responsible for the massacre in the Georgian capital. In fact [according to the journalist Roxburgh], Gorbachev 'had categorically stated that the situation in Tbilisi must be resolved by political means and through dialogue'.

> What does Source O reveal about the consequences of the Tbilisi massacre?

Others

Smaller ethnic groups, such as **Crimean Tatars** and **Chechens**, began to push for more freedom, including the end to policies which required them to speak Russian to advance in government positions and in education. There was also violence between groups over territory, as demonstrated in clashes in 1988 between Azeris and Armenians in the Nagorno-Karabakh region that led to at least 30 deaths. Tensions and occasional violence erupted between Ossetians, Georgians, Ingush, Abkhazians and others in the Caucasus Mountains region over disputed territory and perceived past injustices.

The Baltic republics

The strongest nationalist movements were to emerge in the Baltic republics of Latvia, Estonia and Lithuania. Here, there were long-standing nationalist grievances concerning the incorporation of these republics into the USSR by Stalin against their will in 1940, after a brief period of independence after the First World War. By the late 1980s, groups such as the **Sąjūdis** movement in Lithuania began to move beyond their initial stance of pressing for faster implementation of *perestroika* and started to question whether the incorporation of the republics into the USSR was legal to begin with, given that Stalin had later repudiated the **Nazi–Soviet Pact**.

🔑 KEY TERM

Crimean Tatars Turkish-speaking Muslim peoples of the Crimea, located on the north coast of the Black Sea.

Chechens Chechen-speaking Muslim peoples indigenous to the Northern Caucasus, between the Black Sea and the Caspian Sea.

Sąjūdis Political reform movement in favour of sovereignty and independence for Lithuania formed in 1988.

Nazi–Soviet Pact Non-aggression pact signed between Germany and the USSR in August 1939 that included a secret protocol assigning the independent states of Lithuania, Latvia and Estonia to the Soviet sphere of influence.

The political situation was made even more combustible by the fact that all non-Russian republics of the USSR, including the Baltic republics, contained Russian minorities. These were often members of the *nomenklatura* or the military, who fiercely opposed attempts to alter the political *status quo*. Overall, up to 70 million Soviet citizens lived in republics in which they had not been born. In particular, ethnic Russians made up 34 per cent of the population of Latvia and 30 per cent of the population of Estonia.

The secession of the Baltic republics

In 1988, the Estonian government announced its right to veto all legislation passed by the Soviet government and to seize all Soviet property in the republic. Lithuania and Latvia soon followed suit.

In Moscow, the Inter-Regional Group that had formed in the Congress of People's Deputies encouraged nationalist movements and its Baltic representatives in seeking redress for the Nazi–Soviet Pact. Gorbachev approved an investigation into the terms of the Nazi–Soviet Pact.

In 1989, mass demonstrations took place and in August, one million demonstrators formed a 600-kilometre long human chain stretching from Vilnius, the capital of Lithuania, through Riga, capital of Latvia, and then to Tallinn, capital of Estonia. The purpose of this demonstration was to symbolically denounce the fiftieth anniversary of the Nazi–Soviet Pact. The investigative commission admitted for the first time that the secret protocols existed and criticized the pact.

By this stage, nationalists were led by large movements, such as the Sąjūdis in Lithuania that had 180,000 members. In October, in another symbolic act, a faction of the Lithuanian Communist Party formally declared that it was breaking away from the rest of the CPSU. With Lithuanian communists and the Sąjūdis both now supporting full independence, the Lithuanian Supreme Soviet pushed for independence. In March 1990, Lithuania declared its secession from the USSR, which was technically legal under the terms of the 1977 constitution. Latvia and Estonia soon followed suit and announced a transition period towards full independence. The USSR reacted by imposing an economic blockade on the newly independent states along with minor military operations that eventually were called off. Having failed to contain nationalism in the Baltic republics, the political and constitutional unity of the USSR now appeared to be increasingly fragile. Republics in other parts of the USSR also began to assert their right to political sovereignty.

What economic problems did the USSR have by 1989 and how were they addressed?

Crisis in the economy

By 1989, Gorbachev and his advisers were unsure how to revitalize the ailing Soviet economy, while retaining key features of the centralized economy. Plans were put forward by academics and reformers to introduce much greater free-market reforms, including changing prices, control of monopolies, the formation of a central bank and laws governing foreign investment.

SOURCE P

A table of the economic development of the USSR: the official data and G.I. Khanin's assessment from *The Soviet Union: A Documentary History, Volume 2, 1939–1991* by Edward Acton and Tom Stableford, published by the University of Exeter Press, Exeter, UK, 2007, page 389. Professor Acton of the University of East Anglia, UK, and Assistant Librarian Stableford at the Bodleian Library, Oxford, UK, compiled documents from newly available archival material on the former USSR. Their purpose was to provide non-Russian speakers with documents from the Cold War USSR. This table is from the political journal of the Central Committee of the CPSU, *Kommunist*, official sources and *Dinamika*, an economic journal edited by Girsh I. Khanin, a Soviet economist.

Average annual indices	Source	Average annual rates 1971–90 (%)							
		1971–5	1976–80	1981–5	1986	1987	1988	1989	1990
National income growth rates	State Statistical Committee	5.7	4.2	3.5	2.3	1.6	4.4	2.5	−4.0
	G.I. Khanin	3.2	1.0	0.6	1.3	0.7	0.3	−4.3	−9.0
Labour productivity growth rates	State Statistical Committee	4.6	3.4	3.0	2.1	1.6	4.8	2.2	−3.0
	G.I. Khanin	1.9	0.2	0	1.2	0.8	1.3	−3.95	−8.0

> What does Source P suggest about the trend of Soviet growth and labour productivity rates from 1971 to 1990?

In 1990, Gorbachev, despite the opposition of conservative ministers and members of the Supreme Soviet, instituted a dramatic shift to a full market economy with the 500 Day Programme. It involved selling off state enterprises to investors and dissolving collective farms. Control over economic policy was also to be devolved to the republics of the USSR. It was envisaged that there would be a fully functioning market economy within 500 days of the implementation of these reforms so that the state would no longer control prices. The radicalism of the plan may reflect Gorbachev's sense of political desperation by this stage and the depth of the economic crisis faced by the USSR.

Given the dire situation of the economy, Gorbachev proceeded with his economic reforms. However, he now lacked the political support to make such a radical plan work and the Soviet population, 25 per cent of whom were living in poverty, were unwilling to give the plan the time that it needed to improve citizens' standard of living. In addition, the USSR lacked a capitalist culture needed to make such reforms work quickly.

Ultimately, the economic crisis created a sense of political crisis. By 1990, it was clear that the general population was turning against Gorbachev and thousands marched through Moscow on May Day demanding his replacement.

Why was there a coup against Gorbachev in 1991?

🔑 **KEY TERM**

Article 6 The 1977 Soviet constitution article that guaranteed the monopoly of the CPSU as the only ruling party in the USSR.

Democratic Russia A pro-Yeltsin political coalition that began to challenge the political monopoly of the CPSU from 1990 onwards.

Political crisis

By mid-1990, the Berlin Wall had been breached, the Soviet control of eastern Europe was ending (see Chapter 7) and several republics within the USSR were on the verge of outright independence. These events were seen by many conservative members of the *nomenklatura* as almost akin to a political betrayal on the part of Gorbachev.

In 1990, Gorbachev amended **Article 6** of the Soviet constitution and ended the political monopoly of the CPSU. This was hailed by reformers as a liberalizing measure, ushering in genuine democracy for the first time. However, for reactionaries, it was regarded as yet another betrayal of the old Soviet order. With other political parties, such as Boris Yeltsin's **Democratic Russia**, now permitted and winning widespread support, the political dominance of the CPSU was under great threat. The final trigger for a coup against Gorbachev was a new constitutional treaty in August 1991, which gave the various Soviet republics more autonomy. A group of conspirators began to emerge.

The events of the 1991 coup

On 18 August 1991, a self-styled State Committee for the Emergency Situation led by the Vice-President Gennadii Ianev, the Interior Minister Boris Pugo, and the head of the KGB Vladimir Kruichkov, announced that Gorbachev was ill; he was actually under house arrest in his villa on the Black Sea. A state of emergency was declared and Red Army units were brought in to Moscow to seize control of key buildings such as the Russian Supreme Soviet building, known as the White House.

Thousands of civilians surrounded the White House building, led by Boris Yeltsin, to prevent the coup's success. Army units refused to attack the White House as it would mean major civilian casualties and the coup collapsed. Gorbachev returned to Moscow on 22 August, but his political authority had suffered a near fatal blow.

How did the USSR finally come to an end in 1991?

The collapse of the USSR

In the aftermath of the coup, Gorbachev was a weakened figure. In a speech to the Russian Supreme Soviet on 23 August, his attempts to defend the CPSU met with hostility. In a very public humiliation, Yeltsin insisted that Gorbachev read aloud the minutes of the USSR Cabinet of Ministers that revealed that most of its members had supported the coup. Gorbachev's hopes of reviving his constitutional treaty and his hopes that his plan for a loose Union of Sovereign States would resolve the crisis of nationalism and independence of member republics were doomed to failure. Gorbachev also found that the republics were increasingly unenthusiastic about sharing any political power at all with the central government. The Baltic republics and Ukraine wanted full independence and when US President George Bush, as well as Yeltsin, in his new capacity as President of the Russian Soviet Federative Social Republic (RSFSR), recognized them as sovereign states, only the ruthless application of force could have kept these republics within the USSR.

As the Baltic states declared complete independence in September, Gorbachev officially recognized them. Ukraine followed after a referendum demonstrated that 90 per cent of the population wanted independence. In the RSFSR, the largest part of the USSR, Yeltsin was now more powerful than Gorbachev, as were Leonid Kravchuk in Ukraine and Stanislav Shushkevich in Belarus. Following a meeting of the three leaders, a joint statement, known as the Minsk Declaration, was issued in December 1991 stating that the USSR ceased to exist. In its place, a loose grouping of republics known as the **Commonwealth of Independent States** (CIS) was created, destroying what remained of Gorbachev's political power and any lingering hopes that he had of a constitutional treaty to preserve the USSR. On 25 December 1991, all the republics, except Georgia, joined the CIS. Gorbachev announced his resignation from the defunct post of President of the USSR.

 **KEY TERM**

Commonwealth of Independent States
A loose association of Soviet republics formed in December 1991 as a successor to the USSR. It differed from the USSR by asserting that all member states were fully sovereign and independent.

SOURCE Q

Excerpt from *Memoirs* by Mikhail Gorbachev, published by Doubleday, New York, USA, 1995, pages xxiv–xxv.

One of the most powerful states in the world, the Soviet Union, collapsed before our very eyes. The people seemed almost to welcome the event! The Supreme Soviets of the Republics rejected the Treaty on the Union of Sovereign States, drafted by the USSR State Council under the guidance of the country's President … The intelligentsia remained silent. The media were thrown into disarray. My appeals to the deputies of the Supreme Soviet and to the people, my warning that the disintegration of the Soviet Union was fraught with dire consequences, went unheeded – society was bewildered and unable to appraise the crisis. Destructive forces in the country exploited the confusion, usurping the people's right to decide their own future. It was what I had feared most of all … Time is a merciless judge … I am still firmly convinced that the reforms conceived and initiated in 1985 were generated by historic necessity. Once the period of trials and tribulations is over, our countrymen will learn to make proper use of the main achievements of perestroika – liberty, democracy and civil rights.

According to Source Q, what was the result of the dissolution of the USSR?

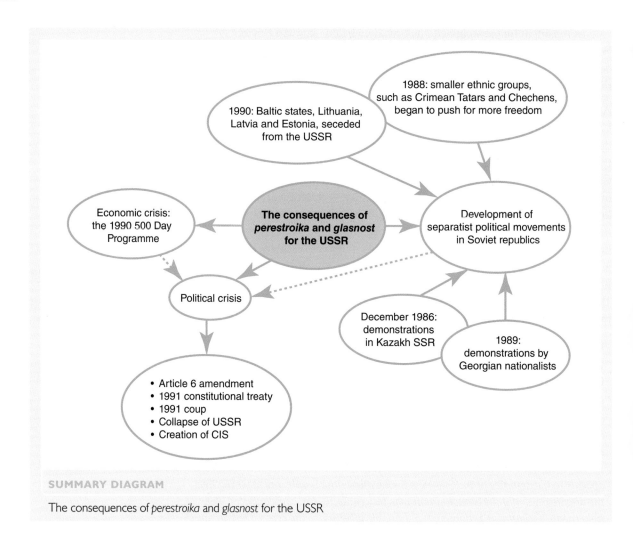

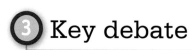

The consequences of *perestroika* and *glasnost* for the USSR

3 Key debate

▶ **Key question:** *To what extent did Gorbachev precipitate the USSR's downfall?*

Gorbachev's weaknesses

For historians such as John Darwin, Gorbachev's policies were instrumental in the decline and fall of the USSR. He argues that *glasnost* and *perestroika* had the effect of weakening the grip of the party bureaucracy on the economy and that this destabilized the political system. The process of decline and fall was therefore more rapid in the case of USSR than in any major empire of the past 500 years. Certainly, it was the case that very few analysts at the time predicted that a gifted politician such as Gorbachev would be the last leader of the USSR.

Character flaws

Historian Martin McCauley presents an interpretation of Gorbachev's political skills. He was described as being unable to delegate effectively. Historian David R. Marples supports this view, explaining how Gorbachev failed to build a working relationship with Boris Yeltsin, whose charismatic populism could have been an important political tool for Gorbachev, had they remained allies. Gorbachev was also something of a political risk taker, which led him to attempt too much political and economic change on too broad a front.

SOURCE R

Excerpt from *Age of Extremes: The Short Twentieth Century 1914–1991* by Eric Hobsbawm, published by Michael Joseph, London, 1994, pages 490–1. Hobsbawm was a well-known British Marxist historian.

The failure of perestroika *and the consequent rejection of Gorbachev by the citizenry were increasingly obvious, though not appreciated in the West, where his popularity remained justifiably high … He was and will go down in history as a tragic figure, a communist 'Tsar-Liberator' … who destroyed what he wanted to reform and was destroyed in the process. Charming, sincere, intelligent and genuinely moved by the ideals of a communism which he saw corrupted since the rise of Stalin, Gorbachev was, paradoxically, too much of an organization man for the hurly-burly of democratic politics he created; too much of a committee man for decisive action; too remote from the experiences of urban and industrial Russia which he had never managed, to have the old party boss's sense of grass-root realities. His trouble was not so much that he had no effective strategy for reforming the economy – nobody had even after his fall – as that he was remote from the everyday experience of his country.*

According to Source R, what were Gorbachev's major failings as leader of the USSR?

Failure to control the RSFSR

Gorbachev had difficulties in controlling the Russian Soviet Federative Socialist Republic (RSFSR), especially after Yeltsin became Chairman of the Russian Supreme Soviet. Some authors have remarked on the strength and dominance of this one republic.

SOURCE S

Excerpt from *Politics, Paradigms, and Intelligence Failures: Why So Few Predicted the Collapse of the Soviet Union* by Ofira Seliktar, published by M.E. Sharpe, Armonk, NY, USA, 2004, page 173. Seliktar is an Israeli Political Scientist who teaches at Gratz College, PA, USA.

While the dramatic events in the republics were front page, the real … change … was taking place in Russia. As already noted, glasnost *initiated the first comprehensive discussion on the costs and benefits of maintaining an internal*

According to Source S, why did some in Russia argue that it should be an independent state?

empire. A growing number of academics and journalists argued that Russia, which held 92 per cent of oil reserves, 85 per cent of coal reserves, and was the only producer of diamonds, platinum and other rare metals, had no need for the republics. Indeed, as a group of scholars pointed out, the Union … took away from Russia its vast resources.

Economic failings

One of the strongest charges made against Gorbachev was that he missed opportunities to provide the economic cures for the Soviet economy as a whole. This point was made by a future Prime Minister of Russia, Yegor Gaidar, who stated in a *Pravda* article that *perestroika* was doomed to failure from the moment in 1985 that Gorbachev allowed a 10 billion rouble gap in public finances to open – an economic consequence of falling tax revenues as a result of the anti-alcohol campaign (see page 138). Historian Robert Service argues that key aspects of *perestroika* simply did not work and therefore Gorbachev's promises of economic rejuvenation were not realized. Martin McCauley's biography of Gorbachev supports this analysis. He argues that Gorbachev had little understanding of market economics and that *perestroika* simply made pre-existing systemic problems worse. A further charge against Gorbachev is that he did not prioritize the economic aspects of *perestroika* until it was too late and therefore an opportunity for an orderly transition to capitalism, as happened in the People's Republic of China, was missed.

Gorbachev's strengths

On the other hand, to argue that Gorbachev was totally culpable for the downfall of the USSR runs the risk of ignoring the great political skill that he displayed in maintaining some semblance of political stability in the late 1980s. Both Robert Service and Martin McCauley persuasively argue that without Gorbachev's reformist policies, which made a sustained military crackdown against nationalism in the republics unthinkable, the USSR may have been plunged into a civil war. David R. Marples corroborates this point, arguing that faced with multiple crises between 1985 and 1991, Gorbachev acted with admirable self-control, preventing the fractious politics of the USSR from descending into conflict. Therefore, it could be argued that *glasnost* might not have succeeded in keeping the USSR together, but it ensured an orderly transition of power, even if not planned. Furthermore, it could be argued that by 1985, saving the USSR was a virtually impossible task, even for a leader of Gorbachev's ability.

SOURCE T

Excerpt from *The Gorbachev Factor* by Archie Brown, published by Oxford University Press, Oxford, UK, 1996, pages 317–18. Brown is Professor Emeritus of Politics at Oxford University, UK, and an expert in Russian and Eurasian studies.

Taking all his mistakes and some undoubted failures into account – along, however, with the almost insuperable obstacles he had to overcome – Gorbachev had strong claims to be regarded as one of the greatest reformers in Russian history … He went along with, encouraged and (in important respects) initiated fundamental rethinking about politics – radically new thinking in the Soviet context about the political and economic system he inherited and about better alternatives. He presided over and facilitated the introduction of freedom of speech, freedom of the press, freedom of association, religious freedom and freedom of movement and left Russia a freer country than it had been in its long history.

> According to Source T, what were the most important aspects of Gorbachev's legacy?

Russian historians have also contributed to the debate – see Source U.

SOURCE U

Excerpt from *Post-Soviet Russia: A Journey Through the Yeltsin Era* by Roy Medvedev, published by Columbia University Press, New York, USA, 2000, pages 3 and 46. Medvedev, a Russian dissident historian during the Brezhnev era, was elected to the Congress of People's Deputies in the Gorbachev era.

Not until the coming to power of Mikhail Gorbachev did the Soviet Union make a decisive turn toward democratization. The totalitarian political censorship of the press was eliminated in 1987 with the advent of glasnost, *and in 1989 a new electoral system brought with it a general parliament (the Congress of People's Deputies) and a multiparty system …*

The failure of Gorbachev's reforms from 1985 to 1990 caused great discontent and disillusion among the people. The reformers themselves were dismayed. Some of them were inclined to abandon the framework of socialism, within which the reforms had remained. Valentin Pavlov, who replaced Nikolai Rhyzkov as premier, admitted later that by 1990 he was firmly convinced that only a bourgeois-democratic revolution could save Russia.

> According to Source U, what was the effect of the failure of Gorbachev's reforms?

Conclusion

There is still a lively historiographical debate about the extent to which Gorbachev's policies directly caused the final collapse of the USSR or merely failed to turn the USSR away from the path of decline it had started on well before 1985. Ultimately, most historians agree with Hobsbawm that it was the scale of the domestic problems facing Gorbachev, and his failure to reconcile *glasnost* with the nationalism in the various republics that eventually led to the collapse of central authority and, with it, the state: an outcome which Gorbachev had certainly not sought or intended in 1985.

Scholars have approached the study of history by focusing on the deeds of 'great men'. How valid is this approach and does it work for the study of the USSR from 1985? (History, Perception, and Reason.)

Chapter summary

Gorbachev's reforms and the consequences for the Soviet state

Gorbachev faced a huge array of social, political and economic challenges when he became the General Secretary of the CPSU in 1985. The USSR was in a state of undoubted crisis. Cautiously at first, and then more rapidly following the 1986 Chernobyl disaster, Gorbachev embarked on a programme of radical reform. His initial intention was not to undermine the Marxist–Leninist system. However, the *perestroika* reforms liberalized the economy and destroyed the power of the gerontocracy that had dominated Soviet politics. It paved the way for political reform and multi-candidate elections to the Congress of People's Deputies, which eventually undermined the very system that Gorbachev tried to save.

With censorship ending, thanks to Gorbachev's policy of *glasnost,* dissidents, such as Sakharov, were able to speak out much more freely. A new political culture was created in which it became legitimate to challenge the authority of the CPSU. Boris Yeltsin embraced this new political culture and was elected Chairman of the RSFSR. He was much more willing than Gorbachev to contemplate the dissolution of the USSR, while Gorbachev remained convinced that a new constitutional treaty could save it.

The gravity of the economic crisis by 1990, and the failure of the 500 Day Programme, coupled with the emergence of vigorous nationalist movements in the Baltic republics in particular, doomed Gorbachev's hopes of preserving the USSR. By 1991, Gorbachev's policies had so alienated the *nomenklatura* that a coup was launched against him by CPSU hard-liners. This was defeated thanks to the ambivalence of the armed forces and the active opposition of Yeltsin and others in Moscow. From this point onwards, Gorbachev's political power was fatally weakened and he now lacked the authority to hold the USSR together. Republics, such as Ukraine, were now determined to push for full independence. Seeing support for his proposals ebb away in many of the republics, including Russia, Gorbachev accepted the inevitable and the USSR came to an end in December 1991.

 Examination advice

Paper 1 Question 4: how to integrate sources and write a good essay

Question 4 is always an essay question. It requires you to write what you know while integrating the sources provided. The sources are there to support your own knowledge. Therefore, it is important that you prepare yourselves for this type of question by knowing and understanding the history of communism in crisis between 1976 and 1989 that we have presented in this book.

Question 4 is always worth 8 marks. This means it is worth about one-third of the overall mark possible. We suggest that you spend 30–35 minutes answering this question, using the first five to eight minutes of this time to summarize the sources and outline your response.

How to answer

Summarize the sources and outline your essay

It is best to first list and summarize your sources to focus your thoughts. This should be done in about five minutes and should be in the form of short bullet points. Once you have summarized the sources, briefly outline your essay's structure. This outline should include some sort of introduction to your essay and a concluding answer to the question. Write your outline down on your examination paper, but put a single line through these pre-writing notes once your essay is finished.

Writing the essay

When you write your essay make sure you follow your outline and use *all* the sources. This should take the remainder of your time, which should be at least 25 minutes.

You need to start with a good introduction to focus your essay and which defines anything that might be open to interpretation. Your introduction should conclude with a definite answer to the question that you will proceed to support in the coming paragraphs. The introduction should serve to focus your essay. Usually, you can introduce one or more of your sources into the introduction to support what you are going to cover.

All sources must be used at least once, but use them multiple times if they will help your essay. Remember the sources should support your essay.

If you write something that you want the examiner to ignore, draw a single line through this and move on. Finally, do not just list the five sources and a couple of bullet points under each in a sort of preamble to a real essay. This is sketchy and will not be credited fully. Sources should be integrated and quoted to support your essay.

Your concluding paragraph should clearly answer the essay question, summarizing your main arguments.

Example

This question uses Sources A, B, D, E and H, found in this chapter:

> Using these sources and your own knowledge, explain the challenges to reform that Gorbachev faced. (8 marks)

Source A: see page 136
Source B: see page 137
Source D: see page 138
Source E: see page 139
Source H: see page 142

First, very briefly summarize the sources just for your own information in five minutes or less.

Source A: Gorbachev tries to convince the CPSU Central Committee reassuring them that he follows Lenin's path and socialism will be upheld.

Source B: Photo of Mikhail and Raisa Gorbachev, friendly, energetic.

Source D: Dealing with bureaucracy in promoting anti-alcohol campaign.

Source E: Failings in agriculture and food production and being able to report it and make speeches about it openly.

Source H: Influential Politburo member Ligachev's scathing criticism of applying market economy reforms.

Second, briefly outline in bullet points the main parts of your essay in five minutes or less.

Introduction
- Challenges Gorbachev faced were from centralized socialist bureaucracy:
  – insistence on following socialism as a system
  – reforms urgently needed in consumer products and food
  – deep-seated reaction against reform in the Politburo.

Paragraph 2: Insistence on following socialism as a system.
- Gorbachev convinced that socialism and the CPSU was the government for the USSR:
  – but realized reform urgent.
- Convincing the politburo of reforms:
  – laws, anti-alcohol campaign
  – reiterating commitment to communism.

Paragraph 3: Reforms urgently needed in consumer products and food.
- Agriculture problems:
  – production, distribution.
- Management:
  – corruption in collectivized system
  – maintaining positions of power.
- Failures in agriculture:
  – food production
  – waste from central planning: Gosagroprom.

Paragraph 4: Deep-seated reaction against reform in the Politburo.
- Ligachev.
- Ryzhkov.
- Seeking reform-minded allies:
  - Yeltsin.

Conclusion: Centralized socialist bureaucracy had great impact, great importance for Gorbachev as a challenge to his reforms, but also:
- Gorbachev's insistence on following socialism as a system.
- Consumer products and food shortages.

Third, write an answer to the question.

When Gorbachev became General Secretary of the Communist Party of the Soviet Union (CPSU) in 1985, he faced many political and economic problems. He realized reforms were needed in order to surmount them, but Gorbachev faced serious challenges from the centralized socialist bureaucracy and the deep-seated reaction against reform in the Politburo. He set about meeting these challenges by insisting on following socialism as a system, yet pushing through the reforms that were urgently needed. Gorbachev's greatest challenge was striking a balance between pushing reform and convincing the centralized bureaucracy to follow through with them.

Gorbachev believed in the strength of the CPSU and communism as a way of governing the USSR, but recognized that reform was needed for economic and political development. In Source A he soothes the Central Committee of the CPSU by saying that he will 'follow this Leninist tradition unswervingly, enriching and developing our Party policy and our general line for social improvement under advanced socialism'. He also used vague terminology in Source A, to tone down the reforms: 'tightening up organization and discipline all around and fundamentally improving the way we do things'. His outgoing, energetic personality helped, as shown in Source B, where he and his wife Raisa enthusiastically talk to workers. Soon Gorbachev convinced enough key members of the Politburo to support him. One such reform was the Law on Co-operatives in January 1988. This legalized co-operatives and some private enterprises. However, state ownership

> The introduction clearly indicates that the centralized socialist bureaucracy posed great challenges for Gorbachev and proposes areas that will be explored in the essay.

> All five sources are utilized in the essay and explicitly mentioned. Some sources are quoted, which demonstrates the importance of particular sources in making a historical argument.

remained predominant. Another campaign was against alcohol, but in Source D we see that it failed because 'the recommendations got lost in the bureaucratic labyrinths of the administrative-command system'.

In the agricultural sector, Gorbachev realized great reforms were needed to face the challenges of consumer and food shortages. To improve the latter, he had production centralized under Gosagroprom, the State Committee for the Agro-Industrial Complex, supposedly to streamline planning. Source E shows that the problems in the agricultural sector were not solved, but they were certainly reported more in the press, such as when a '**Pravda** journalist found tubercular cattle kept in Kazakhstani herds'. Gorbachev was aware of the problems of central planning, as Source E reports: 'the chief of all bureaucrats, speaking … about the failure of the Soviet Union's 50,000 state and collective farms, its rudimentary food processing'. In 1989, Gorbachev dissolved Gosagroprom, and allowed a mix of market and socialist agribusiness. Gorbachev did try and reform the system of collective farming so that peasants could lease land from the **kolkhoz**, or collective, to farm. But farm managers discouraged peasants from accepting this offer as it threatened their positions. Managers controlled farm equipment and supplies and sometimes allowed farm equipment to go to waste, like 'new irrigation pumps rusting out-of-doors in an obscure storage yard', as described in Source E.

To enact major economic reform meant major political reform was necessary and the Politburo, as the strongest ruling entity of the CPSU, needed to be convinced by Gorbachev, or changed. Gorbachev realized that if his economic reforms were to succeed, he would need to break the power of conservatives in the party. He promoted reform-minded politicians who would support his policies, discharging 39 government ministers in his first year in power. Politburo members who opposed reform were replaced. Yegor Ligachev, organization and agriculture specialist, and Nikolai Ryzhkov, an industrial specialist, became key members of the Politburo, as they had supported Gorbachev for General Secretary. He supported active reformers like Boris Yeltsin. Gorbachev also encouraged political participation by young people and women at the local level of the party and increased ethnic diversity at the highest levels of the CPSU. However, he was

The essay makes three strong arguments in three tightly focused paragraphs. Each paragraph focuses on a different topic relating to the challenges faced by Gorbachev.

not always supported by the new appointments. Source H shows that Ligachev strongly opposed Gorbachev's economic reforms by stating that a 'model of a market based on private ownership is fundamentally unacceptable to a socialist system'. Ryzhkov also supported this view and insisted that Gorbachev's reforms should not go beyond the framework of socialism. In Source H, Ligachev also insisted that 'the Party is not going to renounce its leading role'. His support of Yeltsin also turned sour when Yeltsin proposed removing General Secretary privileges. This, and Yeltsin's mounting political enmity with Ligachev, resulted in Yeltsin's removal from the Politburo in 1987. This has been called one of Gorbachev's major political mistakes.

Gorbachev faced serious challenges to reform when he became General Secretary in the USSR. The centralized socialist bureaucracy had great importance in challenging his reforms, by its reluctance to give up the power to control the economic and political aspects of running the USSR. This can be seen in the Politburo's adherence to party predominance. In addition, Gorbachev's insistence on following socialism as a system prevented him from going beyond vague terms and campaigns that did not go far enough to solve Soviet problems, like the enterprise laws and anti-alcohol campaign. Food shortages continued and Gosagroprom had to be dissolved after it failed. Ultimately, the centralized socialist bureaucracy was more than Gorbachev could face and he resigned in 1991. The USSR came to an end.

> The conclusion clearly indicates that the centralized socialist bureaucracy had great importance in challenging Gorbachev's reforms.

This essay utilizes all the sources in an explicit and appropriate manner. The essay also goes beyond the sources to indicate that the student also used their own knowledge and that this knowledge was correct. The response to the question is complex, but balanced in that it demonstrates that Gorbachev faced great challenges.

Examination practice

Below are some exam-style questions for you to practise. Paper 1 exams are one hour long, not including five minutes of reading time at the exam's start when only reading is permitted. You may wish to only practise specific questions, and if this is the case, allow the following amounts of time per question:

Question 1:	5 minutes
Question 2:	10 minutes
Question 3:	10 minutes
Question 4:	35 minutes

These questions relate to Gorbachev's policies of *glasnost* and *perestroika* and their impact on the USSR. The sources used are found within this chapter on the following pages:

- Source B (page 137)
- Source C (page 138)
- Source H (page 142)
- Source M (page 147)
- Source Q (page 155)
- Source R (page 157)

1 a) What, according to Source B, were the qualities which marked Gorbachev out as an effective leader? *(3 marks)*
(For guidance on how to answer this style of question see page 41.)

b) What can be inferred from Source C about the aims of Gorbachev in implementing *glasnost* and *perestroika*? *(2 marks)*
(For guidance on how to answer this style of question see page 37.)

2 Compare and contrast the views expressed in Sources H and Q about the impact of Gorbachev's reforms. *(6 marks)*
(For guidance on how to answer this style of question see page 91.)

3 With reference to their origin and purpose, discuss the value and limitations of Source M and Source R for historians studying the impact of *glasnost* and *perestroika*. *(6 marks)*
(For guidance on how to answer this style of question see page 130.)

4 Using these sources (Sources C, H, Q, M, R) and your own knowledge, analyse the positive and negative consequences of the policies of *glasnost* and *perestroika* on the USSR. *(8 marks)*
(For guidance on how to answer this style of question see page 160.)

 # Activities

1 'Hot seating' is where a member of the class adopts the persona of a historical personality and answers questions posed by other students. Research the career of Gorbachev between 1985 and 1991 and write a list of questions to ask Gorbachev at the following stages of his career: 1985, 1989 and 1991. In your questioning, try to ascertain how and why Gorbachev took the decisions that he did. Alternatively, you could take on the role of Gorbachev and give historically valid answers to the questions posed. One member of the class can take on the role of 'historian' and deliver a final judgement on the accuracy of the answers.

2 To what extent can Gorbachev's political career be regarded as a study in political failure? Debate this question in class. If working on your own, write two paragraphs: one supporting the statement and the other challenging it. Do you find that any events or pieces of evidence can be interpreted in more than one way?

3 Look back through this chapter and select the source that you think comes closest to providing a definitive judgement of Gorbachev. Explain why you agree with the author's judgement, making use of your own knowledge, to substantiate your points.

CHAPTER 7

The collapse of Soviet influence in eastern Europe

This chapter analyses the reasons for the collapse of Soviet influence in eastern Europe in the late 1980s, and looks in depth at the events in Poland, East Germany and Czechoslovakia. It also examines the impact of events in eastern Europe on superpower relations and the end of the Cold War. You need to consider the following questions throughout this chapter:

✪ Why and to what extent did Gorbachev transform Soviet relations with the USA from 1985 onwards?

✪ What were the causes and consequences of the fall of the Berlin Wall?

✪ What were the causes and consequences of the Velvet Revolution in Czechoslovakia?

✪ What were the causes and consequences of the collapse of communism in Poland?

✪ Why did communist rule in eastern Europe collapse at the end of the 1980s?

Soviet foreign policy and superpower relations 1985–9

▶ **Key question:** *Why and to what extent did Gorbachev transform Soviet relations with the USA from 1985 onwards?*

Gorbachev was willing to engage in diplomacy with the USA in a manner that few of his predecessors would have been willing to contemplate. Between 1985 and 1991, he held nine summit talks with US Presidents Reagan and Bush. Gorbachev believed that confrontation between capitalism and communism was not inevitable and that the two systems could benefit each other. He was also genuinely interested in limiting nuclear weapons; in 1987 he addressed a forum in Moscow entitled 'For a Nuclear Free World, for the Survival of Mankind' to this end.

This was a marked change since in the early 1980s, when both the USA and USSR spent enormous and growing sums on military expenses. The US Strategic Defence Initiative (SDI) or **Star Wars**, as it came to be known, also raised the prospect of an even more expensive nuclear arms race. This encouraged Gorbachev to be even more determined to reduce military expense as a way to fund his domestic reforms.

 **KEY TERM**

Star Wars Colloquial term used to refer to President Reagan's Strategic Defence Initiative, designed to set up a missile defence shield to protect against Soviet nuclear attack.

A cartoon by Nicholas Garland which appeared in a British newspaper, the *Daily Telegraph*, 14 March 1985. It shows US President Reagan on the left of the bed and Gorbachev on the right. Garland is a British cartoonist who has worked for many major British publications. The *Daily Telegraph* is a daily British newspaper in publication since 1855, known for its conservative perspective.

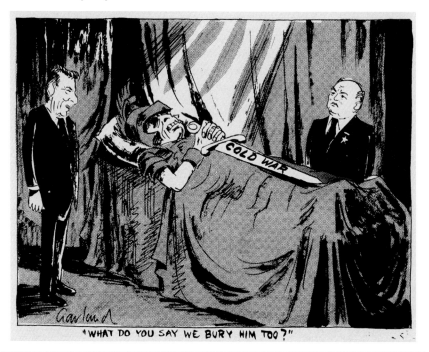

"WHAT DO YOU SAY WE BURY HIM TOO?"

How far was
Gorbachev's foreign
policy a break with
the past?

Gorbachev's foreign policy

Gorbachev replaced long-time Foreign Minister Andrei Gromyko with Eduard Shevardnadze, signalling that Gorbachev's policies would differ from those of previous Soviet leaders. It was assumed that Shevardnadze's appointment indicated that a new era of negotiations was at hand and he was soon appreciated and trusted by the two US Secretaries of State with whom he dealt, George Shultz and James Baker. Another important supporter of diplomatic engagement with the USA was Alexander Yakovlev, former Soviet ambassador to Canada and member of the Politburo responsible for international affairs; he was also one of Gorbachev's closest advisers. A new era of foreign policy was in the making.

A strong motivation for reducing or ending the arms race with the USA was to cut military expenditure in the USSR. Gorbachev urgently needed to allocate those resources to revitalize an ailing economy and improve the standard of living of Soviet citizens. In order to do this, the USSR had to reduce its arms and increase trade with the West.

SOURCE B

Excerpt from *Memoirs* by Mikhail Gorbachev, published by Doubleday, New York, USA, 1995, page 171. In this extract, Gorbachev, as former Head of State, describes his rationale for a new foreign policy on becoming General Secretary.

On taking office as general secretary in 1985 I was immediately faced with an avalanche of problems. It was vital to change our relationship with the West, particularly the United States, and to bring the costly and dangerous arms race to an end. We needed to withdraw from the damaging and costly war in Afghanistan. The Soviet Union faced tremendous internal problems. The process of reform required new leadership and courage. Long-term problems needed to be addressed as soon as possible … A programme that would stop the country's slide toward crisis and prepare to meet the challenge of the future was urgently needed.

According to Source B, what was Gorbachev's motivation for new foreign policies in the USSR?

Germany and eastern Europe

At first, Gorbachev showed little sign of reducing Soviet global influence in general and in eastern Europe in particular. However, within two years he began to subtly signal that he was willing to contemplate changes to the European political order that had prevailed since 1945. For instance, when West German President Richard von Weizsäcker visited Moscow in July 1987, Gorbachev did not dismiss the prospect of **German reunification** categorically, as Gromyko had earlier, allowing that history would decide Germany's future.

In addition, Gorbachev seems to have decided at a fairly early stage that he would not be prepared to uphold the Brezhnev Doctrine (see page 107) in Warsaw Pact countries.

KEY TERM

German reunification
The idea of reuniting East and West Germany into a single state.

SOURCE C

Excerpt from *Politics, Paradigms, and Intelligence Failures: Why So Few Predicted the Collapse of the Soviet Union* by Ofira Seliktar, published by M.E. Sharpe, Armonk, NY, USA, 2004, pages 133–4. Seliktar is an Israeli political scientist. She teaches at Gratz College, PA, USA.

Perhaps the most painful area of revision was Soviet relations with its external empire in Eastern Europe. Following the decision to refrain from intervention in Poland [in 1981], the debate about the future of Moscow's East European satellites had intensified among the top leadership. During his first speech as general secretary, Gorbachev departed from the customary emphasis on 'socialist internationalism,' a code word for a homogeneous commitment to a Soviet-style economy on the part of the satellites. To Gorbachev, already concerned about the price of bailing out the inefficient East European economies, the potential cost of repressing the spreading unrest was too high to contemplate.

According to Source C, why did Gorbachev revise Soviet policy regarding eastern Europe?

This decision was formally communicated to the leaders of Warsaw Pact countries at a COMECON summit in 1986, although it was not yet made

Sinatra Doctrine
A reference to the song *My Way*, made popular by US singer Frank Sinatra in 1969. It meant that eastern European countries would be allowed more autonomy from the USSR as of 1986.

public. Eventually, this determination not to intervene in the internal politics of the Warsaw Pact came to be known as the **Sinatra Doctrine** – in essence, eastern European countries in the Warsaw Pact were to be allowed to do things *their way*. Gorbachev hoped that reforms to the communist system, similar to his own programme of *perestroika*, might be implemented by enthusiastic satellite states anxious to emulate the USSR. He also mistakenly assumed that reform movements in these states would not topple governments.

SOURCE D

Excerpt from 'Continuity and change in Soviet foreign policy under Gorbachev' by Achin Vanaik from *Economic and Political Weekly*, published by Sameeksha Trust, Mumbai, India, Vol. 23, No. 11, 12 March 1988, pages 551–2. Vanaik teaches political science at the University of Delhi, Delhi, India. *Economic and Political Weekly* is a journal published in India since 1949 that features scholarly papers in the social sciences, with critical analysis.

The Soviet weak spot, however, is eastern Europe. Here again, it is Soviet security that is the key consideration. Gorbachev would not be opposed to east European versions of glasnost and perestroika. Indeed, to the discomfort of the conservative sections of the ruling bureaucracy in these countries he would encourage such developments. In this he is unlike his predecessors, and this can only be a positive and welcome development, with respect to the fact that greater pressures for political democratisation will be unleashed. But like his predecessors, Gorbachev will be opposed to any demands following in the wake of détente or glasnost–perestroika for withdrawal from the Warsaw Pact or which challenge the primacy, i.e., 'leading role' of the ruling Communist Parties.

? According to Source D, what will be the effect of Gorbachev's policies in eastern Europe?

Gorbachev's foreign policy changes in eastern Europe would have an important effect on world events, superpower relations and the Cold War.

→ Superpower relations

How far was Gorbachev responsible for the thaw in superpower relations between 1985 and 1989?

Gorbachev's attitude and personality became a great boon to superpower relations. In the hostile diplomatic environment of the mid-1980s, his open disposition contrasted with previous Soviet leadership, although he did not immediately depart from the military policies of his predecessors. At the end of 1985, the superpower leaders met and continued to do so several times in the next five years.

The Geneva Summit 1985
Reagan and Gorbachev met for the first time at Geneva in November 1985. Gorbachev had prepared carefully, having created a negotiating position in consultation with the Politburo, the KGB, the Ministry of Foreign Affairs and the International Department of the Central Committee. He entered the talks with the key aim of getting an agreement that neither superpower would launch a nuclear first strike, but Reagan saw this as removing a powerful deterrent in the event of a Soviet invasion of western Europe.

Reagan went into the summit determined to make no concessions whatsoever on SDI. Gorbachev regarded this stance as provocative, since he believed that it ran the risk of creating a new arms race in space. Gorbachev was surprisingly honest with Reagan, telling him that the USSR was in no economic position to sustain a new arms race. By the end of the summit, a real rapport had developed between the two leaders, as well as a strong commitment to ease tensions and begin nuclear disarmament in earnest. The CPSU approved.

SOURCE E

Excerpt from a report of the Central Committee Politburo from Moscow TASS in English, 25 November 1985, *Daily Report* (USSR), 26 November 1985 from *From Brezhnev to Gorbachev: Infighting in the Kremlin* by Baruch A. Hazan, published by Westview Press, Boulder, CO, USA, 1987, page 192. Hazan is a Bulgarian historian who teaches at the Institute of European Studies in Vienna, Austria.

The results of the talks in Geneva can have a positive effect on changing the political and psychological climate in present-day international relations and their improvement, and lessen the risk of outbreak of nuclear war. The meeting has marked the beginning of a dialogue with a view to achieve changes for the better in Soviet–American relations and in the whole world. … The Political Bureau of the CPSU Central Committee fully approved the work done by Mikhail Gorbachev.

> According to Source E, what would be effects of the Geneva Summit?

The Cold War was a long way from being over at this stage. Soviet troops had yet to be withdrawn from Afghanistan (see page 121) and Soviet influence in eastern Europe remained very much intact. The USA continued to maintain and support NATO and supported anti-communist organizations around the world, including *mujaheddin* rebels in Afghanistan.

The Reykjavik Summit 1986

At the beginning of 1986, Gorbachev proposed that all nuclear weapons be eradicated by the year 2000. In April 1986, the Chernobyl disaster occurred (see page 147) and Gorbachev became more committed to ending any danger of nuclear war. He entered the Reykjavik Summit in October 1986, determined to have Reagan renounce SDI and nuclear weapons altogether. It was agreed in principle that all intermediate-range missiles would be withdrawn from Europe and that there would be a 50 per cent reduction in intercontinental ballistic missile (ICBM) numbers. In addition, an agreement to phase out nuclear weapons entirely was briefly considered by both sides.

The main difficulty was that Reagan was determined to keep SDI. On the other hand, Gorbachev favoured making all other agreements conditional on keeping to the terms of the 1972 **ABM Treaty**, which Gorbachev interpreted as meaning that SDI would remain a purely theoretical project. The end result was that, once again, no major diplomatic breakthrough occurred, but

KEY TERM

ABM Treaty An anti-ballistic missile treaty preventing the development of anti-missile defence systems, signed by the USA and the USSR in 1972.

important groundwork had been done that would bear fruit in 1987, in the form of the **Intermediate-range Nuclear Forces Treaty** (INF Treaty) (see page 173).

(see page 173)

KEY TERM

Intermediate-range Nuclear Forces Treaty
A treaty that eliminated Soviet and US nuclear missiles with a range of between 500 and 5000 km.

German question During the Cold War, this term referred to issues emanating from the sovereignty and potential reunification of East and West Germany.

? What information is conveyed by Source F?

? According to Source G, what will bring peace?

SOURCE F

Joined by their interpreter (centre), President Ronald Reagan (left) and Soviet leader Mikhail Gorbachev (right) face each other uneasily at the end of their 1986 summit meeting in Reykjavik, Iceland.

After the summit, strategic and ideological tensions between the USA and USSR remained. This was illustrated by Reagan's visit to Berlin in June 1987.

Far from praising Gorbachev for his reforms, Reagan dramatically called on Gorbachev to end the physical divide between West Berlin and East Berlin: the Berlin Wall. Coming eight months after meeting at Reykjavik, this seemed like an open challenge. Gorbachev, however, had already repudiated the Brezhnev Doctrine and relations between the two countries were moving in a more positive direction despite the rhetoric.

SOURCE G

Excerpt from US President Reagan's address at the Brandenburg Gate in West Berlin, Germany, 12 June 1987 from the US National Archives and Records Administration at www.archives.gov.

*Behind me stands a wall that encircles the free sectors of this city, part of a vast system of barriers that divides the entire continent of Europe … Standing before the Brandenburg Gate, every man is a German, separated from his fellow men. Every man is a Berliner, forced to look upon a scar … As long as this gate is closed, as long as this scar of a wall is permitted to stand, it is not the **German question** alone that remains open, but the question of freedom for all mankind …*

General Secretary Gorbachev, if you seek peace, if you seek prosperity for the Soviet Union and Eastern Europe, if you seek liberalization, come here to this gate.

Mr. Gorbachev, open this gate!

Mr. Gorbachev, tear down this wall!

The Washington Summit 1987

At the Washington Summit in December 1987, both Reagan and Gorbachev agreed to phase out all intermediate-range nuclear missiles. This was the key term of the Intermediate-range Nuclear Forces (INF) Treaty which was signed on the first day of the summit. As in previous summits, Reagan refused to abandon his commitment to SDI. However, Gorbachev shifted his approach and did not make nuclear disarmament in Europe conditional on the abandonment of SDI. Gorbachev was willing to make this diplomatic concession as he had been informed by leading Soviet scientists that SDI had only a small chance of ever operating. Against the fading background of SDI, the summit meetings between Gorbachev and Reagan became increasingly productive.

The Moscow Summit 1988

From 29 May to 2 June 1988, Reagan visited Moscow. The major political item on the agenda was the ratification of the INF Treaty on 1 June 1988. Relations now so cordial that Reagan sent Gorbachev a note in which he wrote 'To Mikhail from Ron'. At the summit, the two leaders paved the way for the Strategic Arms Reduction Treaty (**START**) to be signed two years later. They also discussed human rights and regional issues.

The end of the Cold War

By 1988, it was clear that the Cold War was coming to an end. At home, Gorbachev embarked on an ambitious programme of political liberalization (see page 141), while abroad, troops were being withdrawn from Afghanistan (see page 122). In an address to the UN General Assembly, Gorbachev rejected class struggle and the superiority of socialism as ideological precepts of Soviet foreign policy. Instead, he stated that all peoples should have the right to choose their own form of government and that universal human values should encompass both the capitalist and socialist blocs. In the same speech he also announced a reduction of half a million Red Army troops, prompting the resignation of head of the military, Marshal Sergey Akhromeev. This failed to deter Gorbachev, and in 1989 he went further by removing 500 **tactical nuclear weapons** from eastern Europe.

Such actions and rhetoric signalled to eastern Europe that Gorbachev was a unique Soviet leader and that the Brezhnev Doctrine was finished. Indeed, Gorbachev supported reform movements in Warsaw Pact countries like Hungary, the first state within the Soviet political orbit to move towards multi-party elections and political liberalization under Prime Minister Miklós Németh.

The symbolic end of the Cold War arrived with the demolition of the Berlin Wall in November 1989, encouraging the reunification of a divided Germany. In December 1989, at the Malta Summit with US President Bush, Gorbachev agreed to begin withdrawing Soviet troops from eastern Europe. This marked

 **KEY TERM**

START Strategic arms reduction treaty between the USA and USSR limiting the amount of nuclear weapons that both superpowers could deploy.

Tactical nuclear weapon Small nuclear device intended for use on the battlefield.

What political message is
conveyed by Source H?

Gorbachev and Reagan in Red Square during the 1988 Moscow Summit.

the end of Soviet military dominance in the Warsaw Pact and is taken by
many historians to mark the real end of the Cold War.

Soon, communist governments in Bulgaria, Czechoslovakia and Romania
collapsed, with Poland following suit. Finally, in 1992, Albania ended 47 years
of communist rule following elections. The following sections examine the
different experiences of three of these Warsaw Pact members in their
transition from Soviet satellite states, namely:

- East Germany
- Czechoslovakia
- Poland.

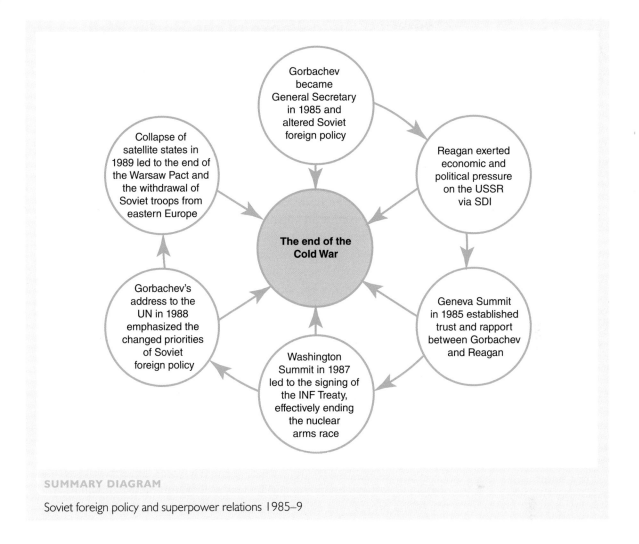

SUMMARY DIAGRAM

Soviet foreign policy and superpower relations 1985–9

2 The fall of the Berlin Wall and the collapse of the East German state

▶ **Key question:** *What were the causes and consequences of the fall of the Berlin Wall?*

On 9 November 1989, the East German government gave permission to open gates in the Berlin Wall that had separated East and West Berlin since 1961. Crowds surged through the gates, climbed on the wall and began tearing it down. This event has become a symbol for the end of the Cold War and this section examines the events leading up to it and its consequences.

<table>
<tr><td>

What was the nature of the communist regime in East Germany in the 1980s?

</td><td>

Causes of the collapse of the Berlin Wall

As we have seen in Chapter 1 (page 15), in 1949, the Soviet occupation zone of Germany was formally reconstituted as the German Democratic Republic (GDR), although it was also known as East Germany. It developed as a Stalinist state, dominated by the **SED** until 1989. The 1968 constitution formalized the SED's leading role, although other minor non-communist parties such as the DBD, a farmers' party, were tolerated and even had small numbers of seats assigned to them in the East German parliament.

</td></tr>
</table>

KEY TERM

SED Socialist Unity Party of Germany. The Marxist–Leninist party in East Germany established in 1946 by the merger between the Socialist Party (SPD) and the Communist Party (KPD).

Basic Treaty Treaty between the FRG and the GDR in 1972 that led to the exchange of permanent diplomatic missions between the two countries and to both joining the UN.

Lutheran Church The main Protestant Church in East Germany.

New Forum Pro-democracy movement founded in East Germany in September 1989 which led to public demonstrations that accelerated the end of barriers between East and West Berlin and the end of communist government in East Germany.

East Germany was governed until 1971 by SED leader Walter Ulbricht, who admired Stalin. Under his leadership, agriculture was collectivized and there was an emphasis on central planning and the development of heavy industry. Ulbricht was finally replaced as leader of East Germany and First Secretary of the SED in 1971, by Erich Honecker. Besides attempting to stabilize East Germany economically, Honecker also eventually accepted diplomatic contact with West Germany. In 1972, he agreed to the **Basic Treaty** with West Germany (see page 109). This improved relations between East and West during the 1970s, but Honecker did little to alter the political and social *status quo* in the GDR. He remained convinced that only the SED should govern East Germany.

East Germany under Honecker

By the mid-1980s, Honecker was much less willing than Gorbachev to contemplate significant political changes. He hoped that the relatively high standard of living in East Germany, compared to other Warsaw Pact countries, and the prestige his regime derived from its success in international sporting events, including the Olympic Games, would act as stabilizing influences. In essence, he was a strict communist, unwilling to consider a programme akin to *perestroika* and *glasnost* in the USSR.

This gradually alienated East German citizens, even the 20 per cent of the population who were members of the SED. The **Lutheran Church,** one of the very few non-communist organizations to occupy a prominent place in East German society, provided moral and institutional support to nearly 200 dissident groups that developed during the 1980s. Many focused on environmental problems or the issue of nuclear disarmament. One of the most prominent dissident groups was **New Forum**, led by Bärbel Bohley and Jutta Seidel, which claimed, in 1989, that the SED had lost touch with ordinary citizens.

The elderly Honecker and his regime declared New Forum illegal, but to no avail. The wide base of the movement, which included young and old, Christians and atheists, as well as workers, artists and students, gave it the impetus to survive.

SOURCE I

Obituary for Bärbel Bohley in 'East German opposition leader remembered: autumn of 1989 unimaginable without Bärbel Bohley' by Daryl Lindsay in *Der Spiegel*, 13 September 2010, Hamburg, Germany, published by Spiegel Online International, www.spiegel.de/international. Lindsay is a US journalist for *Der Spiegel*, the largest news magazine in Germany and Europe.

The woman known as the 'mother of peaceful revolution' who embodied the political awakening that happened in the final days of East Germany, has passed away. Bärbel Bohley died at 65 on Saturday. She will be remembered as an opposition leader who helped to topple the communist regime.

Bärbel Bohley's place in the fall of communism is secure. An important player in East Germany's pro-democracy movement, she helped found the New Forum in Berlin, a mass protest movement that was the most prominent opposition group in the days leading up to the fall of the Berlin Wall on Nov. 9, 1989. She rose to become an important symbolic figure in that movement.

> According to Source I, how did Bohley affect the politics of the GDR?

SOURCE J

Excerpt from a table of basic economic data on eastern Europe, the USSR and selected western countries from 'Symposium on economic transition in the Soviet Union and eastern Europe' by Peter Murrell in *The Journal of Economic Perspectives* Vol. 5, No. 4, Autumn, 1991, published by the American Economic Association (AEA), Nashville, Tennessee, USA, page 6. Murrell is Professor of Economics at the University of Maryland, USA. The AEA formed in 1885 with the purpose of publishing academic articles on economics and promoting discussion of economics.

> According to Source J, how did East Germany compare economically to other Warsaw Pact states?

Country	Current inflation	Per capita GDP as % of USA	Cars per 1000 pop.	Telephones per 1000 pop.	Meat consumed (annual kg per capita)
Bulgaria	50	25	127	248	60
Czechoslovakia	10	17	186	246	76
East Germany	2	36	214	233	90
Hungary	29	13	156	152	78
Poland	690	9	112	122	64
Romania	25	16	NA	111	60
USSR	4	25	46	124	55
West Germany	2.7	99	459	650	83
USA	5.3	100	565	789	67
Note: Compiled in 1991. Data for East Germany are for 1989.					

The economy

Honecker was convinced that no reforms were necessary in the GDR because the country was the most prosperous Warsaw Pact state. East German agriculture was much more fully mechanized than in neighbouring Poland and the GDR was virtually self-sufficient in food.

The situation was not as idyllic as Honecker imagined. The GDR remained reliant on the USSR for oil imports. The standard of living in East Germany lagged far behind that of West Germany and a wide assortment of consumer goods could only be purchased using **hard currency** in so-called **Intershops**. Part of the higher standard of living in the GDR is also explained by the hidden subsidies provided by West Germany and its citizens, such as remittances to relatives in East Germany. East Germany's economy was also burdened by $26.5 billion of foreign debt.

Censorship

Most East Germans were fully aware of life in the West through watching West German television. Within East Germany, censorship was imposed and intellectuals critical of the regime were punished. Restrictions on freedom of thought and action were enforced by the state security agency, the *Stasi*. Up to 25 per cent of the population co-operated with the *Stasi*, informing on others.

Why did the Berlin Wall come down in 1989?

The fall of the Berlin Wall

Despite the relatively prosperous economic development of East Germany, its citizens were aware that life in the West was easier. Above all, they were conscious that their country lacked the basic freedoms and civil rights of western democracies. Many East Germans responded to conditions by trying to move to West Germany. In September 1989, Hungarian Prime Minister Miklós Németh (see page 173) ordered that the barbed wire fence between Hungary and neutral Austria, which he regarded as an expensive irrelevance, be dismantled.

Refugee crisis

Discontented East Germans began to emigrate to the West through the newly opened border between Hungary and Austria. Németh accepted 500 million German marks from the West German government to facilitate the movement of East Germans ostensibly on holiday, to the Austrian border, in defiance of a treaty from 1969 between Hungary and East Germany not to allow East Germans to move to the West through Hungarian territory. The Hungarian government took the decision to revoke this agreement with the implicit approval of Gorbachev, who had made it abundantly clear that the Brezhnev Doctrine was over.

By the end of September 1989, there were 130,000 East Germans in Hungary waiting to cross the border into Austria and almost 25,000 had reached West Germany. Thousands of East Germans also took refuge in the West German

KEY TERM

Hard currency A strong currency unlikely to lose its value; traded on global markets.

Intershops Special stores in select East German cities that sold products from the West for hard currency.

Stasi Abbreviation from the German for Ministry for State Security. Through collaborators, informers and full-time *Stasi* secret police officials, the government controlled civil unrest and anti-communist activities.

embassy in Prague, Czechoslovakia. They would be allowed to travel to West Germany by train through East Germany, but during their transit, riots erupted in Dresden as others attempted to board. This led to the total closure of East Germany's border with Czechoslovakia.

SOURCE K

A cartoon by Nicholas Garland that appeared in a British newspaper, *The Independent*, on 12 September 1989. Garland is a British cartoonist who has worked for many major British publications. *The Independent* is a daily British newspaper in publication since 1986.

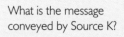

What is the message conveyed by Source K?

THE ONES THAT GOT AWAY

Gorbachev's visit to the GDR

The catalyst for the crisis that led to the fall of the Berlin Wall was Gorbachev's visit to the GDR on 6 October 1989. The purpose of the visit was to mark the fortieth anniversary of the East German state's foundation. Gorbachev was confronted by demonstrators from the communist youth movement carrying placards with slogans like *'Perestroika! Gorbachev! Help us!'* (see Source L, see page 180). This indicated that even many young communists felt alienated from their own government which rejected liberalization and reforms. Gorbachev made it clear to Honecker that reforms were necessary, commenting that 'life punishes harshly anyone who is left behind in politics'.

Gorbachev also asserted that he would not sanction the use of the 380,000 Soviet troops stationed in East Germany to maintain Honecker's grip on power. Honecker was reluctant to accept this new political reality and seemed determined to crush dissent. He was encouraged by Deng Xiaoping's actions in China (see page 85), which the chief of the *Stasi* praised as a firm way to control civil disturbances.

The day after Gorbachev left the GDR on 9 October, Honecker authorized the security police to shoot into crowds of protesters, 70,000 of whom demonstrated against the government in Leipzig. Daily protests in the city had been co-ordinated by the Lutheran Church. However, a massacre on the scale of Tiananmen Square did not occur, mostly due to the opposition of other senior SED figures like Egon Krenz.

? According to Source L, what was the significance of Gorbachev's visit to Berlin in October 1989?

SOURCE L

Excerpt from *Memoirs* by Mikhail Gorbachev, published by Doubleday, New York, USA, 1995, pages 524 and 526. In this extract, Gorbachev, as Head of State at the time, describes his visit to East Germany in October 1989.

Columns of representatives from all the regions of the republic filed past the dais where the East German leader and their foreign guests were standing … Participants in the march, I was told, had been hand-picked in advance. They were primarily activists in the Free German Youth Movement, young members of the SED and parties and public organizations close to it. So much the more indicative, then, the slogans and chanting in their ranks: 'Perestroika! Gorbachev! Help us!' … I had sensed that something was wrong when we were driving into Berlin from Schönefeld Airport. Along almost the entire route to the residence there were solid rows of young people chanting 'Gorbachev! Gorbachev!' – even though Honecker was sitting right next to me … Anyone who saw all that would instantly have dismissed Honecker's later statements about his removal from the leadership of East Germany being the result of an intrigue sanctioned by Gorbachev among the apparatus of the SED Central Committee.

Krenz becomes leader

The protests in Leipzig and other German cities undermined what remained of Honecker's fragile political authority and led to his replacement on 17 October 1989 by Egon Krenz. Krenz was a reform-minded communist who did not favour the use of force against protesters. However, he came to power too late to save the GDR and historian Martin McCauley's acerbic commentary describes him as not equal to the formidable political challenges that he faced by the autumn of 1989.

Krenz was tainted by his association with Honecker's regime, so he lacked credibility in the eyes of many East Germans. His appointment was certainly not enough to satisfy growing numbers of demonstrators in cities like Leipzig and Dresden, whose political agenda now included the end of communist rule. By the first week of November, up to 1.4 million demonstrators demanded the recognition of opposition groups, free elections and the right to travel abroad.

Gorbachev's advice to Krenz was to reduce political pressure on his regime by agreeing to the opening of the border with Czechoslovakia for East Germans. A large number of East Germans now fled to the Austrian border.

One of Krenz's final attempts to regain support was to remove two-thirds of the Politburo on 7 November 1989; this had little real impact.

The fall of the Berlin Wall

On 9 November 1989, having visited Moscow for talks with Gorbachev, Krenz decided to relax, but not eliminate, travel restrictions to the West as part of an attempt to stabilize his regime. Temporary visits to the West of up to four weeks a year were to be made more obtainable. When the decision was announced to the media by the poorly informed First Secretary of the SED, Gunter Schabowski, it was stated that all citizens of the GDR were free to cross to the West with immediate effect and that the border was now open.

That evening, thousands of East Berliners began to demonstrate along the Berlin Wall, anticipating that they would soon be allowed to cross unimpeded into West Berlin. As the evening progressed, some East Berliners began to scale the wall itself and security forces, conscious of Krenz's political weakness and the lack of desire for political repression in Moscow, did not stop them. Finally, several border guards at Bornholmer Strasse took the decision to relieve the crush of people at the border crossing and opened the gates.

> Assess the value and limitations of Source M for a historian evaluating the reasons for the collapse of the Berlin Wall. **?**

SOURCE M

East Berliners climbing on top of the Berlin Wall on the night of 9 November 1989.

What consequences did the collapse of the Berlin Wall have for Germany?

The end of the East German state and the reunification of Germany

Egon Krenz's leadership of the SED proved to be short lived and he was replaced on 7 December by Hans Modrow. Modrow initially favoured the idea of a loose confederation of the two states, but this was opposed by West Germany's Chancellor Helmut Kohl, who wanted full reunification. This was one of Kohl's stated political aims that he had expressed in a 10-point plan on 28 November 1989. He informed Gorbachev at the end of January 1990 that most East Germans were not in favour of the concept of two separate German states. This certainly seemed to be the case in cities like Leipzig, where protesters displayed banners with slogans like 'Germany – united fatherland!'

The Malta Summit, December 1989

Gorbachev was reluctant to agree unconditionally to Germany's reunification, fearing that it could alter the European balance of power that had existed since 1945, since it would probably mean that a united Germany would remain in NATO. Gorbachev's fears were allayed at the Malta Summit with US President Bush in December 1989. At the very beginning of 1990, both Helmut Kohl and Hans Modrow visited Moscow for talks during which Gorbachev stated that reunification was probable and that it was up to Germans themselves to decide what sort of state they wanted to live in. He also stated that reunification could not happen in the short term and must not be allowed to undermine international stability.

'Two Plus Four'

In February 1990, US Secretary of State James Baker travelled to Moscow to engineer a 'Two Plus Four' solution. This meant that the external mechanics of reunification would be determined by the four occupying powers from the end of the Second World War. The FRG and GDR (the 'two') would deal with internal affairs. Gorbachev gave his consent to this political formula.

March 1990 elections

Further impetus was given to the reunification process in March 1990 when the reformed SED, now renamed the Party of Democratic Socialism, achieved only 17 per cent of the vote in national elections. By this stage, its membership was less than half that of the former SED. The winner of the election in the GDR was the resolutely pro-unification Alliance for Germany. This led to the replacement of Modrow as premier and the formation of a coalition government under Lothar de Maizière. This government stated its intention to push through reunification with West Germany as quickly as possible. All the while, at least 1000 East German refugees per day continued to leave the GDR for the West and the East German economy began to grind to a halt as state subsidies to industry started to end.

Reunification

Despite Gorbachev's initial reluctance, by July 1990, after another visit by Kohl to Moscow, Gorbachev had come to concede that reunification might proceed and brokered the formal reunification of Germany, which eventually took place on 3 October 1990.

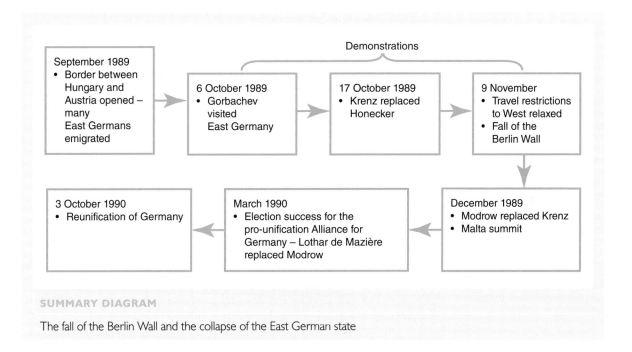

SUMMARY DIAGRAM

The fall of the Berlin Wall and the collapse of the East German state

③ The Velvet Revolution in Czechoslovakia

▶ **Key question:** *What were the causes and consequences of the Velvet Revolution in Czechoslovakia?*

After the Prague Spring in 1968 (see page 108), Czechoslovakia was tightly controlled by the Communist Party of Czechoslovakia (CPC), although this was resented by much of the population. The nationalist aspirations of the Slovak minority also remained unfulfilled.

What was the nature of the communist regime in Czechoslovakia in the 1980s?

Opposition to communist rule

In 1948, a communist regime was established in Czechoslovakia. It remained a totalitarian state for the next 20 years. Alexander Dubček's appointment as CPC First Secretary in January 1968, following a period of economic stagnation, ushered in a brief period of social and economic liberalization, the Prague Spring (see page 108), before Soviet intervention and the arrest of Dubček in 1969. Dubček was replaced by Gustav Husák. Husák remained in power for over 20 years, backed by the implicit threat of another Soviet invasion should the Brezhnev Doctrine have need of being enforced.

Czechoslovakia under Husák

Under Husák, a policy called **normalization** was implemented. This involved the careful management of any political dissent. Intellectuals and writers were forced to repudiate the events of the Prague Spring in order to be published. The secret police, the **StB**, kept a watchful eye on dissidents. The policy of normalization was not greeted with much enthusiasm by most, although there was slightly greater acceptance of the policy in the Slovak part of the country. This may have reflected the large amount of government investment in heavy industry, the bulk of which was located in Slovakia.

Dissent

Despite StB measures, political dissent did not totally disappear. The Helsinki Accords of 1975 (see page 111), in particular the clauses regarding human rights, acted as a catalyst for the emergence of a protest movement. All over eastern Europe, including Czechoslovakia, 'Helsinki Groups' emerged, dedicated to holding their governments accountable on human rights issues.

Charter 77

One prominent example of a 'Helsinki Group' was **Charter 77**. Inspired by Poland's Workers' Defence Committee (KOR) (see page 191), it was established on 7 January 1977, when a group of over 200 Czechoslovak intellectuals, including writer Václav Havel, issued a charter demanding that the Helsinki Accords and the **United Nations Declaration on Human Rights** be fully implemented in Czechoslovakia. The immediate trigger for the issue of the manifesto was the arrest of the members of a dissident rock group named The Plastic People of the Universe.

○━ **KEY TERM**

Normalization Used to describe the period of repression and stagnation in Czechoslovakia in the aftermath of the Prague Spring Movement.

StB Acronym for the State Security Service of Czechoslovakia.

Charter 77 Human rights association of hundreds of Czechoslovak intellectuals and dissidents that advocated democracy; established in 1977.

United Nations Declaration on Human Rights A statement of 30 human rights adopted by the UN in 1948.

? According to Source N, what was the importance of Charter 77?

SOURCE N

Excerpt from 'The politics and power of humiliation' by Jan Urban in *After the Velvet Revolution: Václav Havel and the New Leaders of Czechoslovakia Speak Out*, Tim D. Whipple, editor, *Focus on Issues*, No. 14, Freedom House, New York, USA, 1991, pages 279–80. Urban is a Czech historian and journalist, signatory of Charter 77 and persecuted by the StB.

It is in the arts that our deepest politics are played out in Czechoslovakia; and it was out of a battle in the arts that the movement which mobilized a further generation of Czechs, including myself, came into being. When the clash came, the pretext was the imprisonment of the musicians of the underground pop group

'The Plastic People of the Universe.' A broad coalition professing the most varied political opinions and beliefs, from former functionaries of the CPC to Catholics who spoke out in defense of these musicians' rights to free artistic expression.

In this way, in January 1977, Charter 77 came into being. It was a historic moment. People, humiliated to the point of desperation about their own powerlessness, were no longer able to remain silent and hide.

Charter 77 and another dissident group, the Committee for the Defence of the Unjustly Prosecuted (known by its Czech acronym of VONS), never threatened to overthrow Husák's regime. Their memberships were small and mostly confined to the intellectual élite; the bulk of the Czechoslovak working class, unlike in Poland (see page 190), remained passive supporters of a regime that ensured reasonable living standards for workers.

Moral opposition

In the West, these groups' moral opposition to totalitarianism received widespread publicity. Intellectuals like Havel laid bare the ideological and moral bankruptcy of the ruling élite. Another source of moral opposition was the Catholic Church, which by the 1980s was becoming a powerful institution once again. An indication of this is that when Cardinal Tomásek, the Archbishop of Prague, issued a petition in 1988, entitled 'Suggestions of Catholics for the Solution of the Position of the Faithful,' it was signed by 600,000 people.

Czechoslovakia under Jakeš

In 1987, Husák was succeeded as First Secretary of the CPC by Miloš Jakeš. He was also unwilling to emulate Gorbachev's *perestroika* programme. Jakeš faced increasing economic problems. Compared with the West, Czechoslovakia's industry was outdated and uncompetitive. The combination of economic weakness, dissident opposition and the communist regime's lack of legitimacy dating back to 1968, created a crisis situation for the CPC by 1988.

The end of communist rule in Czechoslovakia

> **Why did the communist regime collapse in Czechoslovakia in 1989?**

The twentieth anniversary of the Prague Spring in 1988 was marked by student demonstrations in Prague involving up to 10,000 protesters. Most had nothing to do with Charter 77. This suggested that the base of opposition to the regime was beginning to widen beyond the intellectual élite. Protests continued into January 1989, and led to the arrest of Václav Havel. Security forces began to use water cannon and tear gas against the protesters. Events in the GDR in 1989 (see page 179) further radicalized the youth and as several thousand East Germans fled to the West German embassy in Prague, there was increasing awareness of growing political volatility across the Warsaw Pact nations. The fall of the Berlin Wall in November 1989 acted as a catalyst for opponents of the communist regime.

Demonstrations, 17 November 1989

On 17 November, the tense political atmosphere worsened. Students gathered in Prague to mark the fiftieth anniversary of the death of a student killed by Germans in the Second World War. Speakers at the rally called for the removal of First Secretary Jakeš. As 50,000 protesters made their way to Prague's Wenceslas Square, they found their way blocked by the police and soldiers. These forces used their batons to try to disrupt the demonstration. In the confused political situation, a false rumour circulated that a student had been killed by the security forces and this prompted further student demonstrations on 18 November.

According to Source O, what were the political views of university students in November 1989?

SOURCE O

'A proclamation of the university students to the workers and peasants of Czechoslovakia' issued on 20 November 1989 from *The Velvet Revolution: Czechoslovakia, 1988–1991* by Bernard Wheaton and Zdeněk Kavan, published by Westview Press, Boulder, Colorado, USA, 1992, pages 198–9. The students were from the University of Prague. Wheaton is a British historian at Charles University, Prague, Czech Republic, and Kavan is a Czech Professor of International Relations at the University of Sussex, UK.

We, the university students of Czechoslovakia, protest most strongly against the brutal breaking up of the peaceful demonstration which took place on November 17ᵗʰ 1989 … this was not an attempt to restore public order but the meting out of physical punishment and with very serious consequences. This course of action is in contradiction to the function of the security forces, to current Czechoslovak law, and to accepted international treaties. Please understand that this was not simply an attack on students but at the same time an attack on your children, on the children of workers' and peasants' families …

We therefore demand the formation of a suitable parliamentary commission of inquiry with the participation of the university strike committees and the subsequent punishment of the guilty, regardless of their present position and office. As we see no other way of expressing our disagreement and alarm at the present internal political situation in our country, nothing remains for us but to embark upon a week-long protest strike …

KEY TERM

Civic Forum Czechoslovak non-violent civic association that quickly became a political force in November 1989.

Civic Forum

Protests and the government use of violence gave impetus to the establishment of **Civic Forum** on 19 November. Its initial political demands included the replacement of the older generation of hard-line communist leaders like Miloš Jakeš and the release of all political prisoners. Civic Forum became a co-ordinating group for all the different protest factions that emerged, such as students, Catholic priests and even Marxists disillusioned with the process of normalization. The Slovak equivalent of Civic Forum was called the Public Against Violence and demonstrations began in the Slovak city of Bratislava.

Final collapse of communist rule

On 22 November, up to 250,000 demonstrators, the majority of them students, protested on the streets of Prague in favour of free and fair elections. They were addressed by Václav Havel. Within two days, this number had grown to 350,000 and slogans appeared on placards such as 'Truth will triumph' and 'We've had enough'. When Alexander Dubček appeared in public for the first time since 1968 in Bratislava, he was given a rapturous reception. With Gorbachev as leader of the USSR, this time there was no prospect of a repeat of the Soviet invasion of 1968.

A military crackdown similar to that carried out by Jaruzelski in Poland (see page 193) was discussed in the CPC Central Committee, but rejected. There was some doubt as to whether conscripted soldiers would be prepared to attack fellow citizens. Pragmatic members of the CPC hierarchy now favoured negotiations with Civic Forum. The CPC did attempt to maintain its political grip on the provinces by censoring news about the events in Prague, but this could not be sustained.

On the evening of 24 November, the entire Politburo, including Jakeš, resigned. The party's hope was that the removal of those most associated with the policy of normalization would reduce the scale and intensity of the opposition movement. Václav Havel, who had emerged as the leading political voice within Civic Forum, denounced what he saw as a ploy by the CPC to maintain a hold on power.

> Assess the value and limitations of Source P for a historian studying the Velvet Revolution. **?**

SOURCE P

Demonstrations in Prague during November 1989.

Continuing demonstrations

Demonstrations of up to 800,000 people continued in Prague and Civic Forum remained determined to extract further concessions, such as the abandonment of Article 4 of the Constitution that guaranteed a leading governing role for the CPC. Seventy-five per cent of the population participated in a general strike on 27 November, a clear sign that the CPC's hold over the working class was ending.

Faced with these developments, Prime Minister Ladislav Adamec agreed to share power and on 29 November, Article 4 of the Constitution was formally removed. Adamec had made a quick trip to Moscow to consult with Gorbachev, but received only reiteration of the USSR's role as a bystander. The CPC was on its own.

Havel as President

A new coalition government, mostly consisting of non-communists, was announced on 3 December 1989. Adamec resigned three days later when it became clear that his presence in the new government would provoke a fresh round of strikes and demonstrations. The decisive political moment came on 29 December 1989. Václav Havel was appointed as President of Czechoslvakia by a unanimous vote in parliament, replacing Husák. On 1 January 1990, the old regime was clearly over when President Havel gave amnesty to 16,000 political prisoners and soon abolished the StB. Havel ensured that the transition to democracy was a peaceful one, hence the name Velvet Revolution.

Czechoslovakia after 1989

Democratic parliamentary elections were held in June 1990 under a system of proportional representation. Civic Forum reaped the benefits of its prominent role in the overthrow of the old regime and won most seats, forming a coalition government. However, Civic Forum, which had always been a very broad coalition of interest groups, soon split up into five competing political parties.

Czechoslovakia did not remain a united polity and in 1992, the Velvet Divorce took place. Czech and Slovak national elements of the state were constitutionally separated into the Czech Republic and Slovakia.

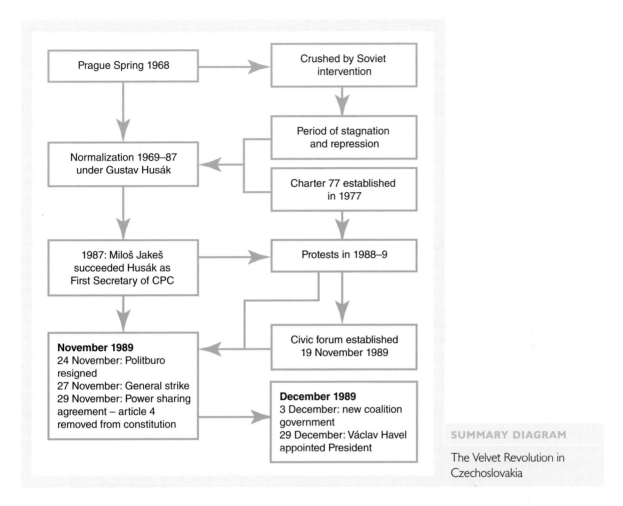

The Velvet Revolution in Czechoslovakia

 # The collapse of communist rule in Poland

▶ *Key question*: What were the causes and consequences of the collapse of communism in Poland?

Following the Red Army's expulsion of German forces at the end of the Second World War, in 1948 a totalitarian state was established and Marxism–Leninism became the official state ideology under the single-party rule of the Polish United Workers' Party (**PUWP**), as the Communist Party in Poland was called.

 **KEY TERM**

PUWP The Polish United Workers' Party, the main Marxist–Leninist Party in Poland between 1948 and 1990.

Excerpt from *The Cold War: A New History* by John Lewis Gaddis, published by Penguin Books, London, UK, 2006, pages 21–2. Gaddis is a Professor of History at Yale University, USA.

The offenses [of the Soviet Union against Poland] included the 1939 Nazi–Soviet Pact, which had extinguished Polish independence, together with the subsequent discovery that the Russians had massacred some 4,000 Polish officers at Katyn Wood in 1940 – another 11,000 remained unaccounted for … Stalin's insistence on taking a third of Poland's territory after the war further embittered the nation … Because Poles would never elect a pro-Soviet government, Stalin imposed one – the cost, though, was a permanently resentful Poland …

> **?**
>
> What does Source Q convey about relations between Poland and the USSR?

> **What was the nature of the communist regime in Poland?**

Communist rule in Poland

Following Khrushchev's 1956 denunciation of Stalin (see page 15), Polish workers began to strike and riots broke out in the city of Poznań. The demonstrators felt vindicated in their condemnation of Stalin, who had perpetrated so many offences against the Polish people (see Source Q). Workers demonstrated, carrying slogans like 'Russians go home'. The resulting political crisis led to Wladysław Gomułka being reappointed as Party Secretary. He had been jailed by Stalin in 1948 for being too much of a Polish nationalist, to the detriment of socialism. Khrushchev freed him and agreed to Gomułka's reinstatement.

Gomułka maintained Poland as a Marxist–Leninist state within the Warsaw Pact, with some concessions to his fellow countrymen. For example, Cardinal Wyszcyński, head of the Roman Catholic Church in Poland and outspoken critic of the regime, was released from prison. Collectivization in the countryside was reversed. Even so, Gomułka was very far from being a political liberal and the PUWP continued to be the dominant force in Polish politics.

In the 1960s, Gomułka lost popularity as significant improvements in the standard of living failed to materialize and censorship was strengthened. In 1970, the government's decision to increase food prices by 20 per cent led to strikes in the shipyards of the port of Gdańsk. At least 50 people were killed as the security forces aggressively restored order and the crisis led to Gomułka's resignation and his replacement by Edward Gierek, a communist official.

Discontent in Poland during the 1970s

After an initial period during which Gierek raised workers' wages and extended social welfare benefits to farm workers, the 1970s saw growing dissatisfaction with the PUWP. The new economic programme failed to deal with the fundamental problem in the Polish economy: military expenses and food shortages. Strikes and protests acted as a catalyst for the development of opposition groups, similar to those that sprang up elsewhere in eastern Europe.

The most important of these opposition groups was the Workers' Defence Committee (KOR). Illegal periodicals such as KOR's *Kommunikaty* were circulated by hand from person to person.

The Catholic Church

Another reason for the growing unpopularity of communism was the role played in the national life of Poland by the Catholic Church, which remained an extremely influential, independent, nation-wide organization following the imposition of communist rule.

In the 1970s, over 20 million Poles attended church services on a regular basis and 95 per cent of the population was baptized. Catholics received a massive boost in 1978, when Cardinal Karol Wojtyła became the first Polish-born Pope, known as John Paul II. This spurred many Poles to assert their commitment to Catholicism as opposed to Marxism. In June 1979 the Pope visited Poland. For a brief moment, ordinary Poles were given the opportunity in public to demonstrate their loyalty to something other than Marxism–Leninism and they seized the moment with enthusiasm.

SOURCE R

Excerpts from *The Crystal Spirit: Lech Wałęsa and His Poland* by Mary Craig, published by Hodder & Stoughton, London, UK, pages 154–5. Craig is a British writer and biographer.

Gierek and the Party had hovered between delight and dismay at the time of his [the Pope's] election, but had finally settled for a cautious chauvinistic pride in this 'son of the Polish nation, which is building the greatness and prosperity of its Socialist fatherland with the unity and co-operation of all its citizens.'

… Miners, the darlings of the regime, defying a government ban, turned out in their thousands, wearing their traditional dress. The regime knew the baffling humiliation of a quarter of a million miners singing: 'Christ has conquered. Christ is king, Christ commands our lives' at full throttle.

The media did their best to play down the visit, to give it a minor place in the evening TV bulletins … But nobody was fooled, … [Pope] John Paul spoke to the whole of Poland, giving voice to truths that had too long been silenced, convincing the people that social renewal was possible only at the price of their own moral renewal.

According to Source R, were the reactions of the government and the people of Poland to the Pope?

By 1980, the Polish government was in a very weak position. Gierek's authority had been undermined both by the Pope's visit and by his failure to successfully address the economic crisis. By this stage, Poland's debt to the West had risen to $25 billion, which necessitated exporting as much as possible in order to generate hard currency. This, in turn, compounded shortages at home.

The Solidarity Movement

In September 1980, the Solidarity trade union (see page 108) was formally established on a legal basis. As the movement developed, its demands became more explicitly political and it became engaged in a power struggle with the communist government.

Strikes in Gdańsk

In August 1980, the government announced an increase in meat prices by 100 per cent. Seventeen thousand shipyard workers in Gdańsk began a strike. The most prominent leader of the protests and the chairman of the shipyards' strike committee was electrician Lech Wałęsa. Within a week, the strike spread to more than 250 factories and over 150,000 workers were involved.

On 31 August 1980, the government agreed to Wałęsa's demands for wage increases, the establishment of independent trade unions, the relaxation of censorship and the release from prison of civil rights activists. General Secretary Gierek resigned on 6 September 1980 and was replaced by Politburo member Stanisław Kania.

SOURCE S

Lech Wałęsa being acclaimed by Gdańsk shipyard workers in 1980.

? Assess the value and limitations of Source S for historians studying the development of Solidarity during the 1980s.

Solidarity's challenge to the communist regime

Solidarity hoped to avoid a Soviet invasion of Poland by accepting the leading political role of the PUWP. Solidarity's very existence, however, was a challenge to the communist regime; its political agenda was different from the PUWP as it called for democratic reforms. Solidarity soon had the support of the majority of manual workers in the country. In December 1980, this prompted the Soviet Politburo to authorize Red Army troop manoeuvres on the border with Poland, a sign that military intervention, as had happened in Hungary in 1956 and Czechoslovakia in 1968, was being considered. The Soviet Politburo, however, decided not to sanction an invasion of Poland, a crucial break with the past, partly due to the fact that Soviet forces were already heavily involved in Afghanistan. US President Carter also cautioned the Soviets that intervention would heighten global tensions.

In addition, Kania persuaded Brezhnev that a Soviet invasion would trigger a national uprising. Other senior Soviet Politburo figures, such as Gromyko, were convinced that military intervention would be a disaster. By 1981, Solidarity was a mass movement with 10 million members out of a population of 38 million. Emboldened by the relaxation of censorship, in September it sent a 'Message to Working Class People in Eastern Europe', offering to help establish independent trade unions.

The economy continued to lurch from crisis to crisis with both inflation and food shortages, especially meat, creating hardship. By the end of 1981, a political stalemate between Solidarity and the government was reached. Negotiations between the two sides had made no significant progress and police prevented Solidarity members from working in certain sectors of the economy, such as the arms industry.

Poland under Jaruzelski 1981–9

In October 1981, the Defence Minister and Premier, General Jaruzelski, became First Secretary of the Polish Communist Party, replacing Kania, in whom the Soviets had lost confidence. Jaruzelski had close ties with the Soviet regime and with Andropov in particular. On 13 December 1981, in response to the Solidarity demand for a referendum on the future of the PUWP and relations with the USSR, Jaruzelski declared martial law and a state of emergency. The Army Council of National Salvation was given power; banning political meetings and imposing strict curfews. As a consequence, Solidarity was banned and its leader, Lech Wałęsa, arrested along with many others. Forty-nine internment camps were created to deal with the influx of Solidarity prisoners.

Jaruzelski maintained the political fabric of the communist state and crushed the wave of Solidarity-led strikes. The economic situation remained extremely severe and Jaruzelski asked the USSR for a loan of $700 million to help it service its debts. This was not forthcoming but, in 1981, the Soviet government did deliver 13 million tons of petrol, for which the Polish government was charged 90 roubles a ton (the world market price at the time was 170 roubles a ton). This was an example of the Soviet subsidies that were required by the early 1980s in order to stabilize fragile governments of the Warsaw Pact. However, the USSR had economic problems of its own and was unable to continue subsidizing Poland and other eastern European countries for much longer.

Stagnation

Under the rule of Jaruzelski, Poland stagnated in similar fashion to the USSR under Brezhnev. The country's economic problems remained severe and in 1986, the government defaulted on $1.4 billion of debt repayments to the West. Martial law was not relaxed until 1983 and by 1986 most political prisoners had been released. Solidarity was banned, but it continued to circulate illegal newsletters and journals that condemned the military coup. It received support from the West.

Gorbachev visited Poland in July 1988 and admitted that there were difficulties in the history of interactions between the two countries. This was a coded reference to Stalin's massacre of Polish army officers at Katyn in 1940 – a long-running grievance for Poles. In 1990, the Soviet government admitted responsibility for that crime.

How did the communist regime in Poland collapse in 1989?

→ The end of communist rule in Poland

In 1989, the Poland's economy entered another crisis and its debt now stood at $56 billion. The cost of food had gone up by an average of 48 per cent in 1988, leading to further strikes.

Jaruzelski, acting on the advice of the Catholic Church, began talks with Wałęsa and Solidarity in February 1989. Wałęsa persuaded workers to end their strikes and, even more significantly, agreement was reached for new elections in June 1989. Solidarity was made legal. Jaruzelski mistakenly believed that he could win these elections. Solidarity re-emerged as by far the most popular political movement in Poland and it won 99 out of the 100 seats that it was permitted to contest in the **Senate**. In the lower house of parliament, the **Sejm**, Solidarity was permitted to contest 35 per cent of the seats and won 160 out of 161 seats where it fielded candidates. This was a spectacular victory.

 **KEY TERM**

Senate Upper house of the Polish parliament.

Sejm Lower house of the Polish parliament.

Talks were held about the formation of a power-sharing coalition government. Gorbachev intervened by informing Mieczsław Rakowsi, the new First Secretary of the PUWP, that Poland could no longer function as a single-party state. Rakowksi was pragmatic enough to accept this political reality and so a negotiated transition ensued. In August 1989, a coalition government formed, with a member of Solidarity, Tadeusz Mazowiecki, as the first non-communist Prime Minister in more than 40 years. The PUWP's leading role and the compulsory alliance with the USSR still remained key features of the Polish Constitution, but this soon changed.

In December 1989, the Marxist–Leninist preamble to the Polish constitution was abolished and the name of the state was changed from the Polish People's Republic back to the Polish Republic. In the same month, Wałęsa was elected as President to replace Jaruzelski, although the relatively low voter turnout of 53 per cent suggests that disillusionment with Solidarity had started to develop. Demoralized by the collapse of communism in Czechoslovakia and East Germany, the PUWP dissolved in January 1990. This heralded the end of communist influence in Poland.

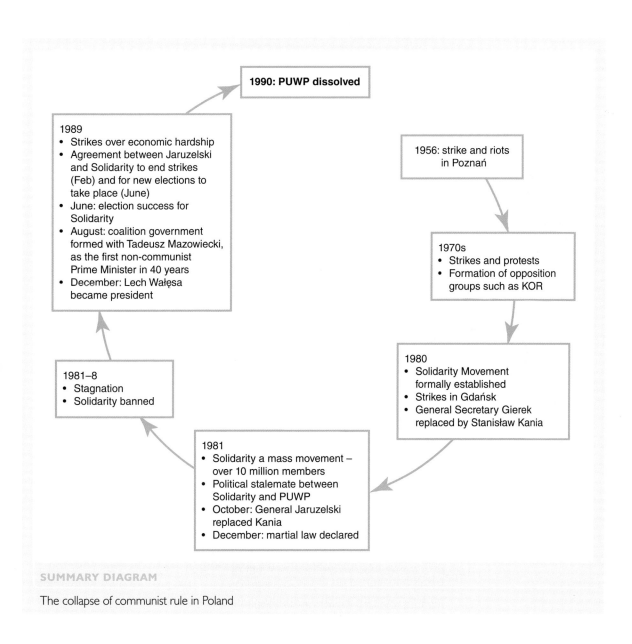

SUMMARY DIAGRAM

The collapse of communist rule in Poland

5 Key debate

> ▶ *Key question:* Why did communist rule in eastern Europe collapse at the end of the 1980s?

Changes in the USSR

The emphasis in the writings of many historians is on changes in the USSR that made a relatively sudden collapse of communist rule in eastern Europe possible. For instance, political scientist and historian Archie Brown makes the point that the communist regimes in eastern Europe were always inherently unstable as they relied not on popular consent or support, but in the last resort, on Soviet troops (see Source T). Therefore, Gorbachev's decision not to implement the Brezhnev Doctrine was always likely to provoke a popular backlash, which the repressive governments of Jaruzelski, Honecker and Jakeš would then find it very difficult to control.

SOURCE T

?
According to Source T, what were the key reasons for the collapse of communist rule in eastern Europe?

Excerpt from *The Gorbachev Factor* by Archie Brown, published by Oxford University Press, Oxford, UK, 1996, page 247. Brown is Professor Emeritus of Politics at Oxford University, UK, and an expert in Russian and Eurasian Studies.

But there is no need to search far to find the main stimuli to change. These were the relative failure of the regimes both in economic terms and in terms of political socialization of the population into acceptance of Communist values. Western Europe presented far more attractive and successful economic and political models than anything on offer from the Soviet Union ... The essential point is that the Communist regimes of Eastern Europe existed because the Soviet Union had put them in place – by force of arms or threat of force – and had been ready to intervene to sustain them in power. The sudden collapse of the systems, accordingly, requires no elaborate explanation, although the internal situation varied greatly from one to another ...

Internal problems

It is certainly possible that communist governments in eastern Europe may still have collapsed, even if Gorbachev had never come to power. This is due to the scale of the problems confronted by these regimes by the 1980s. The governments of Poland, East Germany and Czechoslovakia all lacked democratic legitimacy and this became more of a political issue once the USSR had signed up to the Helsinki Accords (see page 111). An even bigger problem was the stagnant and indebted state of almost all eastern European economies, presided over by self-perpetuating élites who increasingly lacked any sort of real faith in Marxism–Leninism.

SOURCE U

Excerpt from *The Cold War: The Great Powers and Their Allies*, second edition, by John P.D. Dunbabin, published by Pearson Education, Harlow, UK, 2008, pages 577–8. Dunbabin is a former Reader in International Relations at Oxford University, UK.

There had always been fears that the collapse of any one communist state could bring down more … In 1989, the Polish (and more gradually) the Hungarian parties relinquished power, setting off a chain reaction.

Perhaps we need look no further. But one could see other developments converging to promote a general crisis of communism. One factor common to all Warsaw Pact members except Czechoslovakia was high hard currency debt. Servicing this led to the squeezing of living standards and corresponding discontent …

It may be, too, that people had always been aware of higher living standards in the West … But images and information were now more readily available than ever before, from Western radio and tapes, from West German, Austrian and (along the Adriatic) Italian television, and, indeed, from the post-glasnost Soviet and Hungarian media.

Alongside this went a collapse in communist belief … By the later 1980s the East European, and Soviet, parties had become ideologically broad churches, still retaining authoritarian Leninists but also people who had essentially become social democrats, plus many who were simply government-oriented politicians and administrators, as ready to operate within liberal capitalism as Marxist socialism.

Finally, there were the changes in the Soviet Union. These do not constitute a sufficient explanation for the passing of communism in eastern Europe, for this occurred also in Yugoslavia and Albania, which had long left the Soviet sphere. But within it, Moscow mattered. …

Gorbachev says that at his first meeting with Warsaw Pact leaders in 1985, he implied that the Brezhnev Doctrine was a thing of the past.

According to Source U, what were the key reasons for the collapse of communist rule in eastern Europe?

The role of the people

Other historians give much credit to the ordinary people of the USSR and eastern European countries who helped to create a crisis of communism as a form of government. Historian John Lewis Gaddis uses the metaphor of a 'sandpile ready to slide' to explain the situation across eastern Europe at the beginning of 1989 and he argues that those responsible for dropping the final few grains of sand which precipitated political change were the ordinary citizens of Poland, East Germany and Czechoslovakia.

?

According to Source V,
what were the key reasons
for the collapse of communist
rule in eastern Europe?

SOURCE V

Excerpt from *The Cold War: A New History* by John Lewis Gaddis, published by Penguin Books, New York, USA, 2006, pages 238–9. Gaddis is a Professor of History at Yale University, USA.

Nevertheless, the upheavals of 1989, like those of 1789, caught everyone by surprise. Historians could of course look back, after the fact, and specify causes: frustration that the temporary divisions of the World War Two settlement had become the permanent divisions of the post-war era … resentment over the failure of command economies to raise living standards … the unexpected emergence of independent *standards for making moral judgements …*

What no one understood at the beginning of 1989 was that the Soviet Union, its empire, its ideology – and therefore the Cold War itself – was a sandpile ready to slide. All it took to make it happen were a few more grains of sand. The people who dropped them were not in charge of superpowers or movements or religions: they were ordinary people with simple priorities who saw, seized and sometimes stumbled into opportunities. In doing so they caused a collapse no one could stop. Their 'leaders' had little choice but to follow.

One particular leader, however, did so in a distinctive way. He ensured that the great 1989 revolution was the first one ever in which almost no blood was shed. There were no guillotines, no heads on pikes, no officially sanctioned mass murders. People did die but in remarkably small numbers for the size and significance of what was happening. In both its ends and its means, then, this revolution became a triumph of hope. It did so chiefly because Mikhail Gorbachev chose not to act, but rather to be acted upon.

Weakness of communism as a system of government

Some historians assign a minor role to internal problems in Warsaw Pact countries and changes in the USSR. Instead, more emphasis is given to a denunciation of communism itself, as an ideology of government.

SOURCE W

Excerpt from *Strategic Vision: America and the Crisis of Global Power* by Zbigniew Brzezinski, published by Basic Books, New York, USA, 2012, pages 42–3. Brzezinski was National Security Advisor to US President Carter from 1977 to 1981 and teaches US Foreign Policy at Johns Hopkins University, USA.

For a variety of reasons – with some rooted in Soviet policy errors and some in domestic ideological sterility, bureaucratic degeneration and socioeconomic stagnation, not to mention the mounting political unrest in eastern Europe and hostility from China – the Soviet Union imploded …

On the other hand, the Marxist school of historical analysis criticizes the moral bankruptcy of communism as a viable system of government. In the end, many party members were playing a role and not really believing in communist rule with conviction.

SOURCE X

Excerpt from *Age of Extremes: The Short Twentieth Century 1914–1991* by Eric Hobsbawm, published by Michael Joseph, London, 1994, pages 488–9. Hobsbawm was a well-known British Marxist historian.

Yet hardly anyone believed in the system or felt any loyalty to it, not even those who governed it. They were no doubt surprised when the masses finally abandoned their passivity and demonstrated their dissidence … At the moment of truth no East European government ordered its forces to fire. All abdicated quietly, except in Romania, and even their resistance was brief. Perhaps they could not have regained control, but nobody even tried. No groups of communist ultras anywhere prepared to die in the bunker for their faith, or even for the far-from-unimpressive record of forty years' communist rule in a number of these states. What should they have defended? Economic systems whose inferiority to their Western neighbours leaped to the eye which were running down, and which had proved to be un-reformable, even where serious and intelligent efforts at reform had been made? Systems which had plainly lost the justification that had sustained their communist cadres in the past, namely that socialism was superior to capitalism and destined to replace it? Who could any longer believe that, though it had not looked implausible in the 1940s or even the 1950s? … In any case, in Europe as in the USSR, the communists who had once been sustained by the old convictions, were now a generation of the past … Even party members among the less-than-elderly were likely to be not communists in the old sense, but men and women (alas, far too few women) who made careers in countries that happened to be under communist rule. When times changed, and if they were allowed to, they were ready at a moment's notice to change their coats. In short, those who ran the Soviet satellite regimes had lost their faith in their own systems or had never really had it.

> Compare and contrast Sources W and X regarding the key reasons for the collapse of communist rule in eastern Europe. **?**

The role of SDI

Right-wing historians have also been tempted to give a lot of credit for the collapse of the Soviet sphere of influence, and indeed of the USSR itself, to US President Reagan's SDI programme. According to this thesis, the costs of trying to match SDI imposed an intolerable economic burden on the USSR and forced Gorbachev into scaling down the USSR's imperial commitments as quickly as possible. There are several flaws in this argument. At first, Reagan's announcement of SDI failed to drive either Chernenko or Andropov to the negotiating table, and, initially, it also seemed to achieve little in terms of prompting a relaxation of the Soviet grip on eastern Europe. Therefore, the threat of SDI on its own was clearly not enough to prompt a reassessment of Soviet foreign policy, especially as Soviet and western scientists rightly doubted the technical feasibility of Star Wars.

> **TOK**
>
> Historians use evidence to make arguments. Review the sources above. What gives evidence value and makes it convincing? (History, Ethics, Language, Emotion, Reason.)

Chapter summary

The collapse of Soviet influence in eastern Europe

Diplomatic relations between the USA and the USSR improved considerably between 1985 and 1989. The signing of the INF Treaty in 1987 removed a large number of nuclear weapons from Europe and illustrated how much diplomatic progress had been made since 1985.

The collapse of communism in Poland, East Germany and Czechoslovakia cannot be understood without reference to this improved international context in which control over satellite states in eastern Europe became less of a strategic priority for the Soviet leadership. The fact that Gorbachev proved unwilling to enforce the Brezhnev Doctrine may have allowed protest movements to develop in eastern Europe.

In East Germany, Gorbachev's visit to the GDR in October 1989 acted as a catalyst for political discontent and he explicitly stated that he was unwilling for Red Army troops to be used in order to maintain Honecker's repressive regime. Already weakened by the exodus of refugees via Hungary, Honecker struggled to contain the demonstrations in Leipzig and was removed in October 1989. His replacement, Egon Krenz, bowed to the inevitable and relaxed travel restrictions for East Germany's citizens. This led directly to the fall of the Berlin Wall in November 1989, a fatal blow to the long-term prospects of the East German state. Krenz (and the SED) soon fell from power and within less than a year the GDR had collapsed and Germany was reunified.

Following the repression of the Prague Spring, Czechoslovakia had endured a period of totalitarian communist rule, euphemistically entitled normalization. However, the political *status quo* was altered in 1989 with the advent of student protests. Václav Havel helped to establish Civic Forum to co-ordinate the disparate opposition movement. The communist government lacked the explicit backing from the USSR and the consent of its own citizens for harsh repressive measures. The CPC felt that they had no choice but to agree to the formation of a coalition government. The symbolic end of the CPC's political dominance came on 29 December 1989, when former dissident Václav Havel became President.

The communist government in Poland was almost toppled in 1981. Solidarity, led by Lech Wałęsa, challenged the regime and was legally recognized. The USSR was tempted to intervene, but failed to do so partly as a result of its involvement in Afghanistan. A military coup by General Jaruzelski in December 1981 drove Solidarity underground, granting the government temporary respite. Economic problems were not solved by the communist government, leading to constant unrest and major debt. Both Solidarity and the Catholic Church remained committed to opposing the PUWP and, with Gorbachev unwilling to sanction military intervention, by 1989 the communist government had decided to negotiate with the political opposition. This paved the way for elections and the formation of a coalition government that ended the PUWP's monopoly of power.

Examination practice

Below are some exam-style questions for you to practise. Paper 1 exams are one hour long, not including five minutes of reading time at the exam's start when only reading is permitted. You may wish to only practise specific questions, and if this is the case, allow the following amounts of time per question:

Question 1:	5 minute
Question 2:	10 minutes
Question 3:	10 minutes
Question 4:	35 minutes

These questions relate to the collapse of communist regimes in Poland, East Germany and Czechoslovakia. The sources used are found within this chapter on the following pages:

- Source C (page 169)
- Source D (page 170)
- Source N (page 184)
- Source O (page 186)
- Source R (page 191)
- Source S (page 192)

1 a) What, according to Source R, were the reactions to the Pope's visit to Poland?   *(3 marks)*
     (For guidance on how to answer this style of question see page 37.)

   b) What is the message conveyed by Source S?   *(2 marks)*
     (For guidance on how to answer this style of question see page 41).

2) Compare and contrast the views expressed in Sources C and D about the reasons for the collapse of Soviet influence in eastern Europe.   *(6 marks)*
     (For guidance on how to answer this style of question see page 91.)

3) With reference to their origin and purpose, assess the value and limitations of Source N and Source O for historians studying the Velvet Revolution.   *(6 marks)*
     (For guidance on how to answer this style of question see page 130.)

4) Using these sources (Sources C, D, N, O, R) and your own knowledge, analyse the key reasons for the collapse of communist rule in Poland, East Germany and Czechoslovakia.   *(8 marks)*
     (For guidance on how to answer this style of question see page 160.)

 Activities

I Make a table summarizing the sequence of events that led to the collapse of communism in Poland, East Germany and Czechoslovakia. Then debate the extent to which the collapse of communism in these countries can be said to conform to a general pattern.

2 When revising this topic, work in groups of three and appoint one person to be the 'expert' on one of the following case studies: Poland, East Germany or Czechoslovakia. The 'expert' should write and present a summary of how and why communism collapsed in the country they are an expert on, and then be tested on their knowledge by the rest of the group.

3 All historical arguments are simply assertions unless they are backed up by evidence. Look at the statements below and decide how far you agree or disagree with them. You may wish to use a 10-point scale, with 10 equating to strong agreement with the statement and 1 equating to total disagreement with the statement. Then make a list of evidence to support your point of view on each statement.

- Gorbachev could have preserved Soviet influence in eastern Europe if he had acted with greater determination.

- The political achievements of both Lech Wałęsa and Václav Havel have been exaggerated by posterity.

- By 1989 the collapse of communist regimes in Poland, East Germany and Czechoslovakia could not have been prevented.

Timeline

USSR

1917	October Revolution
1928–53	Stalin is leader of the USSR
1956–64	Nikita Khruschev is First Secretary of the CPSU
1964	Leonid Breshnev becomes First Secretary of the CPSU
1968	Prague Spring
1970	Moscow Treaty
1972	Basic Treaty
	US President Nixon visits USSR
	SALT I
1973	Brezhnev visits USA
	October War between Egypt and Israel
1974	US President Nixon visits USSR
	Watergate Scandal
1975	Helsinki Accords
1976–80	Tenth Five Year Plan
1977	New Constitution replaces 1936 Constitution
1978	Camp David Accords
1979	SALT II
1979–88	Soviet military intervention in Afghanistan
1980	Solidarity trade union formally established in Poland
1981	General Wojciech Jaruzelski's coup in Poland
1982	Brezhnev dies. Yuri Andropov becomes General Secretary of the CPSU

1984	Konstantin Chernenko becomes General Secretary of the CPSU
1985	Gorbachev becomes leader of the USSR
	Policies of *perestroika* and *glasnost* introduced
	Geneva Summit
1985–8	Anti-alcohol campaign
1986	Chernobyl nuclear explosion
	Reykjavik Summit
1987	Washington Summit
1988	Moscow Summit
	Geneva Agreement
1989	Congress of People's Deputies multi-party elections
	Fall of Berlin Wall
	Velvet Revolution in Czechoslovakia
	Malta Summit
	Collapse of communist regime in Poland
1990	Gorbachev becomes president of the USSR
	Reunification of Germany
1991	Coup against Gorbachev
	Collapse of USSR, creation of Commonwealth of Independent States

PRC

1949		People's Republic of China (PRC) founded
1965		Start of the Cultural Revolution
1972		US President Nixon visits Beijing
1976	January	Zhou Enlai's death
	April	Tiananmen Incident Hua Guofeng becomes Premier
	September	Mao's death
	October	Hua Guofeng becomes Chairman of the Central Committee Gang of Four arrested
1977		End of the Cultural Revolution announced by the Eleventh Party Congress
1978		Start of Ten Year Plan Four Modernizations introduced
1978–9		Democracy Wall Movement
1979		Household responsibility system introduced
	January	Deng Xiaoping visits the USA
	February	PLA invades Vietnam; retreats after 21 days
		First Special Economic Zones established
1980	January	One-child policy becomes law
1980	November	Trial of the Gang of Four

1981		Hua Guofeng resigns as Chairman of the Party and Chairman of the Military Committee
1984		Agreement reached between PRC and UK about sovereignty of Hong Kong
1985		Law of Succession
1986		Student protests start in Hefei and spread to Beijing, Shanghai and Wuhan
1987		Deng's resignation from the Central Committee
1989	15 April	Hu Yaobang dies Protests start in Tiananmen Square
	20 May	Martial law proclaimed
	3–4 June	Tiananmen Square cleared of protesters by PLA
		Full economic links established between USSR and PRC

Glossary

ABM Treaty An anti-ballistic missile treaty preventing the development of anti-missile defence systems, signed by the USA and the USSR in 1972.

Akademgorodok 'Academy Town' in Russian; also known as the Novosibirsk Scientific Centre, built to house scientists and innovators in a pleasant atmosphere to foster creativity.

Apparatchik Usually used in a pejorative sense to describe faceless administrators and bureaucrats.

Article 6 The 1977 Soviet constitution article that guaranteed the monopoly of the CPSU as the only ruling party in the USSR.

Basic Treaty Treaty between the FRG and the GDR in 1972 that led to the exchange of permanent diplomatic missions between the two countries and to both joining the UN.

Bolshevik The Russian Communist Party. It seized power in a revolution in October 1917.

Bourgeoisie The middle class, particularly business interests, who Marx believed benefited most from the existing capitalist economic system.

Brezhnev Doctrine Brezhnev's assertion that if any Warsaw Pact member threatened socialism, it was the right and duty of the rest of the members to engage in military intervention.

Cadres Professional revolutionaries willing to devote all their time and effort to the communist cause.

Camp David Accords Series of agreements regarding borders and military considerations between Egypt and Israel that were signed at US Presidential retreat Camp David in 1978.

Capitalism An economic system in which wealth is largely in private hands, and goods and services are exchanged in order to generate profit.

Capitalist roader The epithet used against those who criticized Mao's interpretation of communism.

CCP Plenum Discussion forums within the Central Committee usually guided by members of the Politburo.

Central Advisory Commission A powerful body of CCP elders, all of whom had been members of the party for at least 40 years. It wielded a lot of political power behind the scenes during the 1980s.

Central Committee A key body within the CCP with membership of up to 300 people meeting at least twice a year, electing new members of the Politburo.

Charge d'affaires An interim diplomat who substitutes for a missing ambassador or minister.

Charter 77 Human rights association of hundreds of Czechoslovak intellectuals and dissidents that advocated democracy; established in 1977.

Chechens Chechen-speaking Muslim peoples indigenous to the Northern Caucasus, between the Black Sea and the Caspian Sea.

Chinese People's Political Consultative Conference An advisory body to the Chinese government made up of delegates from the CCP and other political groups.

CIA Central Intelligence Agency, a US government espionage organization.

Civic Forum Czechoslovak non-violent civic association that quickly became a political force in November 1989.

Client state A country that depends on economic, military and/or political support from a more powerful one.

Colbert A successful French economic reformer in the reign of Louis XIV of France in the late seventeenth and early eighteenth centuries.

Cold War A tense 40-year strategic and ideological confrontation between the superpowers, USA and USSR, after the Second World War. It is named 'cold' because there was never a direct conflagration between the two opposing powers.

Collectivization   Centrally planned and managed farming where peasants farm communally on large areas of land rather than for themselves individually.

COMECON   A communist trading bloc established in eastern Europe in response to the Soviet perception of growing US economic influence in Europe.

Comintern   A communist organization set up in Moscow in 1919 to co-ordinate the efforts of communists around the world to achieve a global revolution.

Commonwealth of Independent States   A loose association of Soviet republics formed in December 1991 as a successor to the USSR. It differed from the USSR by asserting that all member states were fully sovereign and independent.

Communism   Political and economic system in which the working class is the only class, there is no private ownership of property, and usually the government directs all aspects of the economy.

Conventional arms   These include small arms and light weapons, sea and land mines, (non-nuclear) bombs, shells, rockets and missiles. They are not biological, chemical or nuclear, but are explosive.

Counter-espionage   Efforts to prevent spying.

Counter-revolutionary   Political action made in opposition to an earlier political change.

Coup   An abrupt seizure of power, or takeover of a country, by the military or another armed group.

Credit rating   A judgement on the ability of a nation to pay back loans.

Crimean Tatars   Turkish-speaking Muslim peoples of the Crimea, located on the north coast of the Black Sea.

Cult of personality   The active encouragement of intense devotion and adulation of a political leader, for the purpose of maintaining power.

Cultural Revolution   Mao's attempt from 1966 to revolutionize Chinese society and the CCP, while at the same time dealing with political rivals.

Democratic Russia   A pro-Yeltsin political coalition that began to challenge the political monopoly of the CPSU from 1990 onwards.

Détente   A French word meaning relaxing or loosening; refers to the relaxing of tensions in the Cold War.

Developing economies   National economies which are in the process of being developed to raise living standards.

Dictatorship of the proletariat   A term used by Marx to suggest that following the overthrow of the bourgeoisie, government would be carried out by and on behalf of the working class.

Dissident   A person who challenges the political *status quo* in a single-party state.

First strike   A term used to describe a pre-emptive nuclear attack by one superpower on another.

Five Year Plan   A series of economic development plans imposed by Stalin between 1928 and 1941 that concentrated all industry under state control.

Foreign currency reserves   Foreign currencies and precious metals, like gold, that a country holds in its central bank.

Four cardinal principles   Deng Xiaoping's declaration on the nature of the PRC's government that stated that the PRC was a single-party state under the control of the CCP.

Four Modernizations   The set of policies promoted by Deng Xiaoping after 1978 which introduced significant elements of capitalism into the Chinese economy.

FRG   Federal Republic of Germany, a capitalist state set up in 1949, amalgamating the British, US and French zones of occupation.

Gang of Four   A term allegedly coined by Mao himself to describe a group of influential leftist politicians who became powerful as radical activists defending strict Maoism in the mid-1960s during the Cultural Revolution and continued in power until after Mao's death in 1976.

GDP   Gross domestic product, or what a country makes in selling the goods and services it produces in a year.

GDR German Democratic Republic, a communist state established in 1949 in the Soviet zone of occupied Germany.

Geneva Agreement Signed in April 1988 in Geneva by Afghanistan and Pakistan to agree on non-interference and non-intervention, return of refugees and Soviet withdrawal from Afghanistan, with international guarantees by the USA and the USSR.

German question During the Cold War, this term referred to issues emanating from the sovereignty and potential reunification of East and West Germany.

German reunification The idea of reuniting East and West Germany into a single state.

Gerontocracy A state whose political élite is almost exclusively comprised of a narrow circle of elderly men.

Glasnost Russian for 'openness'. Gorbachev's policy of government transparency, where citizens were encouraged to point out ineffectiveness in industry and the economy, in order to work toward solutions and improvements.

GOSPLAN A government committee set up in 1921 which was responsible for centralized economic planning.

Great Leap Forward Ambitious and ultimately disastrous programme of industrialization and social revolution embarked on by Mao from 1958.

Great Patriotic War What the Second World War was known as in the USSR.

Guerrilla warfare Use of the military technique of ambush and the avoidance of open battle, usually in order to avoid defeat against a technologically more sophisticated opponent.

Guomindang A republican and nationalist political party founded by Sun Yat Sen, which controlled the Chinese government between 1926 and 1949.

Hard currency A strong currency unlikely to lose its value; traded on global markets.

Hawk Refers to a person likely to react strongly and even use military force in world conflicts.

Hegemony A term deriving from ancient Greek used to describe those countries which establish political and military dominance over their neighbours.

Helsinki Accords An agreement between the Soviet bloc and the West for acceptance of existing boundaries and for economic, commercial and scientific collaboration. The final clause included respect for human rights.

Hong Kong A colony of Britain from the mid-nineteenth century until 1997.

Household responsibility system From 1980, peasants were allowed to lease land from the state and to generate a profit by selling surpluses.

ICBM Intercontinental nuclear ballistic missile.

Inter-Regional Group Opposition party emerging from the Congress of People's Deputies.

Intermediate-range Nuclear Forces Treaty A treaty that eliminated Soviet and US nuclear missiles with a range of between 500 and 5000 km.

Intershops Special stores in select East German cities that sold products from the West for hard currency.

Isvestia A leading, official newspaper in the USSR.

Joint ventures When two or more parties engage in an economic activity together by sharing control, investment and profits.

KGB State Security Committee or Soviet secret police, founded in 1954, from the Russian *Komitet Gosudarstvennoi Bezopasnosti*.

Khalq A faction of the People's Democratic Party of Afghanistan strongly influenced by Stalinist ideas.

Kolkhozy Collective farms made up of different families who farmed on state land according to centrally planned production directives and quotas, although production surpluses could be sold on the open market.

Komsomol CPSU youth organization which at its peak in the 1970s had tens of millions of members.

Leftist   The more extreme wing of the CCP, typified by the Gang of Four, committed to a radical interpretation of Mao's ideas.

Little Red Book   The informal name commonly used in the West for the pocket-size edition of *Quotations from Chairman Mao Zedong*, where he summarizes his wisdom.

Long March   An evacuation of southern China by the CCP in 1934 as a response to Nationalist attacks. Only 10 per cent of those beginning the march survived when it concluded a year later in northern China.

Lutheran Church   The main Protestant Church in East Germany.

Macau   A colony of Portugal in southern China until 1999.

Maoism   A form of Marxism developed by Mao that advocated development of communism through the peasantry with elements of Chinese nationalism.

Maoist   A dedicated supporter of Mao's radical policies.

Market socialism   China's blend of a communist command economy with capitalist reforms such as a free price system and a mix of state and privately owned businesses and industries.

Martial law   The suspension of civil law and the constitution and its replacement by military rule.

Marxism–Leninism   The original teachings of Marx which were adjusted by Lenin to deal with the economic, social and political conditions of Russia.

Meiji period   A time of economic and social reform in Japan from 1868 to 1912 during which Japan successfully industrialized.

Military Affairs Commission   A key political body which controlled the People's Liberation Army.

MIRV   Multiple independently targetable re-entry vehicle: a nuclear missile equipped with multiple warheads, therefore capable of hitting more than one target.

Most favoured nation trading status   A term used to describe countries, such as China, granted favourable terms of economic exchange with the USA.

Mujaheddin   Islamic warriors, usually guerrilla fighters.

Mullah   A religiously educated leader of a mosque or an Islamic cleric.

Nationalism   Political ideology which favours individuals associating with other members of a nation or national group, in order to promote the interests and coherent collective identity of that group.

NATO   North Atlantic Treaty Organization, a military alliance of the USA, Canada, and much of western Europe.

Nazi–Soviet Pact   Non-aggression pact signed between Germany and the USSR in August 1939 that included a secret protocol assigning the independent states of Lithuania, Latvia and Estonia to the Soviet sphere of influence.

NEP   Mixed capitalist and strict Marxist economic system instituted by Lenin in 1921 to improve food and industrial production in the new communist state.

New Forum   Pro-democracy movement founded in East Germany in September 1989 which led to public demonstrations that accelerated the end of barriers between East and West Berlin and the end of communist government in East Germany.

Nicolai Bukharin   A prominent Politburo member in the 1920s who supported Lenin's NEP and was executed in 1938 during one of Stalin's purges.

Nomenklatura   The powerful class of officials and bureaucrats that emerged during the Brezhnev era.

Normalization   The creation or resumption of regular diplomatic relations usually including an exchange of ambassadors and the establishment of embassies.

Normalization   Used to describe the period of repression and stagnation in Czechoslovakia in the aftermath of the Prague Spring Movement.

One country–two systems A term used to describe Deng's strategy of reunifying China by allowing former colonies such as Hong Kong a measure of political, economic and cultural freedom, within the over-arching framework of the PRC.

One-child policy A policy introduced by the Chinese government to try to force married couples to have only one child to prevent population growth.

Open Door Policy Allowing foreign investment in the PRC.

Ostpolitik A German term meaning eastern policy; a West German effort to improve diplomatic relations with East Germany, eastern Europe and the USSR.

Parcham A moderate faction of the People's Democratic Party of Afghanistan.

Party Congress A representative body of the entire membership of the CCP which usually meets every four to five years to formally elect the Central Committee.

Patriarch The head of the Russian Orthodox Church.

People's congresses Legislative assemblies with limited power for political consultation under the leadership of the CCP.

People's Daily A Chinese newspaper with close links to the Central Committee of the CCP.

Perestroika Russian for 'reconstruction' or 'restructuring'. Gorbachev's policy of economic and political reform within the socialist system, to improve the standard of living and society in the USSR.

Pershing II US intermediate-range nuclear missiles.

PLA The People's Liberation Army, the military force of the CCP, which became the army of the Chinese state in 1949.

Politburo The Political Bureau of the Central Committee of the Communist Party of the Soviet Union whose members made most of the key policy and political decisions in the USSR.

Prague Spring Name given to the 1968 attempt by Czechoslovakia's Communist Party leader Alexander Dubček to liberalize socialism by allowing freedom of the press, expression and political reforms. The Warsaw Pact nations under the leadership of the USSR invaded the country and deposed Dubček.

Presidium Dominant, policy-making body within the CPSU formed by the Council of Ministers, renamed the Politburo in 1966.

Proletariat Marx's term for the industrial working class, primarily factory workers.

Proxy wars Name given to military conflicts during the Cold War in which the USA and the USSR participated only indirectly, avoiding direct confrontation.

PUWP The Polish United Workers' Party, the main Marxist–Leninist Party in Poland between 1948 and 1990.

Red Guards Maoist students who were trained to lead attacks against class enemies. They were the most dedicated supporters of the Cultural Revolution.

Red Rebels During the Cultural Revolution, young people who were not accepted into the Red Guards joined radical splinter groups called Red Rebels.

Rehabilitated Restored to previously held party and government positions.

Remittances Money sent back by a worker to a town or village of origin to support family members.

Rightist The more moderate wing of the CCP leadership led by Zhou Enlai until his death and thereafter by Deng Xiaoping.

Sąjūdis Political reform movement in favour of sovereignty and independence for Lithuania formed in 1988.

Satellite state A country which, while theoretically independent, is dominated by another.

Second economy An underground economy of small-scale capitalists and merchants that existed within the USSR.

SED Socialist Unity Party of Germany. The Marxist–Leninist party in East Germany established in 1946 by the merger between the Socialist Party (SPD) and the Communist Party (KPD).

Sejm Lower house of the Polish parliament.

Senate Upper house of the Polish parliament.

Shi'ite A Muslim who follows the Shia version of Islam.

Show trial A trial that is staged for the public, usually with the verdict decided well in advance.

Sinatra Doctrine A reference to the song *My Way*, made popular by US singer Frank Sinatra in 1969. It meant that eastern European countries would be allowed more autonomy from the USSR as of 1986.

SLBM Ballistic missile launched from a submarine with a nuclear warhead.

Socialism Political and economic system in which a nation's resources and means of production are controlled by the government to prevent extremes in wealth or poverty.

Socialism with a human face A term used to describe the less repressive and more liberal political and social system developed by Alexander Dubček in Czechoslovakia.

Solidarity Movement Non-communist trade union movement in Poland that used civil resistance to demand economic, social and other changes.

Soviet Union The Union of Soviet Socialist Republics was established in 1922, the biggest and most influential of which was Russia. Also known as the USSR.

Sovkhozy Groups of collective farms converted into huge agricultural enterprises run on an industrial model.

Sovnarkhozes New economic planning institutions, often translated as regional economic councils, set up by Khrushchev in 1957 that tried and failed to improve the Soviet economy by giving more autonomy to regions with regard to economic policy.

Special Administrative Region Parts of the PRC, such as Hong Kong, granted a degree of political autonomy in recognition of their colonial past and long history of separation from the rest of China.

Special Economic Zones (SEZs) Designated areas of China, usually on the coast, where foreign investors were encouraged by concessions like tax breaks to invest and set up businesses.

SS-20 Soviet intermediate-range nuclear missles.

SSR An acronym for Soviet Socialist Republic, of which there were 15 within the USSR.

Stagnation A state of inactivity or low economic growth.

Standing Committee A small, élite decision-making body within the Politburo of the CCP.

Star Wars Colloquial term used to refer to President Reagan's Strategic Defence Initiative, designed to set up a missile defence shield to protect against Soviet nuclear attack.

START Strategic arms reduction treaty between the USA and USSR limiting the amount of nuclear weapons that both superpowers could deploy.

Stasi Abbreviation from the German for Ministry for State Security. Through collaborators, informers and full-time *Stasi* secret police officials, the government controlled civil unrest and anti-communist activities.

State Council The main administrative body of the PRC government.

State-owned enterprises (SOEs) Factories and businesses owned and operated by the government in the PRC.

StB Acronym for the State Security Service of Czechoslovakia.

Superpower Term used to denote the USA and the USSR during the Cold War, as these were the first two nations to develop nuclear arms.

Tactical nuclear weapon Small nuclear device intended for use on the battlefield.

Taiwan An island off south-east China to which Chiang Kai-shek retreated when the communists took over the mainland. It has been known as the Republic of China since 1949.

Taizidang A Chinese term used to describe the children of high-ranking officials who used their connections to set up profitable businesses during the 1980s.

Taliban Ultra-conservative Islamic militants who took over a large part of Afghanistan in 1995, and in 1996 overran the capital of Kabul and declared an Islamic state.

Third World Cold War term for countries not in the First World (developed, capitalist countries) or the Second World (socialist and communist countries). The Third World included developing countries in Africa, Asia and Latin America.

Tiananmen Incident Political disturbances in Beijing following the death of Zhou Enlai (not to be confused with the 1989 student protests).

Tiananmen Papers A collection of CCP documents, published in the West in 2001, which include transcripts of key political meetings in 1989 attended by Deng Xiaoping, Zhao Ziyang and Li Peng.

Tolkachi Helpers or facilitators who had the contacts to procure commodities needed by industrial managers.

Town and village enterprises (TVEs) Private businesses permitted by the CCP as part of the Four Modernizations policy.

Trade surplus When a country sells more than it buys from other countries it trades with.

United Nations Declaration on Human Rights A statement of 30 human rights adopted by the UN in 1948.

Urban underclass The lowest socio-economic group in a city of poor, often unemployed, people.

USSR The Union of Soviet Socialist Republics was established in 1922, the biggest and most influential of which was Russia. Also known as the Soviet Union.

Vietnam War Part of the Cold War, this was a conflict that had started in 1954 between non-communist South Vietnam, supported by the USA, and communist North Vietnam. The USA left in 1973 and Vietnam was unified in 1975.

Virgin Lands Scheme Khrushchev's failed plan to farm more than 70 million acres of virgin land in Siberia and Kazakhstan in order to surpass the USA in agricultural production.

War Communism Soviet economic policies applied by Lenin and the Bolsheviks during the Russian Civil War.

Warsaw Pact A military alliance set up in 1955 between the USSR and its satellite states. The member countries were the USSR, East Germany, Poland, Czechoslovakia, Hungary, Romania, Bulgaria and Albania.

Watergate Scandal A general term used to portray an intricate web of political scandals by President Richard Nixon between 1972 and 1974, including the wire-tapping of the Democratic National Committee housed in the Watergate building in Washington, DC.

Whateverists A term used to describe supporters of Hua Guofeng who believed that Mao's economic and political legacy must be maintained.

Zhou Enlai Leading figure in the CCP, premier (1949–76) and foreign minister (1949–58).

Further reading

General background to communism and its place in the modern world

Darwin, J. *After Tamerlane: The Rise and Fall of Global Empires*, 1400–2000, Penguin, 2008
A very scholarly and analytical overview of global history since 1500, which in the final chapter considers the collapse of the USSR and China's rise.

Ferguson, N. *The War of the World: History's Age of Hatred*, Penguin, 2006
An assessment of the key trends in twentieth-century history by a well-known British academic with a talent for seeing the 'big picture' without falling prey to generalization.

Hobsbawm, E. *Age of Extremes: The Short Twentieth Century 1914–1991*, Penguin, 1994
A scholarly history of the key trends in twentieth-century history, from a left-wing perspective, by a celebrated British historian.

McLellan, D. *Karl Marx: The Legacy*, BBC Books, 1983
Lacks hindsight on events like Tiananmen Square and the collapse of the USSR due to its publication date, but still provides a clear and yet scholarly analysis of the development of left-wing ideas in the nineteenth and twentieth centuries; the first 50 pages in particular provide some very useful biographical background on Marx.

Priestland, D. *Communism and the Making of the Modern World*, Penguin, 2010.
One of the best histories of communism as an idea and how it took different forms in different historical contexts.

Service, R. *Comrades*, Macmillan, 2007
A global history of communism by a leading British academic and expert on Soviet history.

Wheen, F. *Karl Marx*, Fourth Estate, 2010
A detailed and yet very entertaining and accessible biography of Karl Marx.

The context of the Cold War

Ambrose, S.E. and Brinkley, D.G. *Rise to Globalism: American Foreign Policy Since 1938*, Penguin, 1993
A very accessible introduction to the US perspective on the Cold War; the chapters on Reagan and the end of the Cold War are particularly useful.

Braithwaite, R. *Afgantsy: The Russians in Afghanistan 1979–89*, Profile, 2011
A detailed and readable account of Soviet intervention in Afghanistan by a former British ambassador to Moscow.

Dunbabin, J.P.D. *The Cold War*, Longman, 1994
A definitive and scholarly analysis of the key events of the Cold War.

Gaddis, J.L. *The Cold War*, Penguin, 2007
One of the most well-argued, well-written and compelling accounts of the end of the Cold War (among other things).

Isaacs, J. and Downing, T. *Cold War*, Transworld, 1998
An accessible and yet scholarly overview of the Cold War, which is particularly strong on events in eastern Europe and the USSR in the 1980s; written to accompany a seminal television series.

Mason, J.W. *The Cold War 1945–91*, Routledge, 1996
A clear, concise and academic overview of the events of the Cold War.

Modern Chinese history

Bailey, P.J. *China in the Twentieth Century*, Blackwell, 2001
An overview of twentieth-century Chinese history, commissioned by the British Historical Association, which is particularly adept at surveying the historiographical debate.

Brown, K. *Friends and Enemies: The Past, Present and Future of the Communist Party in China*, Anthem Press, 2009
A clear and concise narrative of the major themes in Chinese history since 1949.

Chang, J. and Halliday, J. *Mao: The Unknown Story*, Vintage, 2007
A critical biography of Mao Zedong by a biographer with first-hand experience of communist rule, which places Mao alongside Hitler and Stalin as one of the totalitarian monsters of the twentieth century.

Fenby, J. *The Penguin History of Modern China: The Fall and Rise of a Great Power, 1850–2009*, Penguin, 2009
A compelling, brilliantly written and very detailed account of modern Chinese history; the description of the events leading up to the Tiananmen Square Massacre is especially useful.

Gray, J. *Rebellions and Revolutions: China from the 1800s to 2000*, Oxford University Press, 2003
A scholarly, undergraduate-level overview of modern Chinese history.

Hsü, I.C.Y. *The Rise of Modern China*, Oxford University Press, 1995
A definitive and very detailed overview of Chinese history; complex and challenging but places communist rule within the broad sweep of Chinese civilization.

Lawrance, A. *China under Communism*, Routledge, 1998
A concise and accessible introduction to modern Chinese history.

Lynch, M. *The People's Republic of China Since 1949*, Hodder & Stoughton, 1998
Clear, lucid and accessible introduction to the era of communist rule in China.

Mitter, R. *A Bitter Revolution*, Oxford University Press, 2004
An insightful evaluation of contemporary Chinese politics and society.

Moise, E.E. *Modern China*, Longman, 1994
Now slightly dated, but excellent on the factional struggles in the CCP during the 1970s.

Roberts, J.A.G. *A History of China*, Palgrave, 1999
An undergraduate-level overview of Chinese history from pre-history onwards; covers the period from 1949 to 2005 concisely in a single chapter.

Spence, J.D. *The Search for Modern China*, W.W. Norton & Co., 1999
A great work of lucid scholarship from one of the foremost western experts on modern Chinese history. The accompanying documentary reader is one of the best and most definitive of its type.

Zhao, Z. *Prisoner of State: The Secret Journal of Chinese Premier Zhao Ziyang*, Pocket Books, 2010
Memoirs of one of the key reforming members of the Politburo in China in 1989, based on tapes smuggled out of China.

Soviet and eastern European history

Brown, A. *The Gorbachev Factor*, Oxford University Press, 1996
A clear and lucid thematic account of Gorbachev's domestic polices by a prominent British political scientist.

Davies, N. *God's Playground: A History of Poland, Volume II, 1795 to the Present*, Oxford University Press, 2005
The definitive account of modern Polish history.

Gorbachev, M. *Memoirs*, Doubleday, 1996
A fascinating first-hand account by the leading protagonist in the end of the Cold War and the collapse of the USSR.

Hosking, G. *A History of the Soviet Union 1917–1991*, Fontana, 1992
A lively and accessible account of Russian history from the February Revolution up to the collapse of the USSR.

Judt, T. *Postwar*, Heinemann, 2005
A critically acclaimed history of the European continent since 1945.

McCauley, M. *The Soviet Union 1917–1991*, Longman, 1996
A good, detailed overview of communist rule from 1917 onwards; particularly insightful on the reasons for the collapse of the USSR and provides a wide range of interesting case studies and anecdotes.

McCauley, M. *Gorbachev*, Longman, 1998
A detailed biography of Gorbachev featuring a detailed evaluation of *glasnost* and *perestroika*.

Marples, D.R. *The Collapse of the Soviet Union*, Pearson Education, 2004
A detailed and definitive single-volume guide to Gorbachev's domestic policies and the reasons for the collapse of the USSR.

Mazower, M. *The Dark Continent*, Penguin, 1998
A wide-ranging and scholarly survey of European politics and culture in the twentieth century; some fascinating insights into life in the eastern bloc.

Nove, A. *An Economic History of the USSR, 1917–1991*, Penguin Books, 1992
A clear and definitive overview of the Soviet economy by a former Economics Professor at the University of Glasgow; particularly useful on the problems experienced by the Soviet economy during the Brezhnev era.

Service, R. *A History of Modern Russia*, Penguin, 2003
An excellent, academic introduction to the history of the USSR.

Sixsmith, M. *Russia: A Thousand Year Chronicle of the Wild East*, BBC Books, 2011
A lively and very readable overview of Russian history, placing the Soviet system in the twentieth century in a wider context; written by a former BBC foreign correspondent.

Tompson, W. *The Soviet Union Under Brezhnev*, Pearson Education, 2003
A detailed single-volume account of all key aspects of the Brezhnev era, which also contains a wide range of relevant documents.

Wheaton, B. and Kavan, Z. *The Velvet Revolution: Czechoslovakia 1988–1991*, Westview Press, 1992
A detailed, undergraduate-level insight into the overthrow of communist rule in Czechoslovakia.

Internet resources

- The BBC has a useful site that allows you to view news archives to see how events such as the fall of the Berlin Wall were seen at the time: www.bbc.co.uk/archive
- Political cartoons of the period from Britain may be found at the University of Kent's website: www.cartoons.ac.uk
- A subscription website that allows the searching of undergraduate- and IB Diploma-level articles by topic, theme or author: www.historytoday.com
- A vast number of primary documents, including treaties, speeches, letters and so forth can be found at Fordham University's Modern Internet History Sourcebook: www.fordham.edu/halsall/mod/modsbook.asp
- British National Archives contain primary documents of all periods, but can be difficult to navigate given the sheer volume of data available: www.nationalarchives.gov.uk
- US National Archives also contain primary documents in vast quantities, but can also be difficult to navigate given the sheer volume of data available: www.archives.gov

Films

CNN's Cold War DVD series, 2012.
An acclaimed series now available on DVD which thoroughly discusses and analyses the beginnings of the Cold War as the result of the Second World War in Europe.

Days that Shook the World: Series 1–3, 2003.
A series of short docu-dramas outlining key events in history from an eyewitness perspective; in particular, the episode on the fall of the Berlin Wall highlights the experiences of ordinary people in November 1989, on both sides of a divided city.

Goodbye Lenin, 2002.
A sensitive and humorous film about a family coming to terms with the fall of the Berlin Wall; it gently satirizes aspects of life in the old GDR.

The Lives of Others, 2006.
A German-language film which gives an excellent insight into how the *Stasi* and its network of informers warped East German society during the 1980s.

Internal assessment

The internal assessment is a historical investigation on a historical topic. Below is a list of possible topics on Communism in crisis 1976–89. They have been organized by theme.

The PRC after Mao

1 To what extent did the Gang of Four affect the governance of PRC between 1966 and 1976?
2 In what ways and for what reasons did the Tiananmen Incident affect the PRC's political structure?
3 Why did the Gang of Four's power collapse in 1976?
4 How did the economic policies of Mao and Hua Guofeng differ?
5 What was the significance of the failure of Hua Guofeng's Ten Year Plan?
6 Why was Hua Guofeng replaced by Deng Xiaoping by 1981?

Deng Xiaoping

1 To what extent did Deng Xiaoping's economic policies differ from those of Mao and Hua Guofeng?
2 Why was Deng Xiaoping allowed by the Chinese Communist Party to implement economic reforms in the PRC?
3 How did Deng Xiaoping's control of the Chinese Communist Party compare to that of Mao?
4 Which of Deng's Four Modernizations were most successfully implemented?
5 How did the economic development of the PRC's coastal cities differ from that of cities in the interior?
6 What was the impact of Deng's rule on the PRC's non-Han minorities?

Leonid Brezhnev

1 How far did Brezhnev succeed in revitalizing Soviet agriculture?
2 To what extent did relations between the USSR and the PRC improve during the Brezhnev era?
3 To what extent was the USSR's economic crisis during the Brezhnev era the result of Brezhnev's policies?
4 What was the impact of Brezhnev's policies on Soviet relations with Yugoslavia or a member of the Warsaw Pact?

Mikhail Gorbachev

1 Why did Gorbachev introduce the policies of *glasnost* and *perestroika*?
2 To what extent was Gorbachev successful in obtaining concessions from the USA?
3 How did Gorbachev's policies in Afghanistan differ from those of Brezhnev?
4 What was the importance of West and East Germany for Gorbachev's foreign policy?
5 To what extent was Gorbachev personally responsible for the collapse of the USSR?
6 How did *glasnost* affect the governance of Albania?

Index

A

Afghanistan 106, 114–22, 123–26, 127, 131–2, 169, 171, 173, 193

Agriculture 13, 16, 18, 48–50, 62, 76, 98–9, 139, 142, 176, 178

Amin, Hafizulla 116–17, 118, 124, 125, 126

Andropov, Yuri 115, 116, 117–18, 121, 125, 135, 193, 199

Angola 112, 127

April Revolution 114

Asia 15, 72, 82, 103, 107, 117, 124, 128, 139

B

Baltic republics 128, 143, 151–2, 154–5

Berlin
   Blockade 15
   Wall 17, 192, 173, 175, 178–9, 181

Bolshevik Revolution 11

Brandt, Willy 109

Brezhnev, Leonid 17, 40, 95, 135, 139, 140, 141, 147
   changes to constitution (1977) 96–7
   Doctrine 107, 108, 111, 169, 172, 173, 178, 184, 196, 197
   foreign policy 101, 106–13, 193, *see also* Afghanistan
   nationalism within republics 128
   Soviet stagnation 98–101, 104–6, 194

Brzezinski, Zbigniew 112, 121, 123–4, 198

Bush, George 80, 154, 167, 173, 182

C

Cadres 19, 25, 35, 45, 51, 60, 67, 68, 76, 81, 86, 126, 142, 199

Cambodia 72, 107

Camp David Accords 110

Captions 40, *see also* Visual sources

Carter, Jimmy 71, 72, 111, 112, 113, 117, 124, 125–6, 193, 198
   Carter Doctrine 121

Cartoons 39–41, *see also* Visual sources

Catholic Church 185, 186, 190, 191, 194

CCP, *see* Chinese Communist Party

Central Intelligence Agency (CIA) 109, 112, 117, 118, 123, 124

Charter 77: 184–5

Charts 63, *see also* Visual sources

Chechens 151

Chernenko, Konstantin 135, 199

Chernobyl 146–7, 171

China, *see* People's Republic of China

Chinese Communist Party (CCP) 18, 19, 20, 23–4, 28, 31–3, 34, 35–6, 44–5, 47, 48, 51, 53, 56–8, 59, 61, 66, 67, 68–70, 74, 77, 78, 79–80, 81–2, 86, 87, 88, 89–90, *see also* Politburo

CIA, *see* Central Intelligence Agency

CIS, *see* Commonwealth of Independent States

Civic Forum 186–8

Coastal Development Plan 53, 60

Cold War 15, 17, 109, 124, 131, 170–1, 173–4, 175, *see also* Berlin; Nuclear weaponry

Collectivization 13, 28, 48, 190

COMECON 15, 72, 169–70

Comintern 13

Commonwealth of Independent States (CIS) 155

Communism 9–10, 11

Communist Manifesto, The 9, 10

Communist Party of Czechoslovakia 108, 183–5, 187–8

Communist Party of the Soviet Union (CPSU) 95, 135, 136, 141, 142, 143, 145, 147, 152, 153, 154, 171

Congress of People's Deputies 143, 144, 145, 148, 152, 159

Corruption 57–8, 60, 76, 81, 83, 85, 86, 100, 104, 121, 127, 138, 140, 142, 145

CPSU, *see* Communist Party of the Soviet Union

Crimean Tatars 151

Cuba 17, 112, 127

Cult of personality 13, 19, 20, 32, 33, 40, 70, 138

Cultural Revolution 19, 20, 22, 23–4, 25, 26, 27, 28, 30, 31, 35–6, 44, 45, 59, 67, 76, 77, 78

Czechoslovakia 107, 108, 173, 174, 177, 179, 180, 193, 195, 196, *see also* Velvet Revolution

D

Daoud Khan, Mohammed 114, 125

Decollectivization 48

Defence 55–6, 118, 127, 140, *see also* Nuclear weaponry; Strategic Defence Initiative

Democracy Wall movement 66–8, 76

Deng Xiaoping 19, 20, 22, 23–4, 28, 30, 31, 32, 33, 34–6, 44–7, 48, 51–2, 56, 59–60, 61–2, 66–78, 85–6, 87, 88–90, 92, 179, *see also* Tiananmen Incident; Tiananmen Square

Détente 109–13, 115, 116, 117, 118, 124, 125, 170

Dissidents 78–9, 103, 111–12, 148, 176, 184, 185

Dubček, Alexander 108, 184, 187

E

Education 49, 60, 96, 151, 102

Egypt 109–10

Engels, Friedrich 9, 10

Essays 3, 5, 160–5

Estonia 128, 143, 152

Ethiopia 112, 117

Examination paper, appearance 5

Examination questions 3–5
   comparing and contrasting sources 4, 91–3
   how to answer direct questions 3–4, 37–42
   integrating knowledge and sources 5, 160–5
   interpreting visual sources 39–41, 63–4, 132
   origins, purpose, value, limitations 4–5, 130–3

F

Fang Lizhi 78–80, 82

Federal Republic of Germany (FRG) 15, 107, 109, 176–81, 182–3, 185, 195

Five Antis Campaign 18

500 Day Programme 153

Five Year Plans 13, 100

Four Modernizations 31, 44–58, 59–62

G

Gang of Four 22–7, 28, 32, 33, 34, 44, 67

Gdańsk 190
   shipyards 108, 190, 192–3

Georgian Soviet Socialist Republic 151

German Democratic Republic (GDR) 15, 109, 169

Germany
   reunification 169, 172, 173, 176, 183
   Second World War 13, 14, 15, 151, 186,
      189
   see also Berlin; Federal Republic of
      Germany; German Democratic
      Republic
Gierek, Edward 108, 190, 191, 192
Glasnost 146–8, 150, 156–9, 176
Gomułka, Wladysław 190
Gorbachev, Mikhail 40, 60, 72, 135, 156–9
   domestic reforms 135–48, 196–7
   foreign policy 67–74, 121–2, 167–74,
      176, 178, 182–3
   visit to China 83, 84
   visit to GDR 179–80
Graphs 63, *see also* Visual sources
Great Leap Forward 18–19, 23, 28, 34, 59
Gromyko, Andrei 105, 111, 115, 116, 118,
      125, 141, 168, 169, 193
Guerrilla warfare 72, 115, 119, 121, 122
Gulags 103, 147

H

Havel, Václav 185, 187, 188
Helsinki Accords 111, 184, 196
Historians 6, 23, 44, 59, 60, 62, 78, 88,
      89–90, 104, 105, 106, 108, 123, 125,
      130, 156–7, 159, 173–4, 196, 197,
      198, 199
   Acton, Edward 96, 99, 116, 118, 136,
      153
   Brown, Archie 151, 159, 196
   Cheng, Pei-kai 27, 84, 85
   Darwin, John 156
   Domes, Jürgen 49, 61
   Dunbabin, John 111, 197
   Gaddis, John Lewis 190, 197, 198
   Gray, Jack 59, 60, 85
   Hazan, Baruch A. 106, 171
   Hobsbawm, Eric 157, 159, 199
   Hsü, Immanuel C.Y. 51, 57, 59, 60, 61,
      69, 89
   Kavan, Zdeněk 186
   Kissinger, Henry A. 124
   Lawrance, Alan 32, 59–60
   Leonhard, Wolfgang 146
   Lestz, Michael 27, 84, 85
   Linden, Carl 49, 61
   MacFarquhar, Roderick 76
   Marples, David 147, 157, 158
   Mason, John 109
   McCauley, Martin 104, 136, 157, 158,
      180
   Medvedev, Roy 103, 104, 159
   Michael, Franz 49, 61

Moïse, Edwin E. 47, 50
Priestland, David 88
Prybyla, Jan 49, 61
Roberts, J.A.G. 89
Service, Robert 102, 104, 105, 108, 128,
      141, 158
Spence, Jonathan 27, 60, 84, 85
Stableford, Tom 96, 99, 116, 118, 136,
      153
Urban, Jan 184
Vogel, Ezra F. 88
Wheaton, Bernard 186
Honecker, Erich 176, 178, 179–80, 196
Hong Kong 46, 52, 56, 74
Household responsibility system 48–9
Hu Yaobang 31, 32, 33, 68, 69, 77, 79, 81,
      82
Hua Guofeng 25, 27, 28–33, 35, 40–1, 45,
      59, 68
Human rights 78, 103, 111, 173, 184
Hundred Flowers Campaign 18, 79
Hungary 17, 88, 108, 173, 178, 193
Husák, Gustáv 108, 184–5, 188

I

Industry 13, 16, 31, 40, 50–4, 57, 63, 76,
      99–101, 136–8, 176, 182, 184, 185,
      193
Inflation 56–7, 58, 60, 75, 108, 127, 140,
      177, 193
Intermediate-range Nuclear Forces (INF)
      Treaty 172, 173
Israel 40, 109–10, 112

J

Jakeš, Miloš 185, 186, 187, 196
Jaruzelski, Wojciech, General 108, 187,
      193–5, 196
Jiang Qing 19, 20, 22, 23, 24–5, 26–7, 41,
      see also Gang of Four 22–7

K

Kádar, János 108
Kania, Stanisław 192, 193
Kazakh Soviet Socialist Republic 150–1
Khmer Rouge 107
Khrushchev, Nikita 15–17, 95, 104, 105,
      127, 139, 190
Kim Il Sung 15
Kissinger, Henry A. 111, 124
Kohl, Helmut 182–3
Korea 15, 54, 73, 81–2
Kosygin, Aleksey 17
Krenz, Egon 180–1, 182

L

Latvia 128, 143, 152
Lenin, Vladimir 9–10, 12–13
Li Peng 69, 81, 82, 83–4, 86, 89
Ligachev, Yegor 141–2, 143
Lin Biao 19, 27, 34, 35
Lithuania 111, 128, 143, 151, 152
Little Red Book 19
Liu Shaoqi 19, 30, 34
Long March 18, 34, 70

M

Malta Summit 173, 182
Mao Zedong 18–20, 22, 25, 28–9, 34, 35–6,
      59, 66–7, 78, *see also* Deng Xiaoping;
      Gang of Four; Maoism
Maoism 22, 24, 29, 31–3, 67
Marx, Karl 9, 96
Marxism 9, 10, 13, 46–7, 67, 68, 114, 126,
      143, 186, 191, 197, 198, *see also*
      Maoism; Marxism–Leninism
Marxism–Leninism 9–10, 15–16, 35, 46,
      49, 61, 67, 96, 103, 138, 176, 189, 190,
      191, 195, 196
Mass campaigns 18–19
Middle East 109–10, 114, 124
Migration 51, 57, 60
Minsk Declaration 155
Modrow, Hans 182
Mortality 49, 101–2
Mujaheddin 115, 117, 118, 119–22, 124,
      126, 132, 171

N

Nagy, Imre 17
Nationalism 10, 114, 128, 150–2, 154, 158,
      159, 183, 190
Nationalists in China 18, 70
NATO 14, 117, 171, 182
Nazi–Soviet Pact 151, 152, 190
Nepotism 60, 104, 127, 142
New Economic Policy (NEP) 12, 137
Nixon, Richard 20, 70, 71, 109, 111
Nomenklatura 104, 106, 135, 141, 143, 144,
      152, 154
Nuclear plants, *see* Chernobyl
Nuclear weaponry 16, 17, 100, 106–7,
      109, 110, 111–13, 117, 125–6, 167,
      170–2, 173, *see also* Strategic Arms
      Limitation Treaties

O

Oil 29, 51, 100, 101, 121, 124–5, 127, 140,
      158, 178

PROPERTY OF
MULGRAVE SCHOOL
LIBRARY

The publishers would also like to thank the following for permission to reproduce material in this book:
David Higham for *Age of Extremes: The Short Twentieth Century 1914–1991* by Eric Hobsbawm, Michael Joseph, London, 1994. Pearson Education for *The Cold War: The Great Powers and Their Allies* by John P.D. Dunbabin, 2008.

The publishers would like to acknowledge use of the following extracts:
China Daily online (www.chinadaily.com.cn), 2004 and 2010. Doubleday, *Memoirs* by Mikhail Gorbachev, 1995. Baruch A. Hazan, *From Brezhnev to Gorbachev: Infighting in the Kremlin*, 1987. W.W. Norton & Co., *The Search for Modern China: A Documentary Collection* edited by Pei-kai Cheng, Michael Lestz and Jonathan Spence, 1999. Oxford University Press, *The Gorbachev Factor* by Archie Brown, 1996 and *The Rise of Modern China* by Immanuel C.Y. Hsü, 1995 by permission of Oxford University Press, Inc. (www.oup.com). Penguin Books, *A History of Twentieth-century Russia* by Robert Service, 1998 and *The Cold War: A New History* by John Lewis Gaddis, London, 2006. Routledge, *The Rise and Fall of the Soviet Union 1917–1991* by Richard Sakwa, 1999. University of Exeter Press, *The Soviet Union: A Documentary History: Volume 2, 1939–1991* by Edward Acton and Tom Stableford, 2007.

American Association for the Advancement of Science, 'China's 'Four Modernizations' Lead to Closer Sino-U.S. Science Ties,' by Barbara J. Culliton, *Science*, New Series, Vol. 201, No. 4355, 11 August 1978, pp. 512–13. American Economic Association, 'Symposium on economic transition in the Soviet Union and Eastern Europe' by Peter Murrell in *The Journal of Economic Perspectives* Vol. 5, No. 4, Autumn, 1991, p. 6. Australia National University in Canberra, online version of *The Communist Manifesto* from the. Basic Books, *Strategic Vision: America and the Crisis of Global Power* by Zbigniew Brzezinski, 2012. Berg Publishers, 'Reform in the political system: limits and possibilities' by Wolfgang Leonhard in *From Brezhnev to Gorbachev: Domestic Affairs and Soviet Foreign Policy* edited by Hans-Joachim Veen, 1984. Blackwell Publishing, 'Reflections on a partnership: British and American attitudes to postwar foreign policy' by Henry A. Kissinger, *International Affairs*, Vol. 58, No. 4, Autumn 1982, p. 585. China International Publishing Group, 'China's Special Economic Zones' by Xu Dixin, *Beijing Review*, No. 50, 1981. *China Journal*, 'China's New Economic Policy under Hua Guofeng: Party Consensus and Party Myths,' by Frederick Teiwes and Warren Sun, in *The China Journal*, July 2011, Issue 66, p. 23. *China Review International*, 'Reassessing the starting point of the Cultural Revolution' by Hao Ping, *China Review International*, Mar 1996, Vol. 3 Issue 1, pp. 66–86. china.org.cn, Chinese Peoples' Political Consultative Conference, from www.china.org.cn. Columbia University Press, *Post-Soviet Russia: A Journey Through the Yeltsin Era* by Roy Medvedev, 2000. Consultants Bureau, *Peace Détente Cooperation* by Leonid I. Brezhnev, 1981. Danwei, 'Reform Begins With Transgression,' by Wu Xiaobo, Blog MindMeters, www.danwei.org, 30 May 2006. *Der Spiegel*, 13 September 2010, Spiegel Online International (www.spiegel.de/international). *Europe–Asia Studies*, 'The success of a failure: Gorbachev's alcohol policy, 1985–88' by Daniel

Tarschys, *Europe–Asia Studies*, January 1993, Vol. 45, Issue 1. *Every China*, 'Wang Guangmei's Personal Photo Album (III) The Days with Liu Shaoqi' by Luo Haiyan, 20 May 2011 in the online newspaper *Every China*. Foreign Language Press, *Selected Works of Deng Xiaoping (1975–1982)*, 1984. Freedom House, 'The politics and power of humiliation' by Jan Urban in *After the Velvet Revolution: Václav Havel and the New Leaders of Czechoslovakia Speak Out* edited by Tim D. Whipple, *Focus on Issues*, No. 14, 1991, pp. 279–80. *Gender & History*, 'Who Is a feminist? Understanding the ambivalence towards Shanghai Baby,"body writing"and feminism in post-women's liberation China' by Zhong Xueping in *Gender & History*, Vol. 18, No. 3, 2006, p. 641. Hodder Arnold, *The USSR 1945–1990* by John Laver, 1991. Hodder & Stoughton, *The Crystal Spirit: Lech Wałęsa and His Poland* by Mary Craig, 1986. International Studies Association *Foreign Policy Analysis*, Vol. 7, Issue 3, July 2011, p. 219. Internet Modern History Sourcebook Project by Paul Halsall at Fordham University, New York, USA. *Journal of Cold War Studies*, 'Decision-making and the Soviet war in Afghanistan from intervention to withdrawal' by Artemy Kalinovsky in *Journal of Cold War Studies*, Fall 2009, Vol. 11 Issue 4, pp. 49–50. Longman, *Modern China, A History* by Edwin E. Moïse, 2008. *New York Times*, 'Can Gorbachev feed Russia?' by Mark Kramer, *New York Times*, 9 April 1989. Palgrave Macmillan, *A History of China* by J.A.G. Roberts, 2006. Pearson Education, *The Collapse of the Soviet Union* by David Marples, 2004. Pearson/Longman Education, *The Soviet Union under Brezhnev* by William Tompson, 2003. Penguin Books, *An Economic History of the USSR, 1917–1991* by Alec Nove, 1992. *People's Daily*, a speech by Deng Xiaoping (http://english.peopledaily.com.cn), 2012. *Politics, Paradigms, and Intelligence Failures Why so Few Predicted the Collapse of the Soviet Union* by Ofira Seliktar, M. Sharpe, Armonk, NY, 2004. *Pravda*, November 1989. *Rossiyskaya Gazeta*, 'Boris Yeltsin: Ups and downs in the eyes of the world' by Marina Darmaros, *Rossiyskaya Gazeta*, 2 February 2011. Routledge, *China under Communism*, by Alan Lawrance, 1998. Sameeksha Trust, 'Continuity and change in Soviet foreign policy under Gorbachev' by Achin Vanaik from *Economic and Political Weekly*, Vol. 23, No. 11, 12 March 1988, pp. 551–2. M.E. Sharpe, *Politics, Paradigms, and Intelligence Failures: Why So Few Predicted the Collapse of the Soviet Union* by Ofira Seliktar, 2004. State University of New York Press, *Legitimating the Chinese Economic Reforms: A Rhetoric of Myth and Orthodoxy* by Alan R. Kluver, 1996. University of California Press, 'Hu Yaobang: New Chairman of the Chinese Communist Party' by Shu-shin Wang, *Asian Survey*, Vol. XXII, No. 9, September 1982, pp. 811–12. University Press of New England, *A Documentary History of Communism in Russia: From Lenin to Gorbachev* edited by Robert Vincent Daniels, 1993. Westview Press, *China and the Crisis of Marxism–Leninism* by Franz Michael, Carl Linden, Jan Prybyla, and Jürgen Domes, 1990 and *The Velvet Revolution Czechoslovakia 1988–1991* by Bernard Wheaton and Zdeněk Kavan, 1992.

Every effort has been made to trace all copyright holders, but if any have been inadvertently overlooked the Publishers will be pleased to make the necessary arrangements at the first opportunity.